The Book of Beginning Again

EARLYNE C. CHANEY

Offering ways to create well-being on every level of life.

Astara's Library of Mystical Classics

Published by
Astara, Inc.
800 W. Arrow Highway
Upland, CA 91786

CREDITS

Cover: Teodors A. Liliensteins
Photography: Loulie M. Sprague
Acupuncture Drawing: Frances Paelian
Sanford Bennett Photos (Chaps. 11 and 12):
From the book, *Old Age — Its Cause and Prevention*

Copyright © 1981 by Astara, Inc.
Library of Congress Catalog Card Number: 81-65374
International Standard Book Number: 0-918936-09-8

All Rights Reserved

Printed in the United States of America

CONTENTS

My "Ruination" — And My Road to Recovery 1
The All-Important Protein 8
Fruits and Vegetables — The Cream of The Crops 20
The Value of Vegetables 29
Fruits — The Fabulous Cleansers 58
The Three Deadly Whites 77
Coffee, Kelp and Fiber 89
Food Additives, Chemicals, Preservatives and Dyes 100
The Mysterious Magic of the Bee 108
The Famous Honey-Apple Cider Vinegar Cocktail 120
The Man Who Grew Young At Seventy 125
The Lazy Man's Method of Regeneration 140
Natural Wholistic Methods, Old Home Remedies, and Yoga ... 169
The Healing Miracles of Acupuncture 191
Afterthoughts 219
Summation 221

A MESSAGE FROM ASTARA

Since 1951 Astara has been reaching to "the whole person" with printed teachings, audio and visual meditation aids, seminars, workshops and retreats. With each passing year, the *Library of Mystical Classics* (of which this book is one volume) has gained growing favor among students of Mystical Christianity, the Ancient Wisdom Teachings, psychic research, metaphysics and related fields.

A booklet titled *Finding Your Place in the Golden Age* is available without cost to persons interested in Astara's publications. You may obtain a copy simply for the asking. Address your request to: Astara Information Office, 800 West Arrow Highway, Upland, Ca. 91786.

CHAPTER 1
MY "RUINATION"—
AND MY ROAD TO RECOVERY

Everyone in the congregation of Brother Wilson's church always rose during the testimonial portion of the Sunday service to testify concerning what the Lord had done for them. On this particular Sunday, everyone had testified except Brother Smith, who sat on the back pew all gnarled and crippled. In fact, so withered was he, he could hardly walk without his cane.

"Brother Smith," inquired the pastor, "wouldn't you like to rise like the rest of the congregation and testify what the Lord has done for you?"

After a long and thoughtful pause, Brother Smith rose, groaning and wincing.

"Well," he moaned, "He's pert near ruint me!"

And so it was with me at one period of this incarnation. The Lord "pert near ruint me." My "ruination" first came in the form of headaches—violent and persistent.

But before I can enter fully into the story of my ruination—and my ultimate overcoming and return to wholeness—I must flash back to earlier beginnings and episodes so that you may better understand the entire drama of my Beginning Again.

In my book *Remembering—the Autobiography of a Mystic*, I have told the complete and entire story of my birth, my psychic childhood, and my flight to Hollywood to pursue a career as an actress. I also described how, even in the face of unfolding success, there descended upon me strange and enigmatic moments of cosmic loneliness, times when my heart turned from the glamour and glitter of Hollywood to stand weeping beneath the stars, upreaching for Something I could not comprehend.

There were recurring dreams of a pair of eyes, smiling at me, loving me, searching for me. And I came to know that I must seek for and find the man behind the eyes before I could give my heart in true love.

I told how I met the Captain. He was a pilot returning from the hell of World War II. And I gave my heart to Captain Marvin Moore—but only partially. Doubts and perplexities pervaded my consciousness, realizing his were not the eyes of my dreams. But on the day I decided to cast the dream aside as something from a long ago life, and marry Captain Moore, the plane he was flying on an ordinary training flight went down. He gave his life because he would not parachute from his crippled plane and desert a terrified flying companion, too frozen with fear to jump.

When the Captain departed Earth for the Other Side, he took part of me with him—the part that had known laughter and dancing and singing and all the delights of youth. The part that was left was the "other" me that had often wept alone under the night sky, pleading for God to reveal the "why" of my lonely longings for fulfillment of a destiny that kept vanishing before me.

As the inner mystic within me—my "second" self—began to emerge, I turned completely from a career as an actress to plant my feet firmly on a different pathway, a pathway leading into mysticism, esoteric philosophy, yoga, meditation, and Spiritualism. During the two years that followed, relentlessly pursuing techniques for God-realization, I unfolded psychic and healing potentials that prepared me for the coming light.

The light came when the Captain, from his vantage point on the Other Side, led me to find the-man-with-the-eyes—Robert Chaney. And the moment our eyes met, I knew my search had ended. Three months to the day after we met, we were married.

Together in 1951, we founded a spiritual center in California and named it *Astara*—which means *Light*. As the days of our years passed, Astara waxed strong until it became renowned worldwide, as a church, a re-born School of the ancient Mysteries, an institute of psychic research, and a healing ministry. Together, Robert and I wrote the Teachings which came to be known as *Astara's Book of Life*—the Degree Lessons.

And together, too, we became parents of a beautiful daughter. We named her Sita after the Princess Sita of the Hindu epic, *The Ramayana*. The Hindu Sita was the paragon of all feminine virtue. And as our own Sita unfolded into maturity and young adulthood, in our eyes she more than met the measure of her namesake.

I told, too, of our dreams to establish on the Earth plane a center of love and light where Astarians and all new age seekers might find a haven of soul-peace in a troubled world. In a second book, a sequel to *Remembering* called *The Masters and Astara*,* I told how the dream came true when Astara purchased a ten-acre small college campus in Upland, California, about an hour's drive from Los Angeles. I told of our many struggles and the miracles the unseen Masters manifested to establish Astara as a world renowned new age Center of Light in our new location.

I told the details of these happenings —and much more—in *Remembering* and in *The Masters and Astara*. But I did *not* tell the details of my personal struggle to maintain the pace of daily dharma—writing the Degree Teachings under the downflowing inspiration of my unseen spiritual Teacher from the higher planes; meeting the "deadlines;" appearing as co-minister by Robert's side on the church platform as we met our obligations as ministers-healers; traveling all over the world teaching seminars; rising to the requirements of

---

* See back pages of this book for further references.

motherhood. All these fast-flowing missions took their toll on my health as the headaches increased in intensity and became daily occurences.

It seems unnecessary to delve into gross details. Suffice to say that all medical help—sought reluctantly—offered no help at all, except to recommend more and stronger pain pills, taken almost daily so that the pace of carrying on the *Great Work* might proceed. Suffice, too, to say that the day of final collapse came. The pain-killing drugs had taken their toll.

On the day I was taken to a hospital, Robert and Sita—then about thirteen—actually did not know whether or not I would ever come home again. Nor did I.

It was during the weeks that followed, when I actually fought my way back to life, that I realized I must actually write *The Book of Beginning Again*, not only in words on a printed page, but in action in daily life. I worked out my formula for rebirth to cover many modalities.

First, it should be stated that a fine doctor who was very aware of a holistic new age approach to healing, and who was also aware of my spiritual mission, diagnosed the cause of my problem for the first time. Hypoglycemia—low blood sugar. I had long suspected that such might be the cause of the headaches, but because of heavy ministerial responsibilities, I had never paused long enough in my pressing daily program to seek a full understanding of all that was involved in this all-too-common physical complaint. Now I had no choice. I realized that if, in the years ahead, I was to continue my mission as a laborer in the Great Work of the mystical Hierarchy, I must begin a program of total purification and physical transformation.

THE MYSTERIOUS DR. SOM KU

Back in the days of 1945, following the death of the Captain, I changed overnight from an actress seeking a career in the cinema to a mystic seeking enlightenment, Self-realization and God. In the early days of my seeking, my spirit teacher appeared suddenly to me and requested that I become a vegetarian as part of my upreaching pathway toward the light. (Again, see *Remembering*, my autobiography.)

The request left me baffled and bewildered. I hadn't the faintest notion of how to begin. Along with most of humanity, I had been thoroughly brainwashed and programmed to believe meat to be a natural part of existence on Earth. How to eat—indeed how to live—without it, well, it seemed comparable to climbing Mt. Everest without a rope.

Determined to follow the request, however, I set forth to meet the challenge. I bought books on food and diet—there were very few in those days—and I began attending lectures by speakers who offered guidelines toward purification and diet. Few, I discovered, were vegetarians. But one night I found *him*—Dr. Som Ku.

That wasn't his real name. But he has made me swear to withhold his true identity in these writings, so I shall honor his request and use his "spiritual" name. He came by his Oriental name during a phase of his own soul-searching. Having studied Self-unfoldment and Self-mastery under a guru from India, there came the moment of initiation—and it was then that his guru bestowed upon him his new name—Som Ku. It is by this name he shall be known in these writings.

That first lecture sent me reeling. There were no two ways about it, said this feisty little man, everyone in this whole wide world should be a vegetarian!—and on and on! As he spoke on tirelessly, I realized I'd been sent to him—he was to be my guide in numerous ways. Before the lecture ended, I was burning with fervent impatience, anticipating my headlong flight home to tackle my one remaining dastardly hot dog, crush it beneath my foot, and fling it from my household as the contemptible viper it was—and, of course, spray my kitchen, stove and refrigerator with the very most powerful Lysol.

But first I went forward after the lecture to meet Dr. Som. And, as so often happens in my life, there was an instant recognition of two long ago friends meeting once again. Here was a swarthy, sharp-eyed, fiery-tongued little spit-fire of a man, already middle aged, stretching forth his handshake to a frightened, grief stricken little lost soul, trembling on the edge of mysticism, blindly groping for help from any source available that would help her find her way along the new found path of her yet-to-be life and mission.

All I needed to say was that I was interested in becoming a vegetarian. Just as if we were resuming a conversation broken off in some long past life, he immediately launched into a description of his up-coming teaching activities, and just as immediately, it was naturally assumed that I'd be sitting in the midst of these classes and lectures.

And I was.

Turned out he was a chiropractor-naturopath-nutritionist. That quaint little fire-ball knew more about health, healing, diet, purification, vitamin-minerals, and total well-being than anyone alive. The teachings flowed from his lips like a raging river.

And as he spoke at his lectures, I wrote furiously, trying to capture every word. He spoke of diet, naturally, but he also spoke of herbs, exercise, tub soaks, sitz baths, foot soaks, deep breathing, walking, reflexology (long before it became popular), and celibacy. Oh, my, he was long on vegetarianism and celibacy. And he made no bones about it.

"And anybody," he loudly proclaimed, "who doesn't want to follow my program, just needn't come around to take up my time when they get sick. They have to give up that old meat and that old sex if they expect to become whole—and that's the way it is!"

But his bark was far worse than his bite. Very few of his patients became true vegetarians—and far fewer gave up "that old sex," yet he never failed to give his utmost to help any and all who sought his aid. Scolding continuously, he still fervently sought every remedy at his command—as long as it was "natural."

Well, I became not only a follower, but a patient—and close friend. He "took a liking" to this poor little waif, whose eyes so often brimmed with tears, and who sought help and guidance so desperately. Discovering the reason for my grief, and how sincere and eager was my seeking to reach through to the Captain, he offered all the help he could. Like a father-teacher, it was he who pointed me toward out-of-the-way Spiritualist churches, often tiny cubby holes submerged in old houses and strange arcades.

He told me how he, too, once went seeking. He, too, lost a loved wife in death. During the days of his darkness, he saw a vision and heard a voice. He was told to toss away his cigarettes, his liquor and flesh foods—and to devote the rest of his life guiding others toward the same path.

"And, hot damn, I did it," he grinned, his bright brown eyes twinkling with triumph.

And, hot damn, so did I. There wasn't the cigarettes and liquor to discard in my life—just the flesh foods. But that was quite enough. I think I couldn't have done it successfully without the help of this little miracle-maker. From the day we met, I became his pupil. He poured into my pounding ears all his ingathered wisdom—all his secrets of natural healing, all his accumulated knowledge of man, soul, spirit, God and the universe. It infused my consciousness like ink slowly dripping into clear water—until I was filled to overflowing with the outflowing torrent of his thought waves.

"Someday, after I'm gone, you'll write of these things," he said. "You'll gather it all together and carry forward all my years of learning."

And he was right.

But before that, destiny was to take me back to Indiana to meet and marry Robert. When we finally journeyed to Los Angeles to open Astara, Dr. Som was one of the first to join our congregation. When we were forced to give up vegetarianism and return to meat-eating, he it was who stormed and raved at the "grossness" of it. But we had no choice. Vegetarian cooks simply weren't to be had in those days.

"You'll rue the day!" he prophesied. "Robert can handle meat. He's strong. He has the digestive system of a bull. I'm not concerned for him. But *you!* It will destroy you! You're like a frail little flower. Your body was never meant to be so contaminated. You'll see! The day will come when you'll seek me out to help save your life—because meat eating will kill you!"

I listened to his scolding all through the years. I sought him often for chiropractic adjustments and he often attended our church services and classes.

When he learned I was pregnant he absolutely insisted on vegetarianism during my gestation period. And I complied. I didn't bother to tell him that both Robert and I had already decided we'd become vegetarians while I carried our baby. I let him think he persuaded us.

He was constantly on hand, helping, advising, rubbing my back, giving adjustments—as excited as if he were having his first grandchild. Indeed it *was* his first godchild—he was to become the godfather. He knew we planned a home delivery—and he was beating on our door seeking entrance before Sita, our baby girl, was one day old. And it was his loving tender hands that saw me through the early months of Sita's babyhood.

Dr. Som's prophecy came true. I *did* rue the day. When Robert and Sita took me to the hospital, perhaps to die, it was he that stood by waiting for my emergence—waiting to see if I was ready once again to become a vegetarian. It was he who brought me back to life.

And it is his wisdom, his knowledge of health and healing that now goes out to help others through the pages of this book. I take no credit. All I share with you, all I write, all the guidelines, the old home remedies—I learned from this angel-man. Although throughout the book I mention others as sources of information—Dr. D. C. Jarvis, Edgar Cayce and others—I had heard it already from Dr. Som, long before.

So, salute him, reader. Whatever help you may find in these pages, it comes not from me. I am only the amanuensis who put the words on paper. He it was who taught me. He it was who gave and gave and gave—that you might know. He didn't want his learning to die with him. He hoped I'd someday carry it forward. This book, then, is my poor effort to pay tribute to him, his life, and the work of his years

Having so said, we can now proceed. The first thing I'm sure he'd want me to share concerns diet. And so I shall. But first, I must list the complete program of my Beginning Again, the better to proceed.

1. *First, the diet*. And the diet was only the beginning. Other modalities included:
2. *Herbs*
3. *Exercise*— either through yoga or some other form of muscular movements
4. Plenty of *sleep*
5. *Sunshine* on the whole body, nude when possible
6. *Fresh air* and oxygen
7. *Massage, acupressure,* or *polarity therapy,* to stimulate blood circulation and align the positive-negative polarity of the body
8. *Acupuncture*—to unlock the polarity meridians in the body to allow the free flow of pranic life force to recharge the physical and etheric auras
9. *Chiropractics*—to align not only the spine and spinal nerves of the physical body, but to re-align the physical-etheric bodies with all the higher spiritual bodies
10. *Tub soaks*
11. *Reflexology*—to unlock dammed up physical muscles, cells, tissues, and allow nature to restore balance of the positive-negative forces of the entire being
12. *Homeopathic remedies*—to replace the usual drug therapy of allopathic medicine
13. *Daily walks*—a mild form of physical exercise. The walks were an important part of my recovery. They were vigorous. I always set a rapid pace—head up, arms swinging, long strides—and integrated the pace with deep controlled breathing
14. *Meditation*—deep and intensive, including chanting and pranayamic breath control.

To return to the diet. After I returned to meat eating, as the years passed and the headaches gradually increased, I truly did not connect them with my diet. But I should have. I knew the meat diet was not the first choice of my spiritual Teacher and Mentor, but I also knew he understood my dilemma in hiring a vegetarian cook. We had employed a cook-housekeeper who had woven her way into our hearts and who actually became part of the family. Her name was Annie Mae Turner, a dear and beloved black woman who had no idea we ate meat reluctantly. I kept thinking that "someday" I'd ask her to try vegetarian methods of cooking.

Annie was not only serving meats but had gradually brought into the kitchen all manner of forbidden foods— the bologna, the hot dogs, the doughnuts, cookies, chocolate candies, and on and on. And I was foolishly and thoughtlessly giving no thought to the possibility of their contribution toward my headaches. So it was a combination of flesh food plus the preservatives, the additives, the dyes in the "forbiddens" that actually brought about the malfunctioning of the pancreas, the adrenals, and, indeed, the entire digestive system—resulting in hypoglycemia and headaches.

When my headaches became unbearable and I experienced my "ruination," to carry out my program of Beginning Again, we turned our thoughts once again to diet—and, of course, to Dr. Som. Out of our kitchen went the white sugar, white flour, white salt, the pies, cakes, cookies, doughnuts, chocolate candies, frozen T.V dinners, all meats including processed lunch meats, hot dogs, etc., and all canned foods. In their places came the health foods—the honey, date and maple sugar, whole wheat flour, sea salt and vegetable salt, tahini, carob, organically grown fresh fruits and vegetables for daily salads, a variety of grains, but especially millet, a variety of nuts, seeds, all-grain breads, apple cider vinegar, fertile eggs, raw milk, raw sweet butter and raw cheese.

When I first realized I must become a vegetarian again, I pondered at first how Annie would react. I knew she must completely re-organize her kitchen, and also her method of cooking. Many cooks would have flatly refused such a drastic change. But not our Annie Mae. We were "her family" and departing from us was unthinkable. She didn't flick an eyelash. She rolled up her sleeves and plunged into the program like a brave soldier charging into the fray of battle.

"I have to learn to cook health foods and vegetarian," I heard her tell a neighbor one day, "but I'm happy to do it for my lady. Besides, I'll probably get healthier, too."

So we tackled the new challenge together. It was truly the blind leading the blind. I brought home carloads of cookbooks—and Annie spent hours pouring over them. It was good that she loved to cook and soon was thoroughly enjoying the new approach.

I knew I must become a health food advocate or die. Again, the diet was only the beginning—but because food is of paramount importance in maintaining or regaining health, in this present book I shall lay emphasis upon it. Later I tackled all the other modalities, and I'll share my adventures with you because they may act as guidelines for your own approach to well-being.

CHAPTER 2
THE ALL-IMPORTANT PROTEIN

Because so much has been written about protein—the markets are flooded with books and literature stressing its importance—I'm reluctant to dwell too long on the subject. But because I'm pointing my readers toward vegetarianism, and because vegetarians must be aware of an adequate meat substitute in the diet, I must offer information I found valuable as I made my transition from flesh foods to vegetarianism.*

During the early days of my Beginning Again, my digestive system was too imbalanced to handle a wide variety of foods. So for quite a while my daily diet consisted of large raw vegetable salads and millet casseroles.

Having been a vegetarian many years previously, I still remembered the value of raw salads. I remembered, too, that millet was a complete protein food. So for weeks, Annie Mae daily baked a millet casserole with chopped onions, carrots, celery and mushrooms. Each day she added a "surprise" vegetable to these basics.

First, she partially cooked the millet.

Then she partially cooked the vegetables in a wok, and added them to the millet in a casserole and baked it to completion. Usually she served it with mushroom sauce. To this she added a large green salad. I mention the details because if you are on a health or healing program, this is an ideal vegetarian meal.

To the salad I usually added sunflower seeds, sesame seeds and pumpkin seeds (all complete protein). Occasionally I sprinkled it with bee pollen, alfalfa sprouts, rice polish or brewer's yeast (also complete protein). Occasionally, too, I added shredded raw cheese. And I always sprinkled it with powdered kelp—a total mineral food from the sea. Of course, all the greens of the salad—the butter lettuce, red lettuce, romaine, escarole, watercress, endive, spinach, parsley—also contained the all-important protein. To these greens, Annie Mae alternately added shredded carrots, onions, beets, celery, cabbage, green peppers and radishes. I avoided head lettuce—often called iceberg—because it lacked food value and was occasionally difficult to digest.

I make much of the salad because

---

* See my book, "Light and Life Cookbook," offering complete menus and recipes for healthy vegetarian living, available from bookstores or Astara's Book Shop.

with the important protein added, it could suffice as one's total diet for rebuilding health. And that's what this book is all about—a sharing of my own Beginning Again experiences, so that you, my reader, may avoid ever becoming ill or, following my guidelines may, hopefully, totally regain your health as I did.

The vegetarian or health advocate will be aware of protein foods—flesh and otherwise—but I shall list them to aid the awareness, together with helpful comments.

COMPLETE PROTEINS:
Meat (avoid red meat if possible and choose fish or chicken).

Chicken   *Yogurt*
Turkey   *Milk*
Eggs   *Cottage Cheese*

Legumes (some legumes contain complete protein although some are lacking in potency and some are lacking in one amino acid. Legumes include:

   beans (common) peas
   cowpeas   snap beans
   garbanzos   soybeans
   lentils   split peas
   lima beans
     (butterbeans)

Nuts
   almonds   hickory
   cashews   peanuts
   coconut   pecans
   chestnuts   pine nuts
   walnuts
   (14.8% protein) filberts

Most nuts contain complete protein, but since some of the amino acids are in smaller quantities, occasionally nuts should be combined with other protein foods such as whole grains, dairy products or legumes.

Seeds
   Acorn, ground   dill
   aniseeds   figseed
   chia   flaxseed
   cardomon   fennel
   celery   parsley seed
   cucumber   pomegranate
   caraway   pumpkin
   carob   psyllium
   coriander   senna
   cumin   sesame
   sunflower   squash

Grains
   barley   oatmeal
   brown rice   rice
   buckwheat   rye
   corn   (preferably yellow)
   whole wheat (cereal and flour)
   millet   wheat germ

General
   avocados   Irish moss
   bee pollen   kale
   brewer's yeast   mushrooms
   cabbage   okra
   collards   olives
   carrots   potatoes
   corn, sweet   spinach
   yams   turnip greens
   tahini   sprouts, such as
                         alfalfa and wheat

Fruits
   apricots   dates

This is only a partial list of proteins, given to help you gauge your protein intake. Many research reports include all common beans—pink, pinto, red, navy, butterbean—as complete protein. Also most of the grains.

Incomplete protein foods are found among a few grain products, some vegtables, some fruits. These incomplete proteins are extremely valuable in any diet, but the vegetarian should be cautioned to make sure to include complete protein also. Be aware, too, that valuable incomplete proteins become complete when combined with each other. For example, the Mexicans have lived for centuries with corn and beans combined as their principal source of protein—tortillas and beans. These Latin Americans—including many Indian tribes—scarcely eat animal protein. Yet their diet of corn and beans as their basic food has resulted in sturdy health in the majority and remarkable longevity in some. Other combinations creating complete protein are: wheat bread with cheese, apples and cheese, nuts and milk, beans with green salad, grain bread and salad.

Perhaps you should make a list of the basic foods necessary for health and keep them on a kitchen wall, the better to maintain awareness:

1. protein (I've listed many)
2. nuts
3. fruits
4. vegetables
5. grains
6. seeds and sprouts

Although protein is of paramount importance, it is believed by most wholistic doctors and healers that far too much is consumed daily, especially among meat eaters. Four ounces of protein daily has been proven adequate—for instance, a quarter of a pound of cheese, or one and a half ounces of nuts. You may be surprised to learn, too, that protein is not our principal source of energy. Carbohydrates and fats are.

Let me also say that neither Robert nor I are total vegetarians. When we have a choice—for instance, in our home—we are vegetarians. But when we dine out, we occasionally must choose fish or chicken. However, more than once I have been known to carry a large salad in a brown paper bag for my entire dinner.

Because a habit is time honored does not make it right. Americans have been programmed to believe that health and well-being depend on the consumption of flesh products, whereas the rapidly growing advocates of vegetarianism proclaim just the opposite. Early physiologists, like Lilbig and Voit, stressed the idea that meat was necessary to produce muscles—"meat makes meat" was their approach. But this false notion has long since been scientifically refuted. Muscular strength and endurance are not enhanced by eating meat any more than brain functioning is enhanced by eating animal brains. We all know now that our brains increase in cell development principally through mind usage—that is, using mental power itself, such as meditation. Muscle tone and development are likewise maintained and improved by muscle usage—exercise, yoga, tai chi, the martial arts.

Meat has a stimulating effect on the nervous system—but it is a false one. Like caffeine, nicotine, theine and sugar, it temporarily stimulates the nervous system, but such stimulation adds nothing to nerve energy or muscle strength. Actually, it depletes it. Although the body may experience a sense of warmth and exhilaration following a meal of meat, the digestive system is actually under stress to digest and assimilate the food nutrients. Flesh foods ultimately destroy the stomach and kidneys prematurely through the perpetual flow of acidity in the blood and the accumulation of toxins in the system. The result is heart failure, stroke, cancer, arthritis, hardening of the arteries—all at an early age of sixty or so, when man should be living twice that age or longer.

It seems superfluous to add that meat will remain a part of our diet for many years to come, simply because the majority are slow to accept change, and because the meat industry is intricately interwoven into our present social and economic system. Diet reform is an individual matter. We acquire our dietary habits in early childhood and deviations are rare. As we progress in the Age of Aquarius and begin our upreaching toward enlightenment, meat will gradually be relegated to the past as light seekers begin to realize the effect of animal flesh and blood upon not only the physical but the higher spiritual bodies. Higher states of consciousness require a simplicity of diet, and living on natural foods—natural foods being foods as near to nature as possible. When we realize en masse that since we can't lick Mother Nature, we ought to join her, we'll "hit our stride" toward the solution of many of our social and economic problems—but principally we'll realize what it truly means to be "born again" in the Holy Spirit.

It was not until I began my Beginning Again program of regeneration that I turned my full attention once again to research on the subject of vegetarianism. I had always assumed man to be a meat-eater by nature. Much of my research indicated otherwise.

ARE WE MEANT TO BE MEAT EATERS?

I'd like to share some of my findings—realizing full well that the adamant meat eater can supply equally conclusive evidence to point man toward carnivora. Ultimately it is for each soul to decide for himself the way it seems best for him to travel on his long journey of becoming.

My conclusions, however, seem to indicate man's anatomy was not structured for meat eating. Natural carnivores—the lion, tiger, wolf, cat, hyena, etc.—have short digestive tracts, whereas the vegetarian animals—including humans—have long, intricate and winding digestive tracts. The tract of the carnivore is about 1/4 that of the vegetarian in length.

The stomach of the carnivore is heavily saturated with hydrochloric acid to transmit the ingested flesh food into quick energy. The stomach of the human, attempting to digest heavy flesh food, is perpetually in trouble. Even the most powerful digestive tract has not enough hydrochloric acid to properly digest the flesh food that is regularly ingested. That is why man's principal ailment is in the digestive tract—the gas, the bloating, the ulcers, the delinquent pancreas, gall bladder, stomach and liver, the almost perpetual over-the-counter drugs taken in an effort to aid digestive problems.

The carnivore possesses long sharp

claws, powerful jaws and long fang-like canine teeth—all for the purpose of capturing, clawing, ripping, spearing and tearing flesh. The vegetarian—both animal and human—have instead incisor teeth seemingly sufficient for masticating fruits, vegetables, nuts, seeds, grains. In addition, they possess well developed molars for grinding and chewing these foods—which the carnivore does not possess. The molars enable the vegetarian's jaw to move sideways as well as up and down, thus properly masticating his food—a facility not possessed by the carnivore, who has a "hinged" jaw.

Nor can man correctly be assumed to be omnivorous by nature—meaning a capability to handle a "mixed" diet of both flesh and plant. The teeth of the omnivore—the bear, the dog, the raccoon, the wild swine—are still not comparable to that of the human. Again, man is not equipped with the sharp claws and fangs necessary to handle well the mixed diet.

It is obvious that during man's stay on Earth, somewhere along the way, a great cataclysmic emergency caused it to become necessary that he eat the flesh of animals in order to survive. I have taught details of this in my teachings of ancient wisdom in Astara's Degree Lessons. Not only did he need to survive, but he had need to totally integrate his consciousness in the field of matter. Flesh eating seemed a requisite, as it still is for those dwelling in Arctic zones.

But man, being by nature a vegetarian, will slowly revert to his true aspect. If he were forced to kill animals for food—as does the true carnivore—he would soon sicken of the activity, and cease flesh eating altogether. Our inner sensitivities totally rebel at the thought of devouring raw flesh. We must have it first slaughtered for us. Then it must be fired—either through frying, baking, broiling or boiling. Only then can our senses tolerate it. Usually, too, it is saturated with sauces, gravies, seasonings and dips. We could not long endure a raw flesh diet, as is needed by the true carnivore.

This is an oversimplified offering, I admit, but it sums up my findings. I would suggest that those who truly feel that we humans are born by nature to be carnivores, first try a carnivore's diet. Let him attempt to exist for a while on fresh-killed flesh—the muscle, the blood, the entrails, the brains and all the undesirable anatomical parts—all so relished by the carnivore. Confronted with such a diet I think the argument may be quickly settled. The would-be carnivore will surely decide he is innately a higher "primate"—a vegetarian by nature.

MORE ABOUT SOME PROTEIN ITEMS

Although I've listed many protein foods, some bear closer research. I've selected a few upon which to add emphasis:

Fish

Avoid shoreline fish. It is striated with pollutions now filling our waterways. A dangerous chemical known as *polychlorinated biphenyls*—or PCBS—is discharged into many waterways by industrial plants. Fish surviving in these polluted shoreline waters are badly contaminated with this chemical which has been proven to cause reproductive failures, gastric disorders, skin lesions and tumors, which could be cancerous.

Canadians and Japanese refuse to eat such fish. Their food laws prohibit consumption of fish with such a high level of contamination. *Both Canada and Japan ship their contaminated fish to America where it is purchased and eaten by Americans!* Choose the deep sea variety. Also avoid frozen fish. Always choose fresh. Let me share an experience I had with frozen fish.

Some years ago, to celebrate my birthday, Robert, Sita and I dined in a plush Hollywood restaurant. I ordered fish. The following morning I wakened so dizzy I couldn't leave my bed. I called a doctor friend.

"Before I prescribe anything, let me ask a few questions. What did you have for dinner last night?"

"Fish."

"Where?"

"At Such-and-Such Restaurant."

"Ah! That explains much! You ate frozen fish—but the frozen fish was contaminated. That particular restaurant flies their fish in from the East coast. It is packed in dry ice. Sometimes the dry ice "melts" and its gasses and toxic substances are absorbed by the thawed fish. Dry ice usually is only carbon dioxide, but there are more chemicals in certain brands. You've been poisoned by these dry ice chemicals and thawed fish. I know—because last week my wife and I dined there. She was so dizzy she couldn't walk for three days afterward. I called the restaurant and discovered they *do* serve this thawed fish often. Just stay in bed until your system discards the toxins."

It was a dismal experience—but from it, I learned not ever to eat frozen fish again. If I cannot get fresh fish in a restaurant, I simply don't order fish. Actually, I eat very little fish anyway, since then.

Eggs

Choose the fertile variety usually from health stores. Supermarket eggs are often old, lacking in nourishment and polluted with contaminated chicken feed. Eggs from the supermarket come usually from hens confined to tiny cages in windowless buildings. There they spend their entire lives, unable to exercise, unexposed to fresh air and sunshine, and denied the company of a rooster, which would make their eggs fertile. These creatures are more like machines than living animals. They are fed tranquilizers to keep them pacified, and chemicalized feed to force egg production.

Eggs from the health stores, on the other hand, are from "barnyard" hens who run free, exposed to sunshine, fresh air, unpolluted feed, ground-scratching and the company of a rooster. So do choose the latter.

Many tests have been made over the past fifteen years in an effort to prove eggs to be the culprits in raising cholesterol levels in the blood and causing heart attacks. In no test has such proof manifested. Instead, just the opposite occurred. The two eggs eaten daily did not in any way raise cholesterol levels—to the astonishment of researchers.

But these same researchers—seeking to discover the *real* culprit—found it to be sugar. Sugar almost doubled the amount of blood cholesterol. Sugar also determined the amount of triglycerides in the blood—it increased enormously and may indeed turn out to be the real cause for alarm over heart attacks, especially among prosperous inactive professionals who are not inclined toward any kind of physical exercise or activity. Among those tested, those who deliberately walked daily—at a brisk pace—showed normal cholesterol and triglyceride blood levels, even though the diet contained eggs and normal fat intake.

The conclusive evidence of all these tests indicates a necessity to avoid any kind of sugar and to engage in some form of daily exercise.

Many prefer to take raw eggs beaten in drinks as part of their protein program. It is fine to include the yolk, but raw egg whites should be avoided. Their albumin contains a protein called *aviden* which is toxic. Aviden also destroys the B vitamin *biotin* in the body. If you insist on eating the whole raw egg, then add a biotin supplementary tablet to your vitamin intake.

BACK TO CHOLESTEROL

Cholesterol is a fat-like substance which the body manufactures. The liver produces three to four grams a day! It is found in every cell. It is a normal constituent of blood and tissues. You need cholesterol! The body eliminates excess cholesterol in the bile through the intestines. Ultimately, the trouble seems not to be the intake of eggs and other cholesterol-foods, but the inability of the body to excrete excessive cholesterol as waste. And what causes the organs of elimination to malfunction? Sugar is the principal culprit. Of course, a few patients develop an intolerance to cholesterol intake, but in the majority, if the digestive system is not imbalanced through unnatural foods—principally sugar—the body can certainly handle two eggs a day with all their ingested cholesterol.

Several things help the body excrete cholesterol. They are lecithin, alfalfa sprouts, vitamin A, B-complex vitamins, raw protein, vegetable oils and fiber. Necessary minerals are zinc, chromium, and especially magnesium. Do make sure of alfalfa sprouts, magnesium and lecithin—forget sugar—and prepare to live to a vigorous old age. At least you may escape dying of an early heart attack.

Cheese

Raw unprocessed cheese is an almost perfect food. It provides excellent protein, plus B-complex vitamins and the minerals calcium and phosphorus. Cheese protein is concentrated so eat it in moderation. Two ounces provides protein equal to two ounces of steak.

There is now available a rennetless cheese. *Rennet* is an enzyme from the lining of a cow's stomach, used usually to make cheese. Many prefer the more natural rennetless. Try it. It is delicious.

Do avoid the usual processed cheeses found in supermarkets. Again, find the raw unprocessed variety in your health store. Before eating any cheese, do trim away the outer "peeling" which may have been waxed.

When a recipe suggests adding cheese to a baked dish, do not add it until the dish is removed from the oven to serve. Topping the food at this time provides sufficient heat to melt the cheese, which is all that is required. To cook the cheese into the food makes it stringy, too oily and too rancid. Cooked cheese is not healthy—and not necessary.

For a healthy snack, do try an apple with a slice of raw cheese. This is excellent, especially for a snack so necessary for the hypoglycemic. It provides excellent protein together with natural fruit sugar.

Yogurt

Always choose plain. Avoid that with added fruits. The processed cooked fruits are devoid of enzymes and filled with sugar.

Yogurt lowers the level of cholesterol in the blood—probably due to its calcium content.

Yogurt—especially if it contains viable *lactobacillus bulgaricus*—supplies the necessary intestinal natural flora bacteria to keep the intestinal tract free of harmful bacteria.

Milk

Never, never use pasteurized. It causes arthritis, inflammation and dental problems. Always choose raw unprocessed milk and drink even that in great moderation. The human body cannot handle heavy milk calcuim, which crystallizes as arthritic deposits and causes problems in the absorption of natural calcium in the body.

Always purchase milk in cardboard or fiberboard containers. Avoid plastic containers. The fluorescent light used in display cases, piercing the plastic, destroys many nutritional qualities and adds dangerous radiation to the milk.

Some cannot digest milk because their intestines lack the enzyme *lactase*, which breaks down milk sugar, *lactose*, into a form the body can absorb. If you cannot tolerate milk, you probably must eliminate fresh milk entirely from your diet. Instead, use the cultured form—the yogurt, kefir, and acidophilus milk. Such items are predigested foods, thus require no lactase in the intestines.

Or you can take lactase tablets which are sold in health stores.

Or you may wish to avoid all milk products and get your protein totally from a variety of grains, seeds, nuts, vegetables and fruits—especially millet, almonds, pototoes, buckwheat.

Milk lowers cholesterol levels. Its orotic acid content suppresses the liver's ability to manufacture cholesterol. But since the body needs some cholesterol, milk should never be used to excess.

Never use condensed milk. It has 15% sugar added to it to create a thick liquid. The sugar accounts for 40% of the content, with no vitamins added.

There is a controversy over whether or not we should mix cereal with milk. Those opposed believe the mixture prevents thoroughly chewing the grains, which absolutely must be chewed and mixed with saliva before they enter the digestive tract. Those approving believe this problem can be overcome simply by being aware of the need of thorough chewing. The benefits are that milk is rich in calcium while grains contain phosphorus—a most important mineral combination. Also, since grains are "incomplete" proteins—that is, lacking in one essential amino acid—mixing cereals with milk makes the meal an excellent protein choice.

Those who oppose cows' milk should make milk of sesame seeds or almonds or soybeans, any of which are a source of complete protein. Almond milk is made by mixing the nuts with water and honey in the blender. Use it over cereal for a meal both delicious and nutritious.

Ice Cream

Do avoid commercial ice cream, a milk derivative. Time was when homemade ice cream was the major family treat. Made with whole eggs straight from the nest, raw unprocessed milk and raw sugar, it was laboriously cranked in an ice filled freezer until it hardened—an excellent food indeed.

Today, in our synthetic age, it is far removed from the "good old days." The "ice creams" of now are synthetic from beginning to end. Here is the usual analysis:

Diethyl Glucol—the chemical used in antifreeze and in paint removers, is used as an emulsifier instead of eggs.

Piperonal—a chemical for killing lice, is used as a substitute for pure vanilla.

Aldehyde Cl_7—an inflammable fluid which is a basic chemical in aniline dyes, plastic and rubber, is used to flavor cherry ice cream.

Ethyl acetate—a chemical for cleaning leather and textiles, is used as a substitute for pineapple flavoring. Its vapors cause chronic lung, liver and heart damage.

Butyraldshyde—an ingredient in rubber cement, is used in nut flavored ice cream.

Amyl acetate—an oil paint solvent, used for its banana flavor.

Benzyl acetate—a nitrate solvent, is used for its strawberry flavor.

Formaldehyde—a substance used in embalming the dead, is frequently added as a preservative.

Eat a dish of this "ice cream" at your own risk!—and risky it is. Eaten with any regularity it has been known to cause so many digestive and intestinal problems, they are "unlistable!"

Do seek natural ice cream recipes from natural food cookbooks. There is an excellent one in Astara's *Light and Life Cookbook*, of which I was co-author.*

May I suggest making a milk substitute for your ice cream using almonds, honey and water in a blender, to which a thickener—arrowroot or slippery elm powder—may be added if needed. Honey may also be used as a sweetener for the entire recipe, or fruit juices—rather than sugar. Other thickeners or sweeteners include carob powder or ground nuts.

Top your homemade ice cream with carob sauce—instead of "hot fudge." Just mix the carob with milk, vanilla, honey and heat only until well blended. Add a thickener if desired.

Or make banana ice cream. Use ripe bananas. Peel them and place them flat, or layer deep, in a plastic bag. Place them in your freezer. After they are frozen, remove them from the plastic bag and put them through a blender. You may want to blend with them other fresh fruits such as berries, peaches, grapes—or add chopped nuts.

---

* See back pages of this book for further references.

Butter

Always use raw sweet butter. It is rich in vitamins A, D and E. Use all butter in moderation. The usual butter is processed and the salt content is detrimental and excessive.

You may want to dilute your intake of butter by mixing butter with your favorite oil, such as sesame. Or you may wish to make your own butter. Here is a recipe (from Dr. Som's kitchen):

Olive Butter

Open, drain, rinse and drain again 1 can Graber Olives. Pour in blender enough vegetable oil such as corn, soy, olive (one oil or two mixed)... enough to cover blades. Pit olives and drop in blender. Keep turning blender on every dozen olives or so until thick butter is formed. If too thick add more oil. Pour in glass jar and refrigerate.

Cottage Cheese

Always choose the raw type. Eat all cottage cheese in moderation since even the raw has been processed. Its asset is that it is an excellent protein and a good source of vitamin A, riboflavin (vitamin B2) and calcium—and low in calories.

Almonds

Always choose unblanched almonds. Almonds are 18% pure complete protein. They also contain salicylate—the active pain-killing agent in aspirin. So for a headache or other pain, chew a handful of raw almonds—four or five is equivalent to one aspirin. They do not upset the stomach lining as do aspirin.

For almond preserves, mix 1 pound of finely ground almonds with 1 pound of honey. Cook slowly until thick. Serve as preserves, or add two tablespoons to a glass of water for a quick energy drink.

Cashews

These nuts should be eaten in great moderation. They have been exposed to extremely high heat, to remove *cardol*, a poisonous oil in the shell. Before removal, the cashew contains properties similar to poison ivy, poison oak and poison sumac. The high heat required to destroy the poisonous oil also destroys many of the nutrients of the nut and renders it rancid even before it begins its long journey to America—usually from India, Brazil, Mozambique, Tanzania or Pakistan.

Its asset is that it is a complete protein and contains phosphorus, fat, iron and niacin in substantial quantities.

Peanuts

Always eat them raw, and in great moderation. Limit yourself to six a day. Thus taken, they can eliminate liver problems. Taken beyond that, they increase liver problems and cause other digestive upsets.

Never eat roasted salted nuts. The roasting has released toxic oils and the salt is excessive for the entire system.

Sesame Seeds

Sesame is called a food for the gods. So they should be equally beneficial to mortals.

At any rate, mortals have made much use of them since the days of antiquity. Today they are more important than even for the ancients. The seeds are sprinkled liberally over salads, the ground meal is used in baking, the oil is used for untold purposes (including cosmetics), and sesame butter—known as *tahini*—is of paramount importance in many diets, especially that of the vegetarian.

It is perfect protein. It also contains B-complex vitamins, especially niacin, and is an excellent source of calcium, phosphorus, potassium, vitamin E. Do eat it in liberal portions. It is excellent as a topping for chopped fruit, thus combining protein and fruit sugars. It also contains lecithin which lowers cholesterol. Its protein content compares to that of beef.

Sunflower Seeds

These miniature dynamos contain every known vitamin except vitamin C—and even develop this one when they are sprouted. They are also a perfect protein. Their vitamin D content is especially potent.

They are equally power-packed with minerals and trace elements, especially potassium.

One cup of sunflower seeds contains 34.8 grams of protein; 174 mg. of calcium; 1214 mg. of phosphorus; 10 mg. of iron; 1334 mg. of potassium; 2.8 mg. of vitamin B1; 33 mg. of B2; and 7.8 mg. of B3.

So eat abundantly!

In addition, their pectin content binds radioactive strontium 90, found in the intestinal tract, and carries the toxin out of the system. Their natural oil coats the intestinal wall for further protection.

Soybeans

Soybeans possess all the qualities of other beans—high in perfect protein, rich in vitamins and minerals—but they possess an added treasure, a substance called *lecithin*, described below.

They also contain a substance called *protease* that aids in preventing cancer. Tests have proven that protease protects against skin and breast cancer. It acts as an inhibitor which prevents the protein in beans and seeds from deteriorating.

Use soybeans in numerous ways—cooked like other beans, sprouted for salads, ground into flour, or liquified as soymilk. A by-product called *Tofu*, a curd cheese, is excellent in many versatile preparations.

Lecithin

Lecithin (pronounced *less*-e-thin) is a natural substance found in every cell in the body—and necessary to the health of that cell.

Research indicates lecithin restores deficient cells to normal, which means the intake of lecithin could retard aging, since damaged cells and tissues contribute to aging.

Lecithin dissolves incrustations of plaques, cholesterol deposits and other hardened debris lining the walls of the arteries. Since "hardening" of the arteries is a major cause of most illnesses, and certainly of old age, again lecithin may be important if one expects to remain youthful.

It lowers blood pressure. It feeds the brain cells with choline and inosital, two needed elements to insure mental alertness, sharp memory and mind power. It provides protection against infections. It feeds the skin needed acids which destroy the bacteria causing eczema, acne, and psoriasis.

This incredible substance is a natural tranquilizer, containing many elements necessary for healthy nerves.

Lecithin is necessary for proper functioning of the sex organs. The seminal fluid of both sexes contains a rich supply of lecithin—or should if the sex glands are functioning at peak performance. Lecithin should be taken to insure glandular hormones and to maintain a generous flow of lecithin-rich semen.

Brewer's Yeast

Many would like to make brewer's yeast a part of their diet since it is proclaimed to be a "wonder food." But they experience distress in the digestive tract—excessive gas. To overcome the problem of gas, always take the yeast on an empty stomach, never with meals.

Begin the yeast intake gradually, a half teaspoon at a time. Work up to a tablespoon. The body gradually becomes accustomed to the intake of yeast and responds with the necessary acids and digestive enzymes if the intake is gradual.

To aid this process, mix the powder or flakes with an acid fruit juice, such as grapefruit, lemon or pineapple. Or add the yeast to a glass of water with a tablespoon of apple cider vinegar.

As with grains, the yeast and liquid mixture must be chewed thoroughly, never drunk. It should mix with saliva in the mouth, which contains the enzymes necessary for proper digestion.

Brewer's yeast, being a high protein food, needs hydrochloric acid in the stomach to be properly digested. Any of the above mixtures should supply this stomach acid. If distress is still experienced, take a hydrochloric acid tablet when you take your yeast.

Much more could be said about proteins but, to repeat, the information is widely available elsewhere. This book must focus on many things, so I shall hold the protein parade to a minimum and move on to other items in the diet which are equally vital.

CHAPTER 3
FRUITS AND VEGETABLES— THE CREAM OF THE CROPS

Being neither by his physical nor his moral constitution of the order of the carnivora, man can be the best that he has in him to be only when his system is cleansed and built up anew of the pure materials derived from the vegetable kingdom, and indicated by his structure as his natural diet. The soul of the beatific vision is the intuition. And not only is the system, when flesh-fed, repressive of this faculty, but the very failure of the individual to recoil from violence and slaughter as a means of sustenance or gratification, is an indication of his lack of this faculty.

"The Virgin of the World"
Hermes Mercurius Trismegistrus

Having touched on the subject of protein, I shall now focus on fruits and vegetables. Because I found them to be all-important in my recovery program, and because I found little literature to help me research their value and content, I shall lay emphasis upon them in these writings. I truly believe the health advocate should be aware of the vitamin-mineral content of fruits and vegetables, and the part they play in healing the body.

When writing of protein, I stated that even though many nutritional experts claim that complete proteins can be found only in animal products, the latest nutritional research reveals that complete proteins can also be found in plant foods. And many plant proteins are superior to those found in animal sources. The vegetable or plants containing all the essential amino acids include soybeans, oats, barley, yeast, peanuts, mushrooms, almonds, buckwheat, millet, sesame seeds, cashews, sunflower seeds—which we covered in the protein lesson. Others in the list include potato, all dark green leafy vegetables, avocado, banana, brown rice, whole rye, wheat germ, watermelon seeds, mustard greens, sweet corn, sweet potato, coconut, garbanzo beans, pecans, pumpkin seeds, peas.

Protein is not our main energy-producing food. The main sources of fuel for energy are carbohydrates and fats. We should be eating 60 to 80% carbohydrates (fruits and vegetables), 20% fats, and only 10 to 25% protein. Women need only 45 grams of protein daily—approximately 1.62 ounces. And men need only 60 grams—approximately 2-1/2 ounces.

ORGANIC VEGETABLES

Organic soils are those which are rich in decomposed plant material—soil that has had the stubs of previous crops plowed back into it, for instance, and which has been fed with natural animal waste or compost. Those which are grown on the natural soils—those fed with plant, human and animal waste matter—are what is known as "organically grown foods." That which is inorganic is soil to which has been applied chemical compounds such as nitrates, phosphates and potash. These are known as chemical fertilizers. Fruits and vegetables grown on these chemically fertilized soils are known as inorganic foods. These foods are less sturdy and cannot resist attack by insects, thus, to protect them they are sprayed with chemical pesticides. Further along in their journey to the market they are dyed or coated with wax or exposed to chemical gasses.

The crops grown in chemicalized soil cannot possibly contain the proper vitamins and minerals needed for human health because the land, highly fertilized with chemicals, is a soil that is sterile. True, the chemicals may temporarily cause increased growth of the produce, but increased growth does not guarantee vital food elements necessary to sustain vital health.

Health has not and never has been a matter of medical care. Physicians and their families get the best medical care in the world but they are just as sickly and die, on the average, at the same age as the rest of us, and with the same complaints—the cancer, the heart attack, the stroke, and all the others. Our health begins and ends with the soil and our future rests with agriculture. With each crop taken off the farms and with the driving rains of each passing year, our farm lands have become poorer and poorer, yielding less nutritious crops and costing more each year to produce.

Our soil depletion is robbing us of a natural proteinaceous diet with its resulting firm joints, sound hearts, fecund capacity, good teeth and resistance to all common infections, and ability to grow and repair the wear and tear of the human body. Physical fitness, with the resulting long and healthy life, with a mind bright and alert to the end, begins and ends with good nutrition. Good nutrition depends upon good muscular tone, good digestive powers and good food. Good food, in turn, depends not only on the way we harvest it, select it, preserve it, process it, cook it and serve it but, primarily and above all, upon the quality of the soil in which it is grown.

Most people think of health in terms of disease. We have been programmed to think of health as a struggle to keep out of the physician's or dentist's office, so we approach health from a negative standpoint. Over the long haul, health can be measured in terms of physical fitness, mental alertness, resistance to disease and the ability to produce healthy offspring. A sound nutritional state is the first requirement to help us meet these demands.

To be sure, our animal farmers know a great deal about nutritional programming for their cattle, pigs, sheep and horses. They seem far more interested in seeing that their food supply is pure and nutritious than in the food we humans eat. They seem much less concerned that humans suffer a lack of essential minerals from the soil as well as the necessary vitamins. The longer the land is farmed, the more it becomes depleted of the minerals and vitamins essential to good health. A great portion of the soil of America has long since been demineralized. Valuable soil nutrients have been lost due to year after year of farming without replacing the nutrients naturally. All this makes it quite impossible to obtain our full quota of minerals from the foods we eat today. We must then include certain products from the sea in our diet.

Every individual should be aware that our soil is our life and that what we do to our soil influences the basic answer to health. Few of us have a direct contact with agriculture. We actually know little about soil and water conservation. But we do know that something appalling is happening to the land and we do know that our very life depends on it. God knew what He was doing when He made soil and seed. Agricultural science most certainly cannot improve on natural nutrition. All it does is disrupt the natural chemical formula that God planned.

CHEMICAL INSECTICIDES

In addition to chemical fertilizers, commercial producers use deadly poisons in the form of synthetic sprays whose purpose is to kill insects. But, sad to say, they also kill the humans who eat the food. The sprays are insecticides which always leave a toxic residue on the plant and toxic absorption into the plant. Thus, when you eat inorganic commercially grown food, you are absorbing such poisons through both the roots and leaves of the plants. Such poisons, absorbed into the body, reduce its ability to respond to normal functioning. Glands and organs are affected. Eventually they cease to be able to eliminate the cumulative poisons from chemical fertilizer and chemical sprays.

Insecticides and pollutions from perpetual smog and atmospheric fall-out found on food have the same deleterious effect as antibiotics on the system except in a less drastic way. Insecticides contain chemicals deliberately selected for their ability to kill insects and bacteria, both bad *and* good.

Entering the body, the chemicals gradually strip the walls of the intestines of its protective villi, eventually leaving the raw walls exposed to acids, alkalines, painful inflammation, irritations, gasses, and the toxins of undigested foods. This is why we suggest organically grown food when possible—foods not raised in chemicalized soil and not exposed to cultural sprays or chemical preservatives. It is admittedly very difficult to obtain such food and often we are forced to compromise.

THE VALUE OF FRUITS AND VEGETABLES

Those not familiar with the proper nutrition declare that it is not possible for humans to thrive or even survive on a vegetarian diet, especially raw natural foods. How then is it that all our horses, cows, sheep, hogs, and domesticated animals thrive better on raw food? If left to their natural eating patterns, they live from six to ten times their age of maturity—whereas man struggles to survive two and one-half times his age of maturity.

A horse matures at three years, 25 years is old for him. Cows also mature at three, usually living to fifteen or twenty years. Hogs mature at one year, ten being their total age. Man, on the other hand, reaches full development usually around twenty. By all rights, he should live at least seven times that number of years—or to 140. Why does not man thrive and survive as well as animals? Could it be that instead of "living by what we eat," we die by what we eat?

The value of raw foods—a salad at least once a day—is that waste matter never accumulates in the system. Waste or phlegm cannot thrive in a physical system that is clean. Bacilli and germs are given no opportunity to penetrate the organs because the body itself will throw them out before they have time. A diet of cooked food causes the membranous tissues to weaken. They are stripped of their dynamic power to combat the bacilli and germs of disease. Those who live mostly on cooked foods and a meat diet lack dynamic energy and internal cleanliness. Waste matter accumulates in organs, tissues and cells. The result is often infectious diseases, arthritis, and the complete gamut of poor health.

Tissue cells can be regenerated completely from fruits, vegetables, nuts and seeds. Such a diet can completely rebuild the body if some form of exercise and deep breathing are also practised. Fruits should be taken in the morning. Vegetables grown above ground should be eaten as a salad at noon. Root vegetables grown below ground should be emphasized at night. Mixed nuts and seeds should be eaten in moderation intermittently with these foods. When this rebuilding program has restored the body to health, there should be added the grains, the legumes, and possibly the eggs, milk and cheese if the individual experiences a need for their nutritional input.

Fruits will digest and be partially removed from the body within 20 to 30 minutes. Concentrated foods of refined starch, sugars and meat require four to six hours, and when leaving the body, leave deposits of waste and toxins. Since these are simply facts in nature, it is obvious that when the body is in the process of healing, fruits and vegetables, nuts and seeds are required. They move quickly and easily out of the body and, since they dissolve mucus, take with them much of the waste, the toxins and debris. They contain natural oils and roughage. The oils dissolve the encrusted debris and the roughage acts as a broom, gathering up the waste deposits and discharging them.

The peristaltic action resulting from eating leafy greens may create increased gas in the beginning since accumulated phlegm will be mixing with the leafy fibers, but continuous consumption of raw greens will eventually sweep the stomach clean of the phlegm and there will be no more flatulence. The gas buildup when eating raw live food is not caused by the food but by the stirring up of accumulated phlegm. Such gas activates the bowels through which the phlegm will gradually be expelled. A small portion of raw potato daily will do much to remove phlegm from the stomach. Also raw apples, carrots and rutabaga aid in such cleansing.

If there is a build-up of gas pressure, drink warm water rather than effervescent preparations which cause belching. The warm water will open the pyloric valve, causing the gas to pass out through the bowels.

Many fanatics, seeking rapid purification, hope to do so through an all-fruit diet. Fruits do act as cleansers of the body and provide the best material needed by the cell tissues. But fruits can form the complete diet only for those who are in no way contaminated by wrong eating, atmospheric pollution or toxic buildup. Such people are rare indeed. Those who are recovering from illness require fruits, vegetables, seeds and nuts. Fruits alone do not possess the proper material for tissue building. Above ground vegetables and roots are required. Vegetables contain the richest earth salts directly from the soil, particularly those grown underground— the carrot, beet, turnip, potato, radish, parsnip.

Since fruits and vegetables are necessary not only in a purification or rebuilding program, but as a regular diet, there are a few general rules to observe:

1. Wash every vegetable and fruit you purchase in apple cider vinegar and water—1/2 cup vinegar to a gallon of water. The vinegar must be apple cider, not white. (One cup of vinegar added to your washer during the rinse cycle cuts through soapy residue and leaves your laundry clean and fresh, removing many of the detergent chemicals often left in clothing which could cause potential allergic reactions).

Although the vinegar solution cannot remove the chemicals grown into the produce through the soil, it can remove much of the insecticides from the sprays and the fall-out of atmospheric pollution. Food should *never* be soaked since water leaches out the B and C vitamins. They should be rinsed in the vinegar water, then immediately rinsed in clear cold water to remove the vinegar.

They should then be dried to remove as much water as possible before storing. Root vegetables may be wiped dry. Leafies must be shaken thoroughly, then whirled in a salad whirler (which are now available in household departments) or whirled in a cloth bag such as an old pillowcase or lingerie bag. A good salad depends on the removal of all water from the greens so that they may absorb the salad oil and herbal seasonings.

2. Never cut up, peel or break vegetables or fruit before using. The moment the skin, the cap, or any protective covering is cut into or broken, exposing the cut surface to air, the loss of vitamins-minerals-enzymes begins, especially vitamin C. Many cooks habitually peel or slice food long before cooking, storing it or allowing it to stand at room temperature.

You know how quickly an apple

turns brown once the skin is removed? The same deterioration happens to all other foods without being obvious. So keep all food intact as nature made it until ready to cook or eat. Potatoes, for instance, develop chemicals known as solanine alkaloids when cut and stored. These are poisonous. Sunlight exposure adds to the poison. Avoid long-standing potatoes, potato salad, etc. To help avoid loss of nutrients, chill before cutting, and use stainless steel utensils to cut them. Then sprinkle the cut edge with lemon juice or apple cider. Once cut, refrigerate or eat immediately. Tear lettuce by hand or cut with clean scissors to conserve nutrients.

3. Never use rusty pots or pans or chipped dishes or cups. Foods absorb dangerous elements from the rust. The chips on dishes or cups immediately attract bacteria. Discard them.

4. Never use aluminum cookingware. Aluminum sloughing off into food is deadly. Choose steel, glass, Corningware or enamel—and do choose a wok vessel if possible, or cook foods covered in a heavy vessel so that their own juices are retained and no water need be added.

5. Never boil vegetables. Almost all nutrition is destroyed in the process. Use a waterless cooking method—vessels with lids which allow no steam to escape. Or choose a double boiler. Add a few tablespoons of water to the upper pan and, placing it above the lower pan, bring it to a rolling boil. Then add the vegatables and continue the high boiling until all water has evaporated from the top.

My favorite method is to steam vegetables in a wok, using just enough water to prevent sticking. This method allows food to cook in its own juice and no nutritional elements are discarded as in the boiling method, when most of the food value is poured down the drain with the discarded water. The wok should never be heated to the smoking point. The wok lid should cover the food to allow it to steam rather than fry. It also protects from exposure to oxygen while cooking, which can destroy vitamins.

In the wok, add as little water as seems necessary for steaming. Occasionally you may feel it necessary to add *a few drops of oil*. Often only oil is used which is a mistake. It means the vegetables are saturated and served with heated rancid oil, and often "stir-fried," which again means the oil-frying has destroyed much of the food elements. So do use more water than oil so that the food is steamed, not fried. To the water add tamari or soy sauce for seasoning. Also chop onion and add herbs, such as marjoram, basil, thyme, dill, etc.

Stir the vegetables with two wooden spoons. The leafy vegetables require only a moment or two and most of the fibrous vegetables require less than five minutes. Harder vegetables, such as carrots and green beans, require longer.

My second favorite method of cooking to preserve nutrients is baking. My favorite method of cooking root vegetables such as potatoes, artichokes, yams, carrots and parsnips is first to scrub the skin carefully or, in the case of artichokes, trim away the sharp points of the leaves. Then I rub them with my favorite cooking oil, such as safflower or sesame, and place them in a paper bag and into the oven for one or two hours at about 350°F.

My next favorite method is simply to secure a heavy baking dish, baking the vegetables the required length in the oven, or mixing vegetables with a basic protein grain, such as millet, and baking the required time.

Steaming—other than in the wok—is desirable only if done properly. If not, it can be the least desirable method of cooking vegetables, because steaming requires greater amounts of water into which many of the minerals and vitamins are lost. If steaming, however, is your method be sure to use stainless steel, pyrex, or pottery. Add very little water and steam over a very low flame saving any of the leftover liquids for adding to your next steaming dish.

To repeat, avoid aluminum cookingware. Diverticulitis and colitis (inflamed colon) have been found to heal rapidly when the patient switched from aluminum cooking vessels to glass or enamel, iron pots or stainless steel. Enamel cookingware is excellent if the enamel is intact. Discard it when it cracks or peels since the cracks tend to rust. Corningware is excellent. Iron cookware is also excellent because foods cooked in them leach the iron which is always beneficial. Also stainless steel may leach a bit of chromium into food which is also beneficial.

When cooking via casserole, always pre-heat the oven so that the dish cooks in less time. The longer the cooking time, the less nutritional the food.

6. Never cook vegetables in a pressure cooker—beans are the only exception.

7. Always choose fresh vegetables rather than canned or frozen. If you must use frozen occasionally, cook while still frozen. Do not allow thawing.

8. Never use baking soda in cooking, even baking. The alkaline of the soda destroys the acids in food, transforming them into useless salts. The soda also destroys the hydrochloric acid in the stomach, so needed for proper digestion.

9. Eat organically grown natural foods as near as possible to the way God made them. Avoid processed foods such as white sugar products, white flour products, crackers, chips, TV dinners and concentrated weight control protein drinks. Processed foods contain many undesirable elements.

One particularly undesirable is *nitrite*, which destroys Vitamin A, causes thyroid deficiency, dizziness, unsteady gait, irregular heartbeat, difficulty in breathing, low blood pressure, lowered body temperature and poor circulation. Nitrates and nitrites are formed when nitrogen fertilizer is used to increase crop yields. Thus, not only is man being poisoned through such food, but also animals who eat the grains—and are then eaten by man. The liver is able to handle many of these poisons unless refined and processed food is consumed, such as white sugar and white flour products.

10. Eat only foods that spoil and eat them before they do. Avoid foods

containing chemical preservatives, artificial colorings (dyes), emulsifiers, sugars and foods which have been waxed. Avoid smoked and charbroiled foods. Smoked meat has been found to cause cancer in populations consuming this type of food regularly. Avoid roasting meats, also. Such a process provides the formation of carcinogenic hydrocarbons—cancer causing elements. Never leave cooked meats standing outside refrigeration for hours, especially chicken. Many undesirable elements form.

11. Choose raw certified milk, raw natural cheese, raw sweet butter. Avoid processed milk products, such as: pasteurized, homogenized, dried, canned milk, cooked preserved cheeses, and processed butter. Make your own yogurt and ice cream if possible.

12. Choose cold pressed oils with no preservatives such as sesame, safflower, olive, peanut or soya. Avoid hydrogenated (hardened) heat-treated oils, such as lard and most margarines. Choose safflower, sesame, or olive oil for frying.

13. Avoid soft drinks with or without sugar. They contain dyes, flavorings, etc., which exhaust the pancreas and adrenals. Choose natural fruit and vegetable juices.

14. Avoid commercial candies containing chocolate, sugar, dyes, flavorings and chemical preservatives. Choose products made with carob, honey, fructose, and other natural products—and eat even these in moderation.

15. Use butter rather than margarine. But to dilute the animal fat in butter, blend 1/2 pound of raw sweet butter with 1/2 cup of sesame, safflower or olive oil.

16. Avocados and tomatoes should be sliced just before serving.

17. Many vitamin-mineral tablets, even in health stores, are covered with colored shiny coatings. Some are natural vegetable coatings, some are artificial chemical coatings, and some are made of plastic. The chemicals used are frequently F, D and C Red #5 Lake, Blue #2 Lake, Yellow #6 Lake. Only in 1978 was a coloring dye called Red #2 removed as a cancer causing chemical. Be sure to scan your vitamin products carefully before purchasing. Make sure the colored covering is not chemical synthetic dyes. There are many products with coatings of natural vegetables dyes. These should certainly be chosen.

18. Do include lecithin in your diet. Lecithin is a natural oil derived from soybeans, whole grains, eggs, sesame seeds. It lowers cholesterol levels and prevents plaques forming on arterial walls, thus improving circulation. It may be taken in granule form or in tablets. Liquid lecithin is an excellent healing balm when applied to exterior ulcers, sores and wounds. Lecithin is necessary for the production of semen in the reproductive organs of both sexes. It also provides choline for superior brain functioning. Anyone needing psychiatric assistance—including hyperactive children—would do well to take lecithin rather than drugs. Lecithin could quickly restore normalcy.

19. Use black pepper sparingly. This is a controversial condiment. When it was tested on mice at the University

of Kentucky, they developed cancer of the liver, lungs and skin. These scientists believe it to be toxic. Others believe it has a stimulating effect upon the digestive organs, which would make it an excellent digestive aid. So you must use your own judgment as to *your* choice.

COMBINING FOODS

Even the raw food diet can cause acid in the system if wrong foods are combined. For instance, never mix fruits with cereals or starches. They will quickly ferment, causing acidosis.

Be particularly aware not to mix fruit with cereal when feeding an infant. Such a combination can create all manner of digestive problems for an immature system, not only during infancy but perhaps later in life.

Often fruits mixed with vegetables also cause acidosis, although there are many cases when it seems not to cause distress. There are also many instances when such a mixture is unwise. One would need to be constantly aware, so why not simply avoid mixing fruits and vegetables, especially acid fruits. To avoid a more lengthy discussion concerning food combinations, we simply reproduce here a chart found in Astara's *Light and Life Cookbook** which completely simplifies a complicated subject. One can tell at a glance the safe combinations.

* Available from bookstores or Astara's New Leaf Book Shop. See back pages of this book for details.

C—Combine well
N—Not acceptable combinations
A—Acceptable combinations with some exceptions
   (Example Rule No. 8)

	Vegetables	Fruits	Melons	Proteins	Starches
Vegetables	C	A	N	C	C
Fruits	A	C	N	A	N
Melons	N	N	C	N	N
Proteins	C	A	N	C	N
Starch	C	N	N	N	C

CHAPTER 4
THE VALUE OF VEGETABLES

Nature has given the body all the necessary parts and innate functions to keep it in excellent condition provided you treat it with care. Have you noticed that the incomparable Mother has provided a thermostat in the body to control its temperature? Whether the atmosphere is hot or cold, the body temperature remains the same.

When you cut your finger, Nature immediately forms a wall around the injury, blockading it so that infections will not spread to the blood stream. The great Mother is always on guard to protect you. She will aid you in every possible way if you will only give her the opportunity. Making vegetables an important part of your diet is aiding Nature in the best possible way.

To obtain their highest benefits, vegetables should be ripened before eating. The following vegetables should be part of every diet: artichokes, asparagus, avocado, beans, beets, beet greens, broccoli, bok choy, brussel sprouts, cabbage, carrots, cauliflower, cucumber, celery, chard, Chinese cabbage, whole kernel corn, eggplant, garlic, kale, kelp, kohlrabi, leeks, lentils, mushrooms, mustard greens, okra, onions, parsnips, peas, peppers, potatoes, radishes, soybeans, spinach, squash, sprouts, string beans, turnips, tomatoes, turnip greens, yams.

The leafy greens should include red leaf lettuce, butterleaf lettuce, romaine, endive, parsley, escarole, and watercress. Choose the green leafed lettuces rather than iceberg head lettuce, because they are richer in chlorophyl, vitamins and minerals. All the green leafies contain rich sources of calcium, iron and potassium. All these vegetables contain mineral salts and fibers necessary for health, such as silicon, phosphorus and iron.

Vegetables—and fruits—contain all the elements in their very purest form, easily assimilated into the tissues and bloodstream. They also contain all the necessary vitamins and minerals. As many as possible should be eaten in their raw natural state. In addition, they are filled to capacity with pranic life force, indrawn from the vital sun rays and through the soil of the great Mother Earth.

ARTICHOKES

Artichokes, high in protein, are a source of vitamins A, B, and C. They also contain calcium, iron, phosphorus, and potassium. They are excellent as a kidney stimulant and for aiding a sluggish liver. Their iron content makes them valuable for anemics. Their bland texture makes them easy to digest. They are good for diarrhea, rheumatism, inflammation of the nerves and malfunctioning glands. Never cook artichokes in a pot of boiling water. They should either be steamed or prepared thusly: remove the outer leaves, most of which will have turned a spotted brown. They will be saturated with pollutions and chemical pesticides. Rinse the vegetable in vinegar water, then in clear cold water, pat dry. Pour a small amount of olive or sesame oil on a paper towel and coat the bottom of an iron skillet. Cut the artichoke in half and turn the flat side down in the skillet and cover it airtight. Place the skillet over heat turned as low as possible and cook until the leaves are tender—possibly an hour and a half. This baking-steaming method saves all nutrients and the artichoke is delicious.

ASPARAGUS

One serving of *asparagus* yields two grams of protein. It is rich in vitamins A and C. It also contains vitamin B sources such as thiamin, riboflavin and niacin, plus essential minerals—calcium, phosphorus, iron, potassium and sodium, making it one of the prime sources of vitamin-minerals in the vegetable kingdom.

Asparagus is especially excellent for those suffering with arthritis, cancer, tuberculosis, rheumatism, neuritis and the threat of kidney and gall stones. It is easy to digest for those with digestive problems. When purchasing, choose stalks that are green, tender and firm, with the tips close together. Avoid white stalks, they may be stringy and tough. Refrigerate as soon as possible and cook while fresh since it toughens rapidly.

Asparagus is best prepared by steaming. Tie it into a bundle and stand it stalk down in enough water to cover the thick stalk ends. Steam until the upper stalks are tender. Or you may chop the edible parts of the stalk and steam them in a wok with a little water, seasoned with herbs, tamari sauce and onions. Do not salt until serving at the table. (No food should be salted until it is served.) Do not immerse asparagus in water and boil it. Asparagus loses 60% of its vitamin C content when it is boiled

AVOCADO

Although the *avocado* is a fruit, it is so generally accepted as a vegetable, we include it here. The avocado is rich in vitamins A, B, and C and its high complete protein content makes it an important part of the diet, especially for vegetarians.

The avocado nourishes all nerve tissues of the brain, thus it could be called a "brain food." It is excellent for those who have a bad memory. It should be added to the diet of all females experienceing weakness of the female organs, and males with prostate problems. Its protein, fat, chlorophyl, potassium and phosphorus combine to make it an extraordinary food. Like the apple, avocado contains pectin which so dramatically reduces cholesterol in the blood. Its bland texture makes it an excellent food for those with ulcers, inflammed mucous membranes and colitis. Avocados should be ripened at room temperature, then refrigerated.

BEANS

Almost all *beans* are excellent food—especially for the vegetarian. To be a continued favored item, however, they must be properly prepared. Otherwise they produce distressing gas on the stomach. The causes of gas are the starches, stacchyasi and raffinose, found in most legumes. To remove these culprits, beans must be soaked overnight, the water discarded, and the beans rinsed again. The soaking also germinates the beans, causing them to become softer, easier to chew, tastier and less difficult to digest. They cook more rapidly also.

Since meat is becoming increasingly prohibitive, expensive and unhealthy, beans should certainly increase as a popular item in every diet. They become "complete" protein when mixed with grains, seeds, nuts or raw salads.

BEETS

Beets are rich in vitamin C. There are 50 milligrams in 1/2 cup of cooked beets—more if eaten raw in a salad. They also contain vitamins A and B. Their minerals are calcium, phosphorus, copper, magnesium, manganese, potassium, sodium, sulphur, zinc, and considerable iron—making it understandable why they should often be shredded or chopped into a raw salad. Beets are renowned as blood builders and blood purifiers because of their iron content. They are equally effective in healing inflammation of the kidneys and bladder, and in dissolving kidney stones. Shredded raw beets are an excellent therapy for leukemia or anemia. Or, if you drink raw vegetable juice, add an ounce of fresh beet juice twice a week. Just twice a week will overcome anemia. It is extremely potent.

Sip beet juice by the teaspoonful all during the day to stimulate the kidneys to release and eliminate kidney stones and other crystallized gravels. Through this beet-juice therapy, the stones are eliminated painlessly along with the urine. Do *not* drink it in large quantities. It will not be effective in this therapy and could make you ill. It must be taken in minute homeopathic portions, as just described, to be effective.

For highest benefits, beets should be eaten raw, shredded into salad. When cooked, the loss of vital force is obvious by observing the color of the cooking water. The water has leached out most of the vitamins, minerals and enzymes. If they must be cooked, then cook them without removing the skin, which may save some of the nutrients. When purchasing, avoid oversized beets—the core may be fibrous and tough. Beets may be kept at room temperature or refrigerated.

BEET GREENS

Beet greens are extremely rich in vitamin A and iron. Beet greens contain more iron than spinach. They also contain vitamins B and C—plus calcium, phosphorus and potassium. They are also high in protein. They are recognized aids for anemia, dysentery, lung problems, gout and gonorrhea. Avoid eating them to excess because of their high oxalic acid content. However, if eaten with the red root beet, they are safe, because the root contains magnesium, the very food necessary to combat oxalic acid in the body—which means Mother Nature intended we should eat the root and the greens together.

BLEU CHEESE

Since no special section concerning dairy products is included in this book, I am inserting this information concerning bleu cheese in the vegetable section because I feel it may be important to you.

Bleu cheese contains a nerve poison, or neurotoxin, called *roquefortine*. In tests performed on mice, this nerve poison caused convulsive seizures—but the mice were fed monumental amounts over a long period of time, considerably larger amounts than humans consume, and humans consume it along with other foods. So it is not suggested that you cease eating bleu cheese-roquefort salad dressings altogether, but hold them to a minimum. They are not necessarily dangerous since the bleu cheese is mixed with a number of other ingredients, diminishing the danger potential. Further reduce any ill effects by mixing a salad dressing of roquefort with a vinegar-oil dressing.

BROCCOLI

The *broccoli* flower and leaf should both be eaten, and together. Both the flower and the leaf are high in calcium, vitamins and copper.

Broccoli is rich in vitamin A. It also contains vitamin B and iron, potassium and phosphorus. It has a high protein content. Broccoli is recommended to reduce high blood pressure, to stimulate digestive glands, overcome constipation and heal neuritis. It is a sulphur food.

When purchasing, select green broccoli and avoid those that are yellowed. The flower clusters should be close together.

BRUSSEL SPROUTS

Brussel Sprouts are very high in vitamin C. They also contain vitamins A and B. They contain a generous supply of calcium, phosphorus, iron, sodium and potassium. They are rich in plant protein. They are noted as a sulphur food. They are often prescribed for arteriosclerosis (hardening of the arteries). They have a mild laxative effect, are excellent for intestinal catarrh and to balance acidosis.

BUTTER BEANS

Butter beans contain vitamins A, B and C. The mineral content is calcium, phosphorus and iron—especially iron. Butter beans are renowned as blood builders. They are equally effective in healing inflammation of the kidneys and bladder, and in dissolving kidney stones.

Butter beans are large white matured lima beans. They are much more easily digested and are much more nourishing than the green limas. Because of their high iron content, they are frequently prescribed for anemia. Butter beans are delicious, not only as a main dish for vegetarians, but also served cold on a salad, providing ample protein.

CABBAGE

There are 50 milligrams of vitamin C in one cup of green raw *cabbage*. Cabbage also contains vitamins A and B. Its mineral content is calcium, iron, sodium, phosphorus and potassium. It is recommended as a blood purifier. Because of its high calcium content, it is excellent for preserving the enamel of the teeth and maintaining strong bones. Nails and hair respond when cabbage is included in the diet.

It is renowned as a sulphur food, making it excellent for diabetes, asthma, all lung complaints, and for kidney-bladder disorders. Its sulphur content also makes it an excellent purifier of the mucous membranes of the stomach and intestines, and for inflammation of the throat, mouth and eyes.

It is good for rheumatism and gout. It is extremely beneficial for pyorrhea when eaten in its raw state and chewed very thoroughly. Cabbage should be in the diet of all cancer patients and those with any kind of tumor, cyst, gangrene, lung infection and any condition resulting from a deficiency of lime and calcium salts. Cabbage compares favorably with any other food in vitamins and minerals, and is considerably richer in all nutrients than most foods.

Cabbage should seldom be cooked because heat destroys the nutrients and makes it a food which becomes "gassy." To obtain the remarkable food value from this amazing vegetable, it should be shredded just prior to serving and eaten raw with salads or in cole slaw. If you must cook it, it should be in the wok, with a small amount of water. Herbs may be added for seasoning. Salt should never be added—especially to cabbage—while cooking, but just prior to eating. Cook no longer than 5 or 10 minutes. Overcooking destroys the sulphur content.

When purchasing, choose the head with the greenest leaves. Immediately after purchase, the head should be washed in cold vinegar water, rinsed immediately, wiped dry and stored in a tightly covered crisper in the refrigerator. To preserve its high vitamin C content, it should never be soaked, since soaking leaches out vitamin-minerals. Contact with air also destroys vitamin C.

Fresh raw cabbage juice therapy is recognized as a cure for stomach ulcers because of its mysterious vitamins U and K, which seem to neutralize the effect of pepsin in the digestive tract—pepsin being a naturally occurring digestive enzyme often too powerful an acid for those with ulcers. Back in 1950, Dr. Garnett Cheney of the Department of Medicine of Stanford University conceived the notion of treating ulcer patients with cabbage juice—raw unheated cabbage juice. No other therapy was given. Each patient—in conjunction with regular meals—drank one quart of cabbage juice daily. Raw unheated juice was required since vitamin U, the mysterious healing factor, was destroyed with heat.

Sixty-five patients took part in this

experiment. Some added fresh celery-pineapple-citrus or tomato juice to their cabbage juice to improve the taste. Although several patients experienced some problems with gas and bloating, all but 3 of the 65 patients were healed of ulcers in 3 to 5 days. Following his experiment, Dr. Cheney placed his patients on a convalescent diet of raw fruit or vegetables at every meal, and raw vegetable juice including more cabbage juice.

Since the fresh cabbage juice therapy may be inconvenient for many peptic ulcer patients who wish to experiment with it, concentrated juice has now been made available in capsule form.

Sauerkraut—a by-product of the cabbage—is splendid as a tonic for the stomach and intestinal tract, the kidneys and urinary bladder, the liver and pancreas. Sauerkraut juice is rich in lactic acid so needed in jaundice, ulcers, anemia and constipation. It is excellent when mixed with tomato juice. Because of its high salt content, however, it should be avoided by those on a diet with salt restrictions.

CAROB

Carob is one of God's finest foods. It is almost identical to chocolate in taste, appearance and texture. It contains calcium, magnesium, potassium, silicon, iron, copper, manganese, phosphorus, sodium, aluminum, carotene—and several important B vitamins—thiamin, riboflavin and niacin.

Its thiamin content compares with that found in dandelion greens, watercress, asparagus and potatoes. Its niacin content compares with that found in dates, lentils, peas, lima beans, and other legumes. Its vitamin A content compares with that found in potatoes, radishes, onions, raisins, asparagus and eggplant.

Thus, its vitamin-mineral content makes it an excellent well-balanced food indeed, offering considerable nourishment, as opposed to chocolate. In addition, carob powder contains its own built-in natural sweetening; it needs no additional sugar. Indeed, carob may well be used in many recipes requiring sugar. The substitution is 3 Tbsp. carob plus 2 Tbsp. water to equal one chocolate square. It makes an excellent sugar substitute. Drink it instead of hot chocolate as a stimulating drink. Sprinkle it over cut-up fruit as a snack. You may wish to add tahini, shredded coconut, or diced almonds. According to Dr. Som, it can also be mixed with raw milk or sesame milk for patients suffering with diarrhea—especially infants and children—because of its high pectin and lignin content. Three and one-half ounces of carob powder contain one hundred eighty calories, while cocoa powder contains two hundred and ninety-nine.

The sugar occurring in carob is a natural sugar, as is the fruit sugar in fruits. It not only satisfies the desire for sweets, but it gives considerable energy. Not only that but, as opposed to refined white sugar, its own supply of B vitamins aid in digestion.

A sad commentary is that Americans—and especially children—eat incredible quantities of chocolate every day, not only in chocolate milk and in cocoa, but in chocolate bars, milk shakes, fudge sundaes, sodas, chocolate cake, chocolate doughnuts, and boxes of chocolate candy bought by the pound. The total amount per day is staggering, not only robbing the body of its needed calcium for bones and teeth, but forming dangerous calcium oxalate—to say nothing of the deadly poisonous white sugar in the chocolate confections, but also in chocolate's caffeine content, a substance called *theobromine*, a stimulant with destructive properties. It raises the blood sugar to a high level, then drops it dangerously low, creating hypoglycemia. The caffeine stimulates the heart and raises the blood pressure. Chocolate is now recognized as one of the major causes of acne in teenagers. There are also innumerable allergies to consider—blinding headaches, upset stomach, colds, itching anus, etc.

The difference between chocolate and carob—which resemble each other so closely—is that chocolate is totally destructive having not one single asset, while carob is a marvelous food, rich in vitamins, minerals, enzymes, protein and carbohydrates.

Carob is sometimes called *St John's Bread* and *Honey Locust*—the implication being that this is the food St. John the Baptist existed on during his sojourn in the wilderness of Jordan. Surely it is more logical to presume he ate these nourishing pods of plant food rather than the desert locust—which, incidentally, would have required not only fleetness of foot, but his undivided concentration on the elusive chase for food.

Carob products are in abundance in all health stores. Search for carob candy bars, cookies, cakes—or for cans of carob powder. Avoid the few brands containing sugar or corn syrup. Do not eat carob powder daily, however. Since it is an excellent remedy for diarrhea, if eaten daily it will tend toward constipation.

Do consider planting a carob tree in your yard. We had one at Astara when headquarters were located in Los Angeles. It grew at our back door and was beautiful. Many varieties are available from the nursery—the Casuda, Amele, Santa Fe, Iyliria, Molino, Conejo.

You may not be enthused about gathering the pods and securing the powder under ordinary circumstances—but be aware it may be a source of survival during disasters. The powder, rich in nutrients, is also a medicine, a remedy as old as history. The pectin and lignin it contains combine with harmful wastes—even destructive pollutions and radioactive elements—and carry them out of the body. Remember, too, its usefulness as a protein food, and as a remedy for all manner of intestinal infections and especially diarrhea. Its full nutritional and medicinal value may not yet be recognized by modern therapists and food researchers. But be aware of its potential.

CARROTS

In addition to their high vitamin A content, *carrots* are rich in all the B vitamins and in vitamin C, D, E, G and K. Their mineral content includes calcium, phosphorus, iron, chlorine, copper, sodium, magnesium, cobalt and zinc. Carrots are excellent to purify the bloodstream of toxins, to correct constipation, to aid in asthma and other lung complaints, to reduce high blood pressure, to soothe inflamed kidneys and bladder, for colitis (inflammation of the large intestine, especially the colon), and to correct poor eyesight.

Carrots contain a slight quantity of natural arsenic, thus are stimulating as a tonic. Their high content of Vitamin A has a tendency to beautify the complexion, the hair and eyes, in protecting against infection, and against night blindness. They are also excellent for nervous disorders and all stomach and intestinal problems. They should be a major item in the diet of every cancer patient.

The best possible way to derive the highest benefit is to eat raw carrots freshly shredded on a vegetable salad, and often—preferably daily. Prepare them just prior to serving or cooking since carrots (and indeed all vegetables) begin losing vitamin C the moment the surface is cut. So do eat carrots immediately after preparing.

Juice therapy is renowned for its healing qualities, and carrot juice is usually the basic ingredient. Carrot juice, being highly concentrated, supplies a rich source of carotene, the substance which reverts into vitamin A inside the body. If a choice must be made, however, it seems wiser to eat the carrot as a complete food rather than the concentrated juice, unless one is in need of high vitamin A intake.

True, drinking the juice releases the needed carotene directly into the blood stream, but, except for occasional juice therapy, it seems best to eat the whole vegetable since chewing the carrot with its fibrous texture stimulates and benefits the teeth and gums, and exercises the jaws.

Like apples, carrots are known as a "detergent" food, which means they help in cleansing the teeth and removing food particles from the mouth. Carrot sticks should be given to young children cutting their first teeth. They not only stimulate gum tissues but, in themselves, provide innumerable nutrients for the growing child. And the habit of eating carrot sticks may hopefully prevail throughout life. Eating the whole food also stimulates the peristalsis action of the intestines, benefiting elimination.

An Oriental method of aiding digestion is to chop and dice carrots and carrot tops, place them in a kettle with enough water to cover, and bring to a boil. Remove from the heat and allow to cool. Strain and refrigerate the tonic immediately and sip a small glass before or with each daily meal. This potion not only aids digestion but flushes the kidneys and bladder.

Dr. Som says carrot soup equals carob as a remedy for diarrhea. (See Astara's *Light and Life Cookbook* for recipe.) What exactly occurs in the case of diarrhea? The circulating body fluids, especially the blood, becomes depleted of water. The cells of the body respond by pouring out their own fluids to offset the deficit. When the body cells are finally depleted, a state of dehydration sets in. Dehydration means that the watery stools have carried out of the body its essential minerals such as potassium, calcium, magnesium, phosphorus and sodium.

If the diarrhea persists, the cells begin to dispose of their protein. If such a state continues, death usually results.

Carrot soup is renowned as a prime remedy. First of all, the liquid of the soup supplies water to the dehydrated body and cells. It immediately begins replenishing the lost minerals. The pectin in the carrot provides an antidiarrheal remedy. The thick, gentle substance of the soup coats the inflamed intestinal walls, not only healing them, but preventing further inflammation.

The consistency of the soup reduces the outflow of watery stools, simultaneously stimulating the growth of beneficial intestinal bacteria. Its destructive effect on undesirable intestinal bacteria prevents vomiting and, because of its effect on the peristalsis movement, it helps to eliminate toxins from the intestine.

After the first 24 hours of treatment, the patient may be given very ripe bananas or scraped apple pulp. The carrot soup diet usually has manifested a healing in about a week. If not, it may be continued indefinitely along with the bananas and apples. Raw milk may gradually be added to supply protein unless there are adverse reactions. If so, almond or sesame milk may be substituted.

The carrot soup treatment is also effective in treating diverticulitis, colitis, and other complaints of an irritated and inflamed intestine or colon, and can be used by both children and adults. Diluted carrot soup may be spoon-fed to infants with diarrhea or, if strained and diluted further, may be bottle-fed.

Carrots should never be peeled because the highest nutritional elements are interlaced and directly under the skin. A good scrubbing just prior to eating is all that is necessary, removing most of the objectionable dirt. Carrots—as well as other vegetables—should never be soaked in water to make them more crisp. The soaking leaches out the natural sugar and most of the vitamin-mineral content. As with other vegetables, they should be washed in vinegar water, dried and refrigerated in an air-tight container.

Or, if you prefer, do not even wash thoroughly until time for cooking. The skin should not be broken even by washing or scrubbing until just prior to eating. Cooking carrots, whether boiled or baked, results in the loss of most food value and all of the enzymes.

When purchasing, avoid the oversized. They are less tender and may have woody, fibrous cores. Check the tops for greenness and freshness. Avoid those whose tops are not fresh. Since carrot tops continually leach nutrition from the carrot, remove the tops as soon as possible. Raw carrot *tops* should be added occasionally to a salad because they are rich in vitamin K and magnesium. Magnesium is especially important in the diet as a recognized prevention of cancer. Carrots may be stored at room temperature or refrigerated.

CAULIFLOWER

Cauliflower is rich in vitamin A and C, and contains some B vitamins. It is high in calcium, iron and phosphorous and, surprisingly, in protein. Since it is a member of the cabbage family, it is a sulphur food, thus excellent as a blood purifier. And it is recommended for asthma, high blood pressure, constipation, and kidney-bladder problems. It is best eaten raw, chopped into a vegetable salad. If cooking is desired, it should be chopped into bite size pieces and steamed in a wok with very little water. Cauliflower should not be included in the diet of the gout patient because of its purine content.

CELERY

Celery, an alkaline vegetable, is rich in vitamins A, B and C. Its mineral content is calcium, iron, phosphorus, potassium, magnesium and sodium. Because of its high calcium content, celery is good for inflammation of the nerves, producing a sedative effect. Because it is alkaline, it is a blood purifier, flushing the inflamed kidney-bladder tract, for arthritis, rheumatism, gout, asthma, high blood pressure, diabetes and for the teeth and gums.

Celery juice is often added to carrot juice as a balanced raw juice therapy. It is excellent because of its magnesium and sodium content. Offer raw green celery sticks to babies cutting their first teeth. Like the carrot stick, the celery provides unnumbered nutrients as well as stimulation of the gum tissues.

Celery salt is an excellent seasoning for soups and stews. It is equally delicious sprinkled over salads and may well be used consistently as a salt substitute.

It may come as no small surprise to learn that all commercially grown celery is usually blanched or bleached. Some is thus processed by shading it completely during growth or blanching by ethylene gas. In the "gas chambers," highly concentrated streams of the gas saturate the celery anywhere from six to twelve days. The process prevents the celery from turning green which, for some strange reason, seems objectionable to the commercial producer. The ethylene gas completely destroys the chlorophyl in the vegetable and, along with the chlorophyl, all the vitamin A and most of the vitamin C and B.

In addition to the bleaching, the celery has, of course, been polluted during growth with poisonous sprays. So seek organically grown celery when possible. All celery should be well washed with vinegar water, rinsed, dried and refrigerated immediately in a closed container. Then, just prior to serving, it should be stripped of its strings which aids in removing at least some of the outer layer of the dangerous insecticides.

In a food such as celery, where the skin is so obviously porous, it is not possible to remove all of the preservatives. When purchasing—hopefully organically grown celery from a health store—choose the greenest stalks. Celery is also high in oxalic acid, but it contains offsetting nutrients.

CHARD

Chard—often called Swiss Chard—is remarkably high in vitamin A, calcium, phosphorous, iron, sodium and potassium. It also contains trace elements of the B vitamins—thiamin, riboflavin, and niacin. Because of its high iron and calcium content, it is excellent in treating anemia and insomnia. It also corrects constipation. High in oxalic acid—which prevents the absorption of calcium in the body—it also contains offsetting supplies of vitamins and minerals which make it an invaluable food. Since oxalic acid is only destructive when food is cooked, try adding raw chard to salads.

CONDIMENTS

Condiments were originally used to camouflage the taste of decaying foods, particularly meat. They are still used somewhat for the same purpose today. How often does the meat-eater reach for the ketchup, the tobasco, the Worchestershire, the A-1, the mustard, the black pepper, the pepper sauce or the gravy? There is an instinctive awareness that condiments add to the "flavor" of flesh food.

Black pepper, mustard, nutmeg and cloves are the worst offenders—excessive pepper is a proven culprit for producing cirrhosis of the liver. Spices which can be used with safety include: thyme, sage, paprika, allspice, cinnamon, mace and carroway seeds.

CORN

Corn is high in vitamin E. It also contains vitamins A, B and C and is high in protein. Its mineral content includes calcium, iron and phosphorus. Rich in magnesium, corn should be in the diet of every cancer patient. In areas where the population eats corn habitually as part of the diet, cancer is relatively rare. Corn is lacking in one essential amino acid—lysine—which prevents it from being a complete protein. But when the whole unprocessed grain is eaten along with a normal diet, the body seems to be able to absorb the lysine from other sources—especially if legumes, such as beans, are included in the diet.

Certainly corn was the principal protein food for unnumbered people in the past. When the Pilgrims first landed on our native soil, they were saved from starvation by friendly Indian tribes who showed them their principal food—corn. Corn eaten fresh and made into the tortilla—together with beans—sustained life for centuries in South American countries.

Like wheat, corn undergoes radical changes in modern processing plants. Before such tactics became available, corn was processed by "watergrinding"—which means it was ground between stones in a mill run by water. This stoneground cornmeal retained all the original food elements, including the corn germ.

But the meal was highly perishable. So a way of "refining" and preserving had to be found—the refining meaning that all the vital live food elements are now removed, including the germ, so that the corn meal has an indefinite shelf life—but no vital life force. Some vitamins and minerals are returned to it in an "enrichment" program, but they are synthetic—which means they are produced chemically—which, again, means they may be more dangerous than beneficial.

Thus, processed corn meal should be avoided, as well as corn starch. Substitute for corn starch natural thickening agents called arrowroot or tapioca flour. Purchase unprocessed or stone-ground corn meal from your health store, or Masa Harina corn meal, which is treated with lime water..

The Masa makes excellent corn tortillas by just adding boiling hot water—no oil. Mix it to the consistency of a thin corn cake. Place it inside a tortilla press and flatten the corn batter. The result will be a thin round tortilla. Place the tortilla in a greaseless skillet over high heat, flop it constantly until crisp. Eat it hot and fresh. You have prepared a most delicious bread substitute. This may be the answer to the bread problems for those who cannot handle wheat or other breads baked with oil.

America's favorite cooking procedure is corn-on-the-cob. Do not remove the corn husks until the moment of cooking. Keep them intact even in the refrigerator. This prevents exposure to the air and preserves the vitamin-mineral content. Remove the husks just prior to cooking. Bring a pot of water to a rolling boil and drop in the freshly husked ear of corn. It should cook at a high boil for *only three minutes*. It only needs to have the milk of the corn kernel heated thoroughly, and three minutes of rapid boiling is sufficient. Cooking beyond three minutes toughens the kernels considerably. The longer corn is cooked, the tougher the kernels become. Corn should never be salted until the time of eating. Avoid cooking in salted water. Corn-on-the-cob may also be steamed in the covered wok with very little water. Delicious!

Try roasting the corn in its husk in an open fire, or place in a hot oven until thoroughly heated. Corn fritters are excellent if they can be cooked in a dry skillet just coated with a touch of oil. Creamed corn can be prepared by adding a spoon of thick cream at the moment of serving.

Corn is one of humanity's basic foods. Corn oil is made from the germ. If you can find a corn oil product that is *cold pressed*, it is a good source of unsaturated fatty acids—linoleic acid. If not, better stay with the oils that are cold pressed—the sesame, the safflower, etc.

Avoid purchasing vitamin C presumably made from corn. Corn is not high in vitamin C, thus a number of chemical elements must necessarily have been added to produce sufficient ascorbic acid from corn. The chemical process will have destroyed every nutrient from the original corn. You should choose your vitamin C product from a source such as rosehips, ascerola berries, green peppers, or citrus fruits.

CUCUMBER

Cucumbers contain vitamins A, B, and C, calcium, iron, phosphorus and potassium. The cucumber is renowned as a natural diuretic stimulating the flow of urine. Its potassium content makes it extremely useful for both high and low blood pressure. It contains particular enzymes that aid in digesting protein. It is high in silicon and sulphur, thus is excellent to stimulate the growth of nails and hair. It is used in many cosmetic soaps and creams because of its benefits for the skin.

Adding cucumber juice to carrot juice is an excellent therapy for rheumatic conditions, because it dissolves excessive uric acid in the system and eliminates it in the waste. Its high mineral content makes it effective in healing pyorrhea of the gums. It is excellent as a liver purifier, and for inflammatory conditions, ulcers and skin disease. Do you see why you should often add thin slices of cucumber to a salad? When purchasing, select those that are long and slender, and are dark or medium green. Avoid those that are yellowed.

DANDELION GREENS

One serving of *dandelion greens* contains more than 15,000 units of vitamin A, and significant amounts of vitamin C, plus three of the B vitamins —thiamin, riboflavin and niacin. They are also rich in calcium, phosphorus, iron, sodium, potassium and are high in protein. They are excellent for purifying the liver and stimulating the gall bladder and spleen. Because of their high iron content, they are also excellent for anemia. They are effective in low blood pressure, constipation, poor circulation, and as a general blood purifier.

Actually, dandelion greens are one of the most splendid green vegetables. They grow wild in almost every yard and are free for the picking. Pick them when the shoots are young and tender, prior to the formation of flowers, and be sure to wash them in vinegar water. Rinse and dry before storing in an airtight container. When cooking, steam them in a wok to preserve their high food quality. You may wish to drain off the first cooking water to remove the bitter taste. Experiment.

EGGPLANT

Eggplant is rich in vitamins A, B, and C, and the minerals calcium, iron, potassium, sodium—and especially phosphorus. Eggplant should be part of the diet of every patient with ulcers, colitis and inflamed intestines. It also is effective as a mild laxative. Because of its thick skin, the "meat" of the eggplant escapes harm from insecticide sprays. The skin, not being porous, repels the chemicals. But, to be safe, the skin should be removed before cooking.

Frying destroys many of the nutrients. They should be baked plain —or sliced, peeled, dipped in beaten egg, then whole wheat flour or wheat germ and baked. Or they may be added to a casserole of other foods. They can be baked covered with chopped onions garnished with herbs and a bit of olive oil. Shredded cheese may be added when removing from the oven just prior to serving. The heat of the food melts the cheese sufficiently. Cheese should never be cooked atop any food —it becomes rancid oil.

ENDIVES

Endives are rich in vitamins A and C, and in calcium, phosphorus and potassium. They contain an average degree of iron. Endives should be added to every salad. They are effective in healing asthma, diabetes, anemia, high blood pressure, arthritis and liver problems. They stimulate the flow of bile through the liver and gall bladder. They are often used simply to decorate other foods—but eat those decorations!

GARBANZO BEANS (CHICK PEAS)

Garbanzos are high in protein. They also contain vitamins B and C, calcium, iron and phosphorus. They are excellent for persons with digestive problems, such as an ulcer or inflamed intestines because of their bland texture and easy digestability. Mashed garbanzos are delicious mixed with tahini (sesame butter). They are often added to a green salad to form a complete protein dish.

GARLIC

Garlic was one of Dr. Som's favorite "healers." He used it in numerous ways. His methods are suggested here.

Garlic contains vitamins A, B, and C, and is rich in minerals, such as aluminum, manganese, copper, sulphur, zinc, iron, calcium, phosphorus and potassium. It is also high in protein. The benefits and blessings from eating garlic or taking garlic perles or tablets are almost endless. In ancient times, when the thaumatergists believed food to be our best medicine, garlic was used as a principal healing agent.

Hypocrates, Galen, Pliny the Elder, St. Hildegard, Paracelsus and a host of other medieval nature healers relied heavily upon the therapeutic powers of garlic. They used it to combat indigestion, old age, skin diseases, respiratory ailments, worms, diarrhea, gas, chronic colitis, colic, headache, heart palpitations, ulcers, hemorrhoids, chronic inflammation of the lungs, swelling of the lymph glands, pains in muscles and joints. They recognized its potential to help polio, ear infection, pimples, open wounds, loose teeth, tartar deposits, typhus, cholera and tumorous growths such as cancer.

The ancient Egyptians, Babylonians, Chinese, Romans, Greeks and Vikings all used garlic as a remedy for practically all ailments, from intestinal disorders to senility.

Garlic compared with our penicillin as an effective antibiotic, except that with garlic there were no side effects. When diphtheria was rampant, garlic was prescribed for the patient to hold in his mouth, sucking upon it from time to time to release the garlic oil. In a very short time, his temperature abated and the symptons slowly disappeared.

Poultices of chopped garlic were also used to heal respiratory infections and skin problems, such as boils and draining sores. It was also used to heal tuberculosis. In tuberculosis sanitariums, the only cure prescribed was diet, rest, exercise, baths—and garlic. Garlic was the only medication employed. Garlic oil was given internally and garlic poultices were applied to the lungs and affected bone structures. Startling cures of this dread disease occured innumberable times— enough to establish garlic as an incomparable antibiotic against infectious disease.

In more recent times, as allopathic medicine and the use of drugs became increasingly pronounced, garlic and other natural food remedies ceased to be regarded favorably. But as we move further into the Aquarian Age, there is increasing acceptance of homeopathy, touch-for-health, acupuncture, herbs, iridology, polarity therapy and other methodologies by the holistic health movement and new age doctors.

A new breed of doctor in the United States, Russia, Germany, France, England — and indeed throughout the world — is beginning to emulate physicians of ancient days, the great healers of antiquity, in declaring food to be our best medicine and recognizing garlic to be supreme among food medicines. Garlic as a therapy is again becoming recognized.

In countries — Spain, for instance — where garlic is prominent in the diet, heart disease and high blood pressure is less than one-third that in the United States.

It has been used in experiments to prove its effectiveness in all the afflictions it aided in earlier decades plus many other disturbances — asthma, low and high blood pressure, diabetes, jaundice, anemia, whooping cough, influenza, heart disease, heartburn, nervousness, muscle cramps, nausea, chills and fever. Its principal function now is as an antibiotic against infections of the respiratory tract and the intestines.

During World Wars I and II, swabs of sphagnum moss were soaked in a garlic solution and applied to wounds to ward off infections.

In experiments conducted, headaches and other symptoms disappeared during the garlic treatment, and a gradual change occurred in the intestinal flora. While the harmful bacteria were slowly decreasing and passing from the body, the beneficial bacteria were increasing. The harmful staphylococcus bacteria were destroyed. In addition, all the symptoms of high blood pressure — headaches, dizziness, chest pains and ringing in the ears — slowly disappeared over a period of one to three weeks — and, strangely, pain in the back between the shoulder blades.

Garlic is now a familiar remedy for aiding digestion, stimulating gastric juices, relieving flatulence, dyspepsia and colic. It is an excellent therapy to prevent pneumonia, influenza, bronchitis, colds and asthma. Not only should it be taken orally in these cases, but it should be applied externally as a poultice. Simply chop garlic on a cloth and apply the cloth to the affected lungs, covering it with a top cloth and allowing it to remain overnight. Or chop garlic into castor oil, soak a cloth in the oil and apply it as a dressing to a wound, covering it with a top cloth.

It benefits chronic constipation, cecolstastis (intestinal obstruction) or chronic appendicitis. Patients suffering from these complaints are unable to completely digest food in the stomach because of subacidity or hyperacidity, and experience extreme toxemia. The undigested food, reaching the secal region, is unable to pass because of a malfunctioning secal valve.

The food wastes, reverting to toxins, are absorbed into the blood stream and toxemia spreads throughout the body, resulting in headaches, fatigue, dizziness, capillary spasms. Garlic therapy is extremely effective in correcting these complaints. Its antibiotic properties destroy the bacteria toxins of the chyme (the undigested food waste).

Garlic taken at meal time increases the natural flow of hydrochloric acid, improving general digestion. It also increases the excretion of bile from the liver and gall bladder. Garlic perles, taken with or following a meal, equalizes the acid-alkaline balance. They prevent flatulence (gas), expelling it from the stomach and intestines. The garlic oil, absorbed by the mucous membranes of the stomach wall, both tones and relaxes the stomach muscles, resulting in a natural flow of hydrochloric acids and all the digestive fluids. The result is relief from gas pains, colic distress, belching, bloating and nausea.

Tests have proven that garlic is effective in preventing or in healing intestinal catarrh, which is inflammation of the digestive tract. Further tests concerning polio indicate that people without the problem of digestive catarrh never contract polio. And in all cases, when polio is contracted, the attack seems to be triggered, or at least prefaced by, digestive catarrh — a damaged, irritated, or inflammed intestinal tract and colon. Thus, garlic is an indirect preventive of polio attacks.

Garlic therapy is equally effective in healing the common cold — performing what antibiotics, sulfa drugs and all manner of other therapies seem unable to do. It is both diuretic and diaphoretic, thereby inducing sweating and increasing urination — which breaks a fever. Not only that, but the garlic brings about healing without attacking the body's own vital organisms, as is often the case with antibiotics and sulfa drugs. As with all antibiotics, garlic can be used to excess in cases of sensitive stomachs. Prolonged usage of large dosage can deplete natural flora in the intestines of some people, increasing problems with gas. It could also cause burning in the stomach, hot belches and burning behind the eyes. Such symptoms only indicate the individual has become oversensitized to the antibiotic properties in garlic and should cease taking it for awhile, or decrease the intake.

The oil of garlic contains, among other things, sulfides and disulfides which combat virus organisms. Garlic therapy, which will abate the oncoming symptoms of a cold, and even influenza, should be started at the first hint of a sore throat or cough. Sinus drainage and cold congestions are often helped by simply inhaling the aroma of a broken clove. Taken internally, it encourages the lymph glands to discharge congested toxins. It may be chopped into castor oil and rubbed on the chest and the soles of the feet. Or cloves may be mixed with honey. Honeyed garlic, sipped a spoonful at a time, is excellent for sore throats. Instead of submitting to routine flu immunizing injections, why not begin each "cold season" by adding garlic capsules or perles to your diet. You may find yourself not only free of colds, flu symptoms, sore throat and chest and nose conjestion, but also of many other problems. (For quick results, wrap a clove of garlic in a small piece of cloth. Beat it. Immerse the cloth with the garlic in a cup of water. Allow it to steep for a few moments. Drink.)

Garlic perles aid in flushing toxins from the kidneys and act as a diuretic. They also stimulate natural perspiration, allowing the body to purify itself through the skin pores. They purify the lymph glands, stimulating the flow of noxious waste matter. They are excellent blood cleansers. They aid in cases of arteriosclerosis (hardening of the arteries), in correcting a malfunctioning thyroid gland, and bacillary dysentery. The natural selenium content — ten times more powerful than vitamin E — is effective in removing heavy metals from the body such as lead and mercury.

Many doctors, Dr. Som included, are convinced that garlic — together with a corrected diet — can heal cancer. Garlic therapy — if the whole garlic is used including the enzyme, plus the substrate — has been known to prevent the growth of cancerous tumors in experiments with rats. The enzyme alone was found not to be effective, nor was the substrate when used alone. (Substrate is the substance with which the enzymes are naturally associated with food.) It requires the whole of the garlic product to obtain the beneficial results, not fragmentized essences. Garlic contains two substances which experiments prove prevent clotting (clumping together) of blood cells that block circulation and cause strokes. These substances are called *allicin* and *mustard oil*.

Allicin, a bactericide, is reported to be effective in inhibiting the growth of enzymes present in tumor cells. Experiments also indicate it will help prevent heart and artery ailments since it reduces blood cholesterol levels. Other experiments proved effective for high blood pressure, which started disappearing within three to five days after garlic oil was taken. Headaches, dizziness and other symptoms decreased. To produce an odor free garlic tablet, the allicin has been extracted. The allicin-free product is called *Kyolic*. Whereas raw garlic — containing allicin — can upset the system if taken in excess, Kyolic does not. Most people prefer the odor-free Kyolic.

One reason garlic is so highly desirable as an agent against aging is because it emits mitogenetic radiation, or rays which stimulate cell growth and regeneration, resulting in a rejuvenating effect on all body functions. In capsule or tablet form, garlic mixed with vegetable charcoal acts as a chelated product, the properties of both the garlic and the charcoal gradually releasing the active substances which, passing through the gastrointestinal tract, perform its miracles.

Do not use garlic salt. It is often mixed with powdered rock — called calcium carbonate. You may use pure powdered garlic. Or make your own garlic salt. Just bury three peeled and pressed garlic cloves in 1/2 cup of sea salt. Let it stand a few days then remove the garlic.

When peeling a clove, use a chilled knife. Hold the point of the clove concave side down against a plate and squash it gently with the thumb. This makes the covering more easily removed. Never keep it longer than four months; it will become too stale. Keep it tightly covered and in a cool place. Prepare tincture of garlic by adding chopped garlic to apple cider vinegar. Let it stand. It can be used as an antiseptic wash for external wounds or taken as a good tonic added to water. It can also be added to oil as a base for salad dressing.

Elephant garlic is a large type variety.

Because it has a mild flavor, it is often preferred in salads, stews, soups, etc. It is more closely related to the leek than to garlic.

KALE

Kale contains 96 milligrams of vitamin C in 3/4 of a cup. It is high in vitamin K which is the vitamin that protects against hemorrahging, prevents abortions, and reportedly protects against cancer-producing substances. Kale is also high in vitamin A, which means it is excellent for the eyes and in combating colds. It contains a high content of calcium, phosphorus, iron, sodium and potassium. Kale should be eaten to aid teeth and gums, arthritis, rheumatism, kidney and bladder disorders and to correct constipation. It is excellent added to salads. If cooked, to preserve its high vitamin-mineral content, it should be lightly steamed in a wok with very little water and perhaps a touch of oil.

LEEKS

Leeks contain 25 milligrams of vitamin C in 1/2 cup. Like garlic, they contain a substance which makes them strongly antibiotic. They contain vitamins A and B, and are high in calcium, iron and phosphorus. They contain many of the same medicinal properties as garlic, and may be substituted for those who find garlic too powerful and too strong. Leeks are extremely effective in cases of nerves, insomnia, bronchitis, and influenza.

LENTILS

Lentils contain vitamins A,B, and C. They are also high in calcium, iron and phosphorus. One serving provides 25 grams of protein, thus they are excellent in the diet of the vegetarian. Because of their high calcium content, they are excellent for the teeth, bones, hair and nails. Because of their iron content, they are useful in cases of anemia and blood purification. Lentil soup is healing and nourishing for patients with ulcers and ulcerated digestive tracts.

LETTUCE

Lettuce is especially high in vitamin C and calcium. It also contains vitamins A and B, iron, magnesium, folic acid, phosphorus and potassium. In certain brands of lettuce, such as romaine, there is a high vitamin E content. Since the green leaf of the lettuce contains a great deal of iron, it is excellent for anemia. Lettuce contains laudanum, a tincture of opium, making it a mild sedative, excellent for insomnia. It is an aid to gastrointestinal disorders. It has a tonic effect inside the intestines, absorbing the toxins of the waste and encouraging their elimination. It has been found helpful in aiding arthritis and rheumatism, and in correcting constipation. Lettuce —every kind of lettuce — is the basis of every salad, including the iceberg head lettuce, butter lettuce, red leaf lettuce, bib lettuce (sometimes called Boston lettuce), and romaine.

The absorbent leaves of lettuce are stripped with insecticides and preservatives to prevent wilting. These chemicals are oily in substance and not affected by water. Thus, lettuce must be washed thoroughly in cold apple cider vinegar water (not soaked, since soaking leaches out vitamins-minerals) and rinsed in equally cold water. To remove the water it should be shaken vigorously, then blotted dry with an absorbent towel. Or better still, dropped into a pillow case and blotted to remove the remaining water (any remaining water will continue to leach out vitamins-minerals).

It should then be refrigerated in a covered container. It is not possible for the vinegar water to remove all the poisonous insecticides because of the porous substance of the lettuce leaf, so be sure to discard the outer leaves.

It is important all year round to add a variety of raw vegetables to every salad, but it is extremely necessary to do so during the summer months, not relying on lettuce as the principal ingredient... because lettuce is usually grown in soil fertilized with nitrates, and the hot sun rays, penetrating the nitrates, transforms them into nitrites, an extremely dangerous substance.

Nitrites ignite with the red pigments in the blood, which is the oxygen-carrying element, thus destroying oxygen in the blood. Due to nitrite danger, when shopping, it is better to choose dark green leaves since the darker leaves have been more thoroughly penetrated with chlorophyl brought about by sunlight.

Of all the lettuces, iceberg head lettuce is least valuable. It is frequently difficult to digest and, being lighter in color, does not contain the nutrients found in the darker green leafed lettuces. Lettuce begins to deteriorate and lose food elements the moment it is picked. It is usually packed in ice on its way from farm to market. If possible, plant lettuce in a backyard garden since it is the basic food for every salad. And, of course, pick it only at the time when a salad must be prepared.

MUSHROOMS

Mushrooms are fungi so cannot rightfully be called a vegetable. They are an excellent food, being rich in all the B vitamins, especially folic acid. They also supply abundant vitamin D which is not usually found in plants. Mushrooms contain vitamin E, and calcium, iron, phosphorus and potassium.

MUSTARD GREENS

Mustard greens contain vitamins A, B, and C and the minerals calcium, iron, potassium and phosphorus. They are also high in protein. The extremely high vitamin-mineral content of this important vegetable has not been recognized, thus they are seldom eaten. But they are valuable for a general cleansing of the blood and the digestive system. They also aid anemia, arthritis, kidney and bladder irritations, bronchitis and constipation. They stimulate the flow of toxins from all the muscles, glands and the blood. They should often be eaten raw in a salad, or steamed lightly in a wok which retains most of their important nutrients.

OKRA

Okra contains vitamins A, B, and C and calcium, iron, phosphorus and potassium. The mucilaginous content of this vegetable makes it excellent for all complaints of the digestive system.

Its thick gelatin substance coats the lining of the inflamed stomach, intestines and colon, bringing healthy benefits. It should be eaten steamed in the top of a double boiler or in a wok to avoid overcooking in water. When preparing, a bit of the stem should remain on it to prevent the escape of the gel substance in the pods. Add vegetable salt when serving and, if desired, a bit of butter or oil.

OLIVE OIL

Olive Oil should be in the diet of all those with hardening of the arteries because the oil is extremely rich in linoleic and oleic acid. Both these natural oils help reduce the accumulation of cholesterol in the blood stream. It is an excellent source of unsaturated fat.

When cooking with oil cannot be avoided, olive oil should be selected. Because of some mysterious element, it seems not to be as affected by heat as do other oils. Also, olive oil is preferred over other oils because the processing is simply that of pressing the oil from the olives. No chemicals are used and no preservatives.

ONIONS

Onions contain vitamins A, B, and C and calcium, iron, phosphorus, and potassium. These bulbous vegetables are expectorants. When there is inflammation of the nose, tonsils or sinuses, they should be eaten raw. They loosen phlegm and drain mucus from the bronchial tubes and lungs, aiding healing in cases of asthma, pneumonia, influenza, tuberculosis and the common cold.

A poultice of crushed onions relieves inflammation of the lung (pleurisy). They are good blood purifiers and glandular stimulants. They are an excellent aid to insomnia and high blood pressure. Chemists analyzing the juice and pulp of onions have identified one of its components as prostaglandin — a substance normally produced in the human body, known to have an anti-hypertensive effect. They destroy worms and other parasites in the digestive system. They are a natural diuretic, stimulating the flow of urine.

Those whose stomachs are not strong enough to digest raw onion should prepare onion soup often. It is an excellent tonic. When purchasing, avoid dry onions with a "neck" growth. They are undesirable. Choose the Bermuda or Spanish for more mildness. All dry onions may be stored at room temperature. The hard, long-keeping varieties are often quite strong. To remove a bit of lingering odor, put sliced or chopped raw onion in a colander and pour boiling water over it. Drain immediately under cold running water. This removes some of its heat and flavor.

PARSLEY

Parsley, as with the turnip, is an excellent bone builder. It is equally excellent for all kidney and liver disorders. It is also good for circulation and elimination of waste toxins from the body.

"Sweet and grateful to the stomach is parsley," wrote Galen, the noted physician of Pergamum some 1775 years ago. This famous Greek physician boiled roots of parsley to heal epilepsy. He employed it also as an effective remedy to remove obstructions from the body. It was labled one of the "five opening roots." He used it as an herb concoction to aid in "women's complaints." In Greek mythology, parsley was regarded as a sacred herb for it reportedly sprung up from the blood of Archemorus, one of the Greek heroes.

First grown in Sardenia and southern Italy and used as a valuable medicinal plant, its fame spread. The physicians of ancient times spoke of the "parsley breakstone" as an effective remedy for gallstones. They boiled it with onions. An ounce of parsley and an onion were boiled in a pint of water and divided into three daily dosages for gallstone patients. It was used also as a remedy for sore eyes.

In modern medicine, parsley is used as a diuretic and to produce an alkaline ash in the system. It is employed as a stimulant to the adrenal and thyroid glands. Parsley contains vitamins A, B, and C, and calcium, iron, phosphorus, potassium, copper and manganese. It is also high in protein. Parsley should be used in cases of nephritis (inflammation of the kidneys), congestion of the liver and gall bladder, inflammation of the urinary tract, arthritis, diabetes, high blood pressure, and anemia. It is recognized as an aid to digestion. Parsley tablets are effective in removing onion and garlic odors from the breath. Parsley juice should be added to carrot and celery juice occasionally even though it requires tremendous pressure and effort to extract the juice. It is well worth the effort, however, because the vitamins and minerals added are invaluable and it stimulates the flow of toxins from the body.

Taken in raw juice form, it aids in dissolving kidney and gallstones. It is of great benefit in treating the genitourinary tract. It flushes stones and calcium deposits from the kidney and gall bladder. It is so potent, it should never be taken in quantities of more than 1 or 2 ounces at a time.

Unfortunately, it is used as a decorative addition to most salads and dinner plates. It is usually casually set aside and never eaten, but it should be added freely to salads and soups. It adds valuable minerals and vitamins and is palatable both cooked and uncooked.

PEAS

Fresh cooked *peas* contain 20 milligrams of vitamin C per cup. They also contain vitamins A and B. Peas are abundant in phosphorus, manganese, calcium, potassium, iodine, copper, sulphur, sodium. They are high in protein. Their rich iron content makes them excellent for anemia and low blood pressure.

Raw peas are excellent in a salad, but the taste must be cultivated. If you must cook them, make sure they are cooked as briefly as possible and in very little water. If you must make a choice between canned or frozen peas, choose the frozen which have been quick cooked. Avoid canned peas, which are extremely dangerous. A detergent has been used to remove a poisonous weed — nightshade — which invariably grows near peas. So both the water and the peas of the canned product are saturated with detergent.

When purchasing, choose pods that are plump, well-filled and crisp. Avoid those that are dried, yellowed and flaky. When cooking, it is better to shell them and discard the pod which contains most of the insecticide residue.

PEPPERS

The *green bell pepper* is one of our most splendid nutrients. Peppers are usually eaten green but are not actually ripe until they have turned red. Extremely high in vitamin C, the red bell pepper contains as high as 300 milligrams of vitamin C as compared to 50 in the average orange. A green pepper of medium size contains 125 milligrams. Peppers also contain vitamins A and P (bioflavinoid), and some of the B vitamins — thiamin, riboflavin, and niacin. They also contain the minerals calcium, phosphorus and iron. When shopping, it is well to select peppers that are half green and half red. The vitamin C content will be richer.

They should be chopped and added to a salad almost daily. Obviously beneficial in all cases aided by vitamin C, they also aid in overcoming high blood pressure and in correcting liver disorders. The smaller hot red peppers are effective in healing colds, asthma, inflamed sinuses, and in correcting digestive problems created by intestinal worms. The hot red peppers should be avoided, however, if there is present any inflammation or irritation of the stomach or intestinal tract.

PLANTAIN

There is a special variety of the banana family called the *plaintain*. It contains vitamins B and C and the minerals calcium, iron and phosphorus. Whereas the banana should always be eaten raw, the plantain must be cooked. They are tougher, more fibrous and starchy than the ordinary banana. They are often used as a substitute for potatoes. They may be baked in the skin until soft, as is a potato, then removed from the skin, mashed and seasoned with vegetable salt and either butter or sesame oil. Or they may be peeled, sliced and baked until golden brown. They are excellent dipped in beaten egg, then in whole wheat flour or wheat germ and baked.

The plantain leaf is also valuable. For bee stings, animal bites and wounds, chew and apply a mashed leaf. Added to a raw salad, the plantain leaf heals urinary organs.

POTATO

A medium sized *potato* contains 2 grams of complete protein and 22 grams of carbohydrates. It contains 36 milligrams of vitamin C, 0.7 of iron, 1.7 of niacin, and 11 of calcium. It also contains vitamins A and B, phosphorus, potassium, cobalt, copper and sulphur. This analysis destroys the myth that the potato is a totally starch food. Certainly it contains all the essential amino acids — a food with complete protein. It forms the basis of the diet in many poverty sticken areas of the world, supplying the people with an excellent nutrient. It also should form the basis of many vegetarian diets, especially if one also consumes at least a portion of the skin.

The rich vitamins and minerals found in the potato are interlaced in the skin. Therefore, after scrubbing to remove the ingrained dirt and pollutions of the outer thin layer of skin, the remaining skin should be eaten. To discard the skin is to discard most of the nutrients. The protein portion of the potato is found in the section just under the skin, while the center of the potato contains the starch element.

The potato is easily digested, making it an excellent food for inflamed intestines, colon or stomach. Where milk and milk products were once first choices in healing an ulcer, many patients have found the milk diet difficult. They cannot digest the unnatural protein and calcium. Potatoes, on the other hand, produce an alkaline effect on the stomach. Thus, they do not require an outpouring of stomach acids so painful to the ulcer patient. They might well form the basis of the diet until the ulcer is healed.

Potatoes not cooked in fat or eaten with fat should be part of every reducing diet. They are low in calories. They should also be added to every diet for fiber, which prevents heart disease, gallstones, varicose veins, diabetes, appendicitis, hemorrhoids and colon disease.

When ordering in a restaurant, always order potatoes baked in the skin. Restaurant fried potatoes are dangerous to health. They are cooked in long standing rancid deep fat which is known to be cancer causing. They have been cut long before cooking and serving. To prevent their turning black, they are stored in containers filled with a benzoate of soda solution and bisulfides, which are preservative chemicals.

Also avoid instant mashed potatoes. The product bears little resemblance to its original name. They are saturated with preservatives, including sodium nitrate. If you order potato salad in a restaurant, and it has a strange metalic taste, do not eat it. It means the salad was prepared earlier and stored in an aluminum container. The acidic action of the vinegar used in seasoning the salad has reacted on the aluminum, absorbing much of its poison into the potatoes. Baked potato is safest. Instead of saturating a baked potato with butter, try vegetable oil, such as sesame, and try vegetable seasoning salt rather than white table salt.

Try the following as an excellent method of serving potatoes: Cover an iron skillet with just enough cooking oil to coat the surface. Cut a potato lengthwise and place the two halves face down in the skillet. Cover tightly and place on heat as low as possible. Bake for about an hour. All the nutrients of the potato will be intact. The flat surface will be browned and crisp. This is one of the most delicious and nutritious methods of serving potatoes. (Try artichokes this way, also.) Also, potatoes will turn a beautiful brown when you scrub the skin well, dry thoroughly and rub with olive oil before baking. Don't wrap them in foil.

Potatoes are excellent eaten raw as well as cooked. The minerals provide a blood purifier and help prevent fermentation in the stomach and intestines.

Try a facial mask of raw potatoes shredded to a pulp. If applied in a thin mask and allowed to dry, it may remain overnight to great advantage. The vitamin C and enzymes feed the cellular tissues, and the acid of the potato pulp dissolves decaying cells on the surface of the skin.

When potatoes are boiled, the water should be drunk either plain or with lemon juice. Never soak potatoes in water since it leaches out the B and C vitamins. If the potatoes sprout during storage, discard the sprouted area before cooking. It contains a substance called solanine which is harmful. When purchasing, avoid potatoes with deep "eyes" since they are not edible. And avoid those with green skins.

RADISH

Radishes contain vitamins A, B, and C, calcium, iron, phosporus and potassium. Radishes have long been known as aids to digestion. Rich in vitamins, minerals and enzymes, these marvelous little vegetables are renowned as stimulators of the gall bladder, resulting in an outflow of digestive bile fluids, making them excellent healers of liver-gall bladder ailments.

Radish therapy — especially black radish tablets — has been known to dissolve hard concretations along the liver-gall bladder, even gall stones. Radishes stimulate the function of the liver and improve the circulation. They also soothe the nerves and are beneficial for teeth, gums, hair and nails. They stimulate the flow of urine from the kidneys. Radishes, including the green tops, should be added often to a salad. When purchasing, avoid the oversized since they may be pithy.

SPINACH

Spinach is high in vitamins A, C, and B (thiamin, riboflavin, niacin, pyridoxine, pantothenic acid, biotin). Spinach also contains the minerals calcium, iron, phosphorus, potassium and magnesium. It also contains vitamin K, important in correcting blood clotting. Because of its high iron content, spinach is excellent for anemia, for blood building and blood purifying. It contains chlorophyl similar to that found in the meoglobin of blood. It stimulates the glands, thus it is excellent for "tired people" with little energy. It is an all-around tonic and anemic persons should eat it often. It also stimulates heart action. It neutralizes acids. It aids cases of insomnia, arthritis, high blood pressure, bronchitis and all other lung related problems.

Spinach is frequently listed as a negative food because it contains *oxalic acid*, a substance that prevents calcium from being absorbed and utilized by the body. Oxalic acid combines with calcium to form a salt compound that cannot be assimilated, resulting in kidney and gall stones. But spinach also contains high magnesium, a neutralizer of oxalic acid. It is better eaten raw in salads, rather than cooked, since cooking destroys much of the magnesium and frees the oxalic acid for destructive action. (We shall have more to explain about oxalic acid later.)

If cooked, it should be only slightly steamed in a wok which preserves all the water containing its vitamins, minerals and important enzymes. Spinach should never be soaked as the water quickly leaches out the nutrients. It should be dipped in vinegar water quickly, rinsed in cold water, dried and stored immediately in a closed airtight container.

SQUASH

Zucchini contains vitamins A, B, and C, calcium, iron, phosphorus and potassium. It's an aid to bladder-kidney problems, high blood pressure and constipation. Because of their bland texture, both zucchini and summer squash are effective in all problems of intestinal disorders — ulcers, inflammed intestinal walls, colitis.

Squash is excellent added to raw salad, but it may also be cooked into a soup for those with digestive problems. Hubbard and banana squash, high in vitamins and minerals, are equally effective in healing inflammation of the colon, ulcers, diarrhea, hemorrhoids. Extremely high in vitamin A, they may be used in problems of kidney and gallstones, not only to dissolve those already present, but to prevent stones from forming. The high vitamin content also makes winter squash an excellent food for eyes and hair.

TOMATOES

Tomatoes are actually a fruit, but since they are generally considered to be a vegetable, they are included here.

Tomatoes are rich in vitamins A, B, C and K. Their B content includes thiamin, riboflavin, niacin, pyridoxine, pantothenic acid, biotin, inosotol, folic acid. Their minerals include calcium, phosphorus, iron, copper, sodium, flourine and cobalt. Surprisingly, small tomatoes yield more vitamin C content than large. The tomato is known as a blood purifier and as a natural antiseptic, making it important in overcoming infection. It aids in cases of arthritis, tuberculosis, rheumatism, gout, high blood pressure and sinus. It also is effective in dissolving gallstones and in healing colds and influenza.

The presence of vitamin D aids in preventing hemorrhages and blood clotting. Tomatoes are excellent for gall bladder difficulties, liver ailments, dyspepsia, inflammation, kidney troubles, constipation and sluggish circulation. They are also lymphatic purifiers. They should be eaten raw. As an acid food, they should never be cooked.

When you buy tomatoes, you should not assume them ripe enough to eat. Tomatoes are picked green, then "gassed" with ethylene gas to give them their red color. But the color is artificial — the tomatoes are still not ripe. They should never be taken home and immediately refrigerated. Instead, expose them to the sun until they are blood red and soft. Avoid buying canned tomatoes. Not only will they have been ripened "artificially" with the ethylene method, but they will be grown in chemicalized soil and filled with insecticide sprays. If possible grow your own tomatoes.

TURNIPS AND TURNIP GREENS

Cooked *turnips* contain 22 milligrams of vitamin C in 1/2 cup, making them extremely rich in this important vitamin. Cooked *turnip greens* contain 130 milligrams of vitamin C in 1/2 cup. Thus, it would seem wise to eat both the turnip roots and the turnip greens. Turnip greens are also rich in vitamins A, C, E, and K. They contain the minerals calcium, phosphorus, iron, sodium and potassium.

Their high iron content makes them an excellent food for anemia, as a blood purifier and to eliminate toxins from the bloodstream. They aid in high blood pressure, bronchitis, asthma, and all lung difficulties. They also purify the liver. They act as a slight diuretic, stimulating the flow of urine and healing irritated bladders.

Turnips — the root — contain not only vitamin C, but A and B, and also calcium, iron, phosphorus and potassium. They are excellent to overcome constipation and to heal tuberculosis. They also are sedatives for the nerves, aiding in relieving nervousness and in overcoming insomnia. Their high calcium content makes them valuable for strengthening bones, hair and nails. When purchasing, avoid oversized turnips which may be fibrous and woody.

WATERCRESS

Watercress is extremely rich in calcium. It is especially high in vitamins A and C. It is also high in phosphorus, iron, sodium and potassium. Add it constantly to salads for its all-around excellence as a food medicine. There is hardly a human ailment that is not benefited by this marvelous plant — especially eye disorders, arthritis, arteriosclerosis, rheumatism, kidney and liver disorders, inflammation of the lungs, influenza, colds, pneumonia, bleeding gums and anemia.

YAMS

Yams — or *sweet potatoes* — contain vitamins A, B and C, and also calcium, iron, phosphorus, and potassium. Yams are among our finest foods, extremely rich in both vitamins and minerals, making them an excellent addition to the diet, especially for those who perform heavy physical labor. They are easily digestable, making them excellent for those with ulcers and colitis. They are useful in raising the blood pressure and stimulating blood circulation. They should be added to the diet of anyone experiencing hemorrhoids or diarrhea.

When purchasing, avoid those that are dark red or dark brown — they may be dyed with coal tar. Choose the Puerto Rico or Nancy Hall variety with rosy skins. They are yellow and tender when cooked. Those with pale skins may be stringy and dry. A few of the yams are dyed with vegetable dyes. The good yam has a very thin skin. All potatoes may be stored at room temperature.

OXALIC ACID

Oxalic acid is an undesirable substance found in some food which, as we have pointed out, mixes with and renders useless the calcium in the body. Foods containing oxalic acid are: rhubarb, chard, dandelion greens, endives, collards, lettuce, escarole, brussel sprouts, broccoli, mustard greens, turnip greens, kale, watercress, spinach, beet greens, parsley, chocolate, cocoa, tea, whole wheat bread and cereals, celery, carrots and beans.

Most of these foods, however, also contain magnesium and vitamin B6 (pyridoxine) which are natural offsets to oxalic acid and render it fairly harmless. Thus, the majority of these foods can be eaten in moderation with some degree of regularity... especially if one takes vitamin B and calcium-magnesium tablets.

The only foods which do not contain offsetting qualities of magnesium and B6 are chocolate, cocoa and commercial tea. These should be studiously avoided. But chocolate is consummed by millions in liberal amounts and its content of oxalic acid is enormous. Also, cocoa is consumed frequently as a substitute for coffee.

Chocolate milk is served to thousands of children for lunch and often for dinner, again forming the basis for calcium-oxalate in the body which, depositing itself in the kidneys and the gall bladder, forms kidney and gallstones. So not only are all those glasses of chocolate milk rendered negative in calcium benefits, but the oxalic acid is combining with the calcium in the milk to form dangerous calcium-oxalate.

Chocolate has become an important and accepted item in the American diet... chocolate candy, chocolate sodas, chocolate cake, chocolate milk, chocolate box candy, hot fudge sundaes, chocolate ice cream and on and on — a standard symbol of Americanism. And cocoa, used to supplement many of the above products, is not far behind. It is from the cocoa bean that sweet chocolate, used in so many products, is obtained —by adding deadly white sugar. The theobromine, the alkaloid in cocoa which acts like caffeine, is a drug.

In addition, both cocoa and chocolate contain caffeine. One bar of chocolate candy contains approximately 78 milligrams of caffeine. Do choose carob candy, carob drinks and carob powder as a complete and perfect substitute for chocolate and cocoa.

As for the plants, the vegetables, eat as many as possible raw. The oxalic content is not as active in raw food.

THE NIGHTSHADE STORY

There is more to be said about the potato, green peppers, tomatoes and eggplants. These are called nightshade plants, the leaves and foliage of which are poisonous and toxic. The vegetables themselves are not, however, if they are properly harvested.

If tomatoes, eggplant or peppers are picked from the vine before they have fully ripened, they will retain some of the toxin of the foliage. Since it is next to impossible to find them vine-ripened, do expose them to the sun before refrigerating if it is possible.

As for the potato, it should *never* be exposed to light. As soon as it is dug from the ground, the potato should be stored in a cellar, or at least in a dark paper bag and then placed in a dark place. If it is exposed to light, the light rays germinate a toxic substance inside the potato called *solanine*. Solanine is the toxic substance found in the roots and foliage of the plant.

There seems to be a mystery about the potato and arthritis. Some claim the potato *cures* arthritis, while others claim it causes arthritis. There really is no mystery. The truth is that potatoes *without* solanine *will* heal arthritis, while potatoes exposed to the light, containing solanine, will *cause* arthritis.

The potato itself is a most remarkable food — and is especially healing for arthritis. Solanine is the culprit. It not only aggravates arthritis, but many other ailments. The poor potato gets blamed when actually the blame should lie with the harvesters who deliberately expose the potato to the light.

Care is no longer taken to store the potato soon after digging. They are uprooted by machines and left afield to dry, then packaged in clear plastic boxes, delivered openly to market, and again exposed to full light on the counters. The result is potatoes often striated with solanine.

Be especially cautious about buying potatoes that are green — the green signals the presence of heavy portions of solanine. Do try to purchase potatoes from health stores which *may* be aware of the necessity to protect them from the light. Also buy other nightshade food — tomatoes, peppers, eggplant — from a health store. Hopefully they just *may* be vine-ripened whereas those from a supermarket assuredly are not.

THE SALAD CONTROVERSY

Nothing is more controversial than the salad-after-dinner or salad-before-dinner argument. Some nutritionists feel that salads should be eaten *after* the main protein meal because, if not, gas and indigestion may develop. They teach that hydrochloric acid is needed to assimilate the protein meal and that eating the salad first does not stimulate a flow of hydrochloric acid. I do *not* agree with this theory — especially if a dressing of oil and apple cider vinegar is added to the salad — or the juice of the lemon. I am reluctant to suggest the protein part of the meal first, because I feel that in so doing the needed raw foods will diminish. Too many will be tempted to abate the appetite with the main dish and allow the salad to be completely secondary. I feel it should be just the reverse.

First of all, the vinegar-oil dressing on the salad certainly supplies hydrochloric acid for the protein meal. Or water may be sipped with the meal (never iced) to which apple cider vinegar or lemon juice is added, either of which assures a ready supply of hydrochloric acid. With all these adjuncts, I really see no reason to switch our standard practice of salad-first.

Before vegetarianism and raw foods became a trend, a salad consisted of a slice of tomato atop a leaf of iceberg lettuce, topped with a dab of mayonnaise. This is not a salad. The salad bowl should include green leafy vegetables — romaine, butter lettuce, bib lettuce, watercress, chard, kale, dandelion leaves, beet greens, celery tops, parsley, spinach. Then there are the other vegetables such as zucchini, cabbage, radishes, beets, cucumbers, green peppers, celery, carrots, onions, garlic. Herbs may be added, such as sweet basil, chives, oregano, or anise in small amounts. Avocado and fresh tomatoes should be added at the very moment of serving. Wheat and alfalfa sprouts add much. Also lentil or bean sprouts, radishes or peas. It is important to prepare the salad in as attractive a fashion as possible. Many of the items — particularly the carrots, beets, zucchini, cabbage — should be shredded. Tomatoes, cucumbers, mushrooms, peppers should be chopped in bite sizes. This makes the salad more appealing. Nothing is more discouraging and disconcerting than to be served a salad piled high with foods too large to handle without chopping and cutting. Shredding makes the salad more palatable and easier to chew.

The dressing is of paramount importance. Do use a variety. Interest in salads quickly wanes if the dressing is monotonous, the vinegar too tart. I like to mix the herbal vinegar-oil dressing with a creamy roquefort or thousand island. Try it. Try whatever sustains the interest in raw food — the true "staff of life."

The current trend toward the salad bar in many restaurants is most fortunate. What is unfortunate is that the basic green is usually iceberg lettuce. One cup of iceberg contains only 96 units of vitamin A compared to 145 for the looseleaf varieties. Watercress, raw spinach, endive and escarole contain even more — from 1650 to 4400 units per serving. Avoid, however, some of the other offerings — the pickled items, including olives, all saturated with salt. Avoid, too, the potato salad, bacon bits, synthetic cheese. Concentrate on the three-bean dishes, garbanzo beans, cheese slices, radishes, celery, cucumber, tomato, cabbage, beets, carrots. Avoid all salad foods which may be ridden with bacteria due to overexposure to open air and over handling. Select only those appearing to be fresh.

CHAPTER 5
FRUITS—THE FABULOUS CLEANSERS

When Nature created fruit, she produced her supreme masterpiece. It is presumed that man's first food in the Garden of Eden was fruit. And it is subconsciously presumed that, as man evolves into the god he is to be, his food again will be only fruit — the food of purification and ultimate purity.

Fruit remains longer in the sun than any other harvesting food, absorbing the beneficial influences of light, heat and air, through which the electric and magnetic forces of the sun are transmitted. In fruits, then, we find the highest manifestation of electro-vital energy and cell vibration — or prana — of all foods.

Fruits may be divided into three classifications:

a. *the tropical* — including bananas, pineapples, papayas, mangoes.

b. *the subtropical* — including oranges, lemons, grapefruit, limes, tangerines, figs, dates, avocados.

c. *temperate zone*, including the rest of the fruit family . . . apples, grapes, pears, peaches, plums, apricots and berries.

There are a few rules which apply only to fruits:

1. If possible, eat fruits that are only tree ripened — that is, ripened in the sun while still on the tree. Such fruits contain a great measure of mineral salts and acids which are necessary to promote good elimination. Eaten daily, fruit contributes considerably toward the cure of constipation.

2. Dried fruits should never be eaten unless dried in the sun's rays and not sulphured. This chemical is most injurious to the system. It also destroys the hygienic value of the food.

3. Fruits may be served whole or cut up into salads or made into juice. The most desirable of bottled juices are pineapple, apple and grape. Avoid artificial juice drinks from the supermarket. They are extremely dangerous — saturated with preservatives, white sugar, artificial coloring, and all manner of dangerous by-products.

4. The natural sugar content of fruit is far superior to white refined sugar. Fructose (fruit sugar) may well be employed as one source of sweetening, a substitute for white sugar, along with honey, maple sugar, maple syrup, molasses, malt syrup, and date sugar. Do not add sugar to fruit.

5. Concerning citrus fruits, much

needs to be clarified. Most healers and holistic physicians frown on drinking citrus juices. They feel the whole fruit itself should be consumed so that the body is supplied with fiber and important *bioflavonoids,* sometimes called *vitamin P* and sometimes called *rutin.* If you insist on drinking the juice, then be sure to eat some of the white meat near the skin before discarding the peels. This is true of oranges, lemons and grapefruit. It is in the white lining of the skin that the bioflavonoids are found. And do choose freshly squeezed juice rather than the frozen concentrates which may have lost much food value during processing —and which may contain a preservative and a dye.

6. Citrus fruits possess certain natural chemicals which, coming in contact with the blood, have the power to alkalize it. Thus, even though they are acid in the mouth, they become alkaline in the system. Fruits such as oranges, grapefruits, pears or lemons never create acid in the stomach. They turn to alkaline a few minutes after eating.

There are those — even doctors and naturopaths — who strongly recommend deleting citrus fruits from the diet. They say that especially those with arthritis should avoid citrus fruits because their substances tend to increase the pain of the joints and muscles. I do not agree. Nor did Dr. Som. We believe the pain is caused because the citrus acids are attacking the uric acids in the inflamed and calcified joints. We believe the increased pain is a "good" symptom, indicating the calcified deposits are being loosened and dissolved and passing out of the system. The citruses should be continued until it can definitely be determined whether the increased pain will continue, or if the citruses are indeed bringing about a cure.

Dr. Som declared that if the arthritic would continue the citrus juices, he may ultimately witness a complete cure. But it is for each individual to decide for himself the way he must go — whether to avoid the citruses altogether and take the pain pills necessary to stay out of pain, or whether to take the citruses, suffer increased pain for a while, and experience the realization that the calcified joints are gradually improving. If your decision is against citruses, then by all means take vitamin C tablets made from rose hips, acerola berries, or some other natural source.

7. Never cook acid fruit. When cooked, the acid is set, and cooked acid fruits are highly dangerous, resulting in what is called *acidosis.* The acid in a cooked lemon is strong enough to blister the tissues of the throat and stomach. While the *raw* acid changes to alkaline a few seconds after it is consumed, the *cooked* acid, fermenting, simply enters the intestines and then the bloodstream as a strong acid, burning and inflaming the tissues.

Acid fruits are: all citrus fruits, pineapple, tomatoes, strawberries. *Sub-acid fruits* (only a small amount of acid) are: pears, plums, sweet apples, peaches, apricots, cherries. These may be cooked — if you insist — with less harmful results. Sweet fruits are: dates, figs, raisins, prunes, papayas, ripe bananas, watermelon, other melons.

THE APPLE

The adage "An apple a day keeps the doctor away" is worthy of its creation. It more than lives up to its reputation.

In health spas throughout the world, the *apple* is now being used as a rapid cure for dysentery and intestinal catarrh. In severe cases, patients are placed on grated raw apple alone. Remaining on this diet for several days sees a rapid recovery of most all digestive tract diseases. On such a diet, apple peelings are consumed as well as the fruit. The patient drinks all the water desired on this "apple cure" diet.

On such a diet, the patient receives usually about three pounds of raw, grated apples a day. Some patients, unable to consume raw fruits, still benefit by stewed apples with a little honey, although the healing is not as rapid. Infants are cured of diarrhea with scrapings of raw apple pulp.

All — even those who feel they cannot eat raw apples — would benefit by the following remedy for digestive problems: to a shredded apple, add honey to taste. Cover with sesame seeds or tahini. Or try cinnamon occasionally. This should be eaten just prior to or with a meal. The apple's minerals, pectin and tartaric acids aid the flow of digestive enzymes. It provides the needed hydrochloric acid.

Its *pectin* is a natural demulcent that coats inflamed digestive walls and absorbs many toxins like a sponge, carrying them from the body. Pectin also helps blood to congeal, which explains its miraculous ability to heal dysentery. Pectin also reduces cholesterol in the blood. By preventing the absorption of cholesterol from the intenstines, the cholesterol passes through and is excreted from the body rather than being assimilated into the blood stream. The peel of the apple should be included, after washing the apple in vinegar water to remove pollutions and paraffin, because most of the pectin is found interlacing the peel.

Eating apple with a meal — or drinking a small glass of apple juice —helps the digestive system to absorb iron from the food, so needed to prevent anemia. Apple cider, drunk regularly, prevents the formation of kidney stones.

Eaten at any time, apples are an excellent blood builder and purifier. For breakfast, baked apples are delicious with a bit of honey, diluted peanut butter and lemon juice. Or stuff the apple with dates, figs or raisins. When you crave a snack, instead of white sugared candy, reach for an apple. Couple it with a handful of nuts or a piece of raw cheese. When dining out, avoid desserts of white sugared pies and cakes and order apple and cheese.

For those with a hypoglycemic or diabetes problem — or also for those who do not — apples are an excellent food because they do not have a high sugar content. Nature's formula for "sugarizing" her fruit is, in most cases, in great moderation. Consider that a chocolate bar contains as much sugar as a dozen apples. Such a concentration of sugar can only send the blood sugar soaring for a scant few moments, then plunge to a dangerous low, with the unhappy result of all the familiar hypoglycemic symptoms — the nerves, the headache, the mental confusion, the crying, the depression, the irritability — and even the hypoglycemic coma. In comparison, the sugar in the apple raises the blood sugar gradually and holds it level for extended periods, especially if it is consumed with protein —a slice of raw cheese, a few nuts, or a glass of raw milk.

One small apple supplies 6 milligrams of calcium, 10 milligrams of phosphorus, 110 milligrams of potassium, 90 units of Vitamin A, along with pectin, lignin and fiber. It aids the body in storing calcium from other sources. Apples not only supply traces of iron, but, again, aid in iron absorption from other sources. Its iron helps protect against anemia. Copper and traces of manganese are also found which combine with the iron to form red blood cells. An abnormal deficiency of sodium-potassium ratio is believed to cause some forms of cancer. The high organic sodium-potassium content in apples could well act as a preventive against malignancies. In addition to iron, calcium, phosphorus, potassium, copper, and vitamin A, apples supply all the B-complex vitamins, including the important thiamin, riboflavin and niacin. The skin is rich in vitamin C.

The seeds of the apple contain *hydrocyanic acid* or *prussic acid*. In medical circles, the acid is called *amygdalin*. And in cancer research circles, it is known as *laetrile*, or *vitamin B$_{17}$*. Although the popular source of laetrile is the seed of the apricot —because it is so high in amygdalin —still the seed of the apple also offers a rich source of this important substance. Ground apple seed therapy should be entered cautiously, however. Amygdalin cyanide taken to excess is poisonous. Taken in minute homeopathic portions, as laetrile, it is renowned in treating cancer and has been highly successful in innumerable cures.

Apples offer a gentle laxative effect, but can be equally beneficial in cases of diarrhea—and this quality is rare in any food. But one of its most amazing features is that, eaten after a meal, the apple cleanses the teeth, acting as a natural toothbrush. Eating a thin slice of apple after each meal produces the same effect as brushing—even better. The low acidity of the fruit stimulates a generous flow of saliva. The fruit substance, combined with the saliva, removes food debris and stimulates gum tissues. The slice of apple is equally effective if eaten between meals. When eating whole apples, for better cleansing effect bite directly into it with your teeth rather than slicing with a knife. It is good to eat an apple before bedtime. It not only cleanses the teeth but helps to produce sound sleep.

Apples contain about 84% water. So eat them for their fluid content—or drink apple juice as a thirst-quencher rather than additive-containing beverages.

Apples are very alkaline when ripe and are most effective in cases of autointoxication such as rheumatism, arthritis, liver and gall bladder ailments, acidosis, gout, and skin problems. A daily apple also aids in preventing lung and asthma problems, inflammation of the bladder, anemia, gallstones and insomnia. Apples will simultaneously stimulate all body secretions and reduce nervous tension. They help prevent bleeding gums, which is a form of scurvy. Indeed, an apple a day keeps not only the doctor, but all he represents, away. When purchasing choose bright red, yellow or green, and select those which feel firm and heavy.

APRICOTS

Apricots are rich in many nutrients. They are high in vitamins A and B, potassium, rutin—and low in sodium. The presence of organic copper and high iron content make them ideal as a builder of red blood cells, thus useful in overcoming anemia. Their splendid mineral content—iron, calcium, copper, phosphorus, potassium—make them an excellent dietary addition for those with asthma, bronchitis, catarrh, toxemia and tuberculosis. They act as a natural laxative. They will destroy intestinal worms.

Hunzakuts, inhabitants of a land called Hunza located near the Himalayan mountains in India, are renowned for their longevity. Most survive in splendid health far beyond the century mark. Apricots are one of their principal foods. They are eaten both raw and dried. Hunzakuts even break open the stones and eat the inner kernel, regardless of the presence of prussic acid—amygdalin—in the seed. Perhaps their consumption of the magical laetrile, so renowned for aiding cancer patients, helps to explain the longevity of these amazing people.

Apricot oil is rich in polyunsaturated fatty acids. It may be used daily to good advantage in salad dressings, cooking, as a food supplement or as a medicine—provided it is cold pressed. It may even be used as a cosmetic on skin and hair. This oil has an advantage over others as it does not so rapidly turn rancid. Dried apricots may be soaked overnight in distilled water and eaten with a bowl of millet. Apricot jams and jellies are both delicious and healthful if honey rather than sugar is used in the preparation.

BANANAS

Bananas contain a generous supply of minerals: calcium, iron, phosphorus, potassium, magnesium, sulphur and chlorine. They are excellent as a source of quick energy and are easily digested. Their content of natural sugar makes them desirable as a snack food, satisfying the need for a quick rise in blood sugar. They are rich in nutrients: all the B vitamins, especially B6, inositol, pantothenic acid, thiamin, riboflavin, niacin and folic acid. One banana supplies 1/5 of the needed daily requirement of vitamin C. Vitamin A is present in abundance. They contain all the essential amino acids, including the important lysine, tryptophane and methionine. They are 1 1/4 percent protein, about the same as mother's milk for a rapidly growing baby.

They are one of God's most excellent fruits and should be part of every diet. Bananas fulfill our nutritional requirements more ideally than any other one food. The list of their benefits is almost endless:

1. They are easily digested. Their natural sugar requires no digesting in the stomach. They are quickly broken down and absorbed through the intestinal villi and into the blood

stream.

2. They should be a major item in the diet of every patient immediately following surgery when the body needs a food to promote rapid healing, quick energy and aid in elimination of wastes. They are high in vitamin C, mildly laxative, bland in nature, and highly nutritious.

3. Because of their bland quality and because they are an ideal food for digestion, and are waste eliminators, bananas should be a major food for colitis and ulcer patients. They soothe and heal inflammation of the colon, ulcerated intestinal wall linings and inflamed mucous membranes.

They act as a buffer against the hydrochloric acid in the stomach, so painful to the ulcer patient, and should be eaten when acid pains irritate. While they neutralize the acids, they also heal the stomach lining. Eaten often—and mixed with protein such as tahini—bananas can form the basis of a long-term healing diet for a wounded colon.

4. A diet of bananas mashed and blended with raw whole milk has been proven effective for heart patients (only trace elements of salt, fat and cholesterol), in diabetes (low in natural sugar and easily digested), those with liver problems, in gout (no purine), in hemorrhoids, and for those with kidney problems—simultaneously providing healing and nutrition, acting as a medicine and, at the same time, as a food.

Because gastrointestinal reactions so often result when uremia is present, bananas are usually prescribed as a principal food. Their soothing, mildly laxative action on the intestines prevents the wounded kidneys from being overloaded in the eliminative process. But a better choice than milk might be tahini or almond milk.

5. They are recognized as the ideal food for infants—the first weaning food. Mashed banana may well form the basic diet, adding additional food as the child's digestive system develops.

6. Bananas are prescribed to heal diarrhea because of their bland pectin content. In the inflamed intestines, the pectin causes the banana pulp to swell, turning the liquid stool substance to gel, and indrawing the offending bacterias and expelling them from the body in soft stools.

7. Bananas contain an important digestive enzyme, so should be eaten as part of every meal by those with digestive problems. Digestive disturbances have often been healed by going on a banana fast—nothing but mashed bananas for several days. Some take a raw vegetable salad for lunch or dinner, and eat bananas the remainder of the day. On such a diet, acid fruits are to be avoided (oranges, lemons, grapefruit, pineapple). Also, no starches, proteins, pastries, wheat or corn products, sugar or milk—just bananas alone with or without a salad once a day. This diet is excellent for even difficult digestive problems.

8. Bananas are an excellent food when one is undergoing food allergy tests. The patient is usually asked to give up all foods for several days, then to begin eating one food at a time until the culprit foods are discovered.

But frequently the doctor, recognizing the nutritional value of the banana and its no-allergy history, will place the patient on a banana fast for several days, then add foods one at a time. This plan is excellent for those who find complete fasting difficult. If you are allergic to wheat or flour, try using banana flour mixed with 5% wheat flour, millet or triticale for your cooking or baking.

9. Bananas are also excellent in reducing diets, one banana containing only 80 to 100 calories, depending on its size. It contains only about 2 grams of fat. Again, they might well form the basis of the diet, since they fill the basic need for protein and carbohydrates. Low in fats, they may be ideal for some dieters. Others, needing fat in the diet, may add tahini to mashed banana. The tahini supplies not only fat but is rich in raw protein.

The banana is ideal for reducing because, due to its low sodium (salt) content, liquids are not held in the cells and tissues of the body. Salt has a tendency to enter the tissues, attracting large quantities of water which, remaining, become part of the overweight syndrome. The banana diet releases the fluids, resulting in a rapid loss of weight without loss of energy or nutrition.

10. Bananas are also excellent for those with anemia because of their high iron content—the iron being easily assimilated into the blood stream, acting as chelated iron—the iron also being in a form easily used for forming hemoglobin.

11. The inner side of banana peels are excellent applied directly to burns.

12. Many are not aware of their function as a natural food laxative—nor their ability to stimulate the growth of lactobacilli flora in the intestines.

13. Although they are best eaten alone, they are one item that can successfully be combined with other sweet or subacid fruits such as raisins, grapes, dates, figs, apples. They also blend well with lettuce and celery.

Bananas have an alkaline reaction in the body, as have most fruits. They are an excellent source of quick energy. Their content of natural sugar makes them a desirable snack food, satisfying the need for a quick rise in blood sugar. To make the banana a more complete healing food, a protein should be added. A wise choice is a spoonful of tahini, a sesame seed cream, available from health stores, or almond butter, mashed with the banana.

Bananas should not be eaten when they are yellow and very firm. They are too acid. They should be eaten only when the skin is brown flecked and the fruit more ripe and soft. Only then will the starch of the banana be changed into completely digestible fruit sugar. When they are green or yellow and firm, they must be considered a starch food and difficult to digest. Only as they ripen does the starch convert to natural sugar, and they become not only completely digestible but one of the most nutritious foods.

Frequently commercial growers use an undesirable gas spray to hasten ripening. Therefore purchase them fairly green and allow them to ripen at room temperature at home. Hot temperatures cause them to liquify into a mush so, after ripening, wrap in a wet cloth or paper and store in a paper bag to prevent shriveling. The skin will continue to darken but the flesh will remain flavorable and firm. They should never be refrigerated—nor should any tropical fruit.

BERRIES

Raspberries are great purifiers, possessing stimulating minerals for therapeutic effects—iron, calcium and phosphorus. They are good for all inflammatory conditions, high blood pressure, intestinal worms, diarrhea, as well as constipation. Raspberry tea is renowned for relieving menstrual cramps, and making childbirth easy if drunk throughout pregnancy and during the hours of labor. To make the tea, pour an ounce and a half of water over an ounce of leaves and simmer for 20 minutes.

Blackberries may be used as a diuretic, flushing toxins from the kidneys and bladder; and as a blood purifier. They are an excellent food for those with arthritis, rheumatism, gout, anemia and constipation. They aid cases of dysentery, inflammations of the intestines and nasal discharges. They contain 66 milligrams of vitamin C per cup. They are also high in A and B, and the minerals iron, calcium and phosphorus.

Elderberries are excellent aids for lung and respiratory problems—colds, coughs, catarrh, asthma, bronchitis, and sore throats. Since the tea induces perspiration, it is excellent to drink while soaking in a hot tub, or when soaking the feet. The berries contain vitamins A, B and C, and iron, calcium and phosphorus.

Blueberries are renowned as blood purifiers and for anemia. They also are excellent for healing inflammation of the intestines. They may be used as an aid to constipation as well as diarrhea, and for soothing menstrual cramps. They are rich in iron, calcium, phosphorus and vitamins A, B and C.

CHERRIES

When purchasing, choose the *black cherry* since they are richer in iron, silicon and magnesium. They are effective as blood purifiers, in cases of anemia, hardening of the arteries, high blood pressure, pyorrhea, asthma, rheumatism, intestinal worms, constipation and catarrh, and should be eaten freely where there may be gravel or stones, such as gall or kidney stones. Cherries contain vitamins A, B and C and iron, calcium, and phosphorus. They also contain malic acid, succinic acid, lactic acid, and linoleic acid.

Black cherries, or black cherry juice, contain an active substance shown to be significantly effective in healing gout and arthritis. The usual portion is from four to six ounces daily. Relief is usually apparent in a few days. *Royal Anne* or *Bing* varieties seem equally effective, and canned are acceptable if a brand can be found that is not loaded with sugar. Pure cherry juice is often available at health stores, free of sugar and artificial colorings. Start with moderate amounts daily to determine your need. The natural sugar content is high so those with hypoglycemic tendencies should experiment cautiously. Cherry juice is recognized as a "spring tonic"—stimulating the liver and the kidneys to discharge congested toxins.

Be very sure to wash cherries with vinegar water to remove the poisonous sprays. And even then, test to see if you have a bad reaction. Thin-skinned cherries absorb great quantities of the chemicals and it is difficult to remove all of them. So if you experience a headache, a stomach upset, dizziness, or any other unusual occurance, discard the cherries.

When they are out of season, you may find it necessary to choose canned ones if you are using them in an emergency to cure a particular ailment, but discontinue as soon after the treatment as possible—too much sugar. And, of course, the canned cherries were probably sprayed.

If possible, locate a source of unsprayed cherries and freeze them. Wash in vinegar water and pit them, being sure to save the juice, and add honey. Choose wide-mouthed glass jars when possible or regular freezing containers. Avoid plastic containers if possible. Freeze the cherries raw. Choose a light colored raw honey. White clover or orange blossom are good selections, and use sparingly because the cherries are already naturally sweet. If the raw honey turns to sugar in the freezer, simply set it in a pan of hot water. Do not heat.

CRANBERRIES

Cranberries are high in vitamins A, B and C, and in the minerals iron, calcium and phosphorus. Cranberries, an acid fruit, are valuable in treating diseases of the skin such as skin cancer, pimples, and scurvy. They aid in all bronchial inflammations, and liver and gall bladder afflictions, high blood pressure and constipation—but especially asthma.

Cranberries, because they contain a bronchial antispasmodic, dilate the bronchial tubes and bring relief to the asthmatic. Once the tubes dilate, the trapped breath is released. Cranberries can be used as an emergency measure for an asthma attack rather than seeking an injection of adrenalin from a medical doctor. Eat fresh cranberries, or, in such an emergency, in spite of sugar and preservatives, eat the canned variety if necessary. Or a pulp can be made by simmering and straining the berries, then refrigerating until needed. One or two teaspoons of the pulp in a cup of warm water usually relieves the attack, says Dr. Som. Honey may be added while simmering the berries to remove tartness. It does not reduce the effectiveness of the remedy.

Cranberry juice is excellent for urinary infections. Four ouces a day until healed should be sufficient since it is highly concentrated; more than that would be excessive. They contain a high acid content—tannic, oxalic and benzoic. Thus, they should be eaten sparingly, especially when cooked with sugar or when overcooked. When preparing for special occasions such as Thanksgiving, simmer in sweet apple cider only until the berries are soft, then add honey, mix well, simmer another five minutes and serve. Try to purchase them at a health store—unsprayed and organically grown.

DATES

Dates are an excellent source of protein. Never eat over five dates at a time; they are too rich in sugars and roughage. The natural sugar of the date—and date milk—makes them an excellent source of quick energy. The skins provide roughage as an aid to overcoming constipation. Substitute date sugar for brown sugar or white sugar. Use in cooking recipes for cookies, cakes and other pastries. Use over cereals and as a substitute for all other sweeteners.

Dates are high in calcium and phosphorus. They contain natural ingredients which lower cholesterol in the blood. They are also rich in iron, copper, chlorine, potassium, manganese, magnesium, vitamins A and B. They are excellent aids to anemia, lung congestion and intestinal inflammation such as colitis, diverticulitis, ulcers, hemorrhoids, low blood pressure and sexual hormone deficiency.

For ice cream without sugar, try the following: Blend pitted dates and raw milk in a blender to a thick consistency, then freeze it.

There is one grave drawback to some dates—the processing procedure. Some are sprayed with a deadly chemical, presumably to destroy insects. But it is extremely harmful to humans. Workers in date factories exposed to the fumigating spray have been poisoned, showing symptoms of headache, dizziness, nausea, difficulty in breathing, blood spitting and even unconsciousness. Though safeguard methods now protect the workers, the dates so fumigated will not be safe for those who eat them. So seek unfumigated dates.

FIGS

Figs are beneficial in all dropsical conditions, also for liver, stomach and pancreatic disorders and ulcers. Fig juice is excellent for coughs and sore throats. They should be in the diet of every cancer victim. They also aid in gangrenous conditions, skin diseases, anemia, colitis and low blood pressure.

They have been used effectively in respiratory illness such as asthma, tuberculosis, pleurisy, bronchitis, in measles, small pox and as a poultice on open wounds and boils. They have long been recognized as natural laxatives. They are seldom obtainable fresh because of their rapid perishability. Usually they are dried. Always buy sun-dried figs—never sulphur dried.

Like papaya, figs contain a protein-dissolving enzyme and could well be used as an aid to digestion, as is papain. They are extremely rich in minerals—iron, calcium, copper, phosphorus, sodium, and potassium—and vitamins A and B. In countries of the Old World, figs have been used to curdle milk, which may make them useful in making homemade yogurt, soured milk, clabber or Kefir.

GRAPES

Grapes supply potassium, sodium, magnesium, calcium, iron, sulphur, chlorine and phosphorus—and vitamins A, B and C. They contain natural fruit sugar and are a source of quick energy. When tired, a small glass of natural grape juice will give an almost immediate upsurge because grape sugar, like honey, is absorbed directly and immediately into the bloodstream. When purchasing juice, choose that which is not processed and is sugar-free.

The grape is an alkaline fruit. Grape sugar is the purest and most beneficial to man's body. Grapes are also rich in iron. They should be eaten often in the case of anemia, low vitality and malnitrution. They are excellent as body cleansers and for cancerous conditions. They are a source of vitamin P—better known as rutin or bioflavonoid, thus grapes are important in the treatment of bleeding gums, cirrhosis of the liver, psoriasis, eczema and glaucoma.

They aid in preventing hemorrhaging, in resisting the harmful effects of x-rays. They quickly reduce uric acid in the blood, thus aiding arthritics, gout victims and rheumatic pain. The reduction of uric acid also relieves the kidneys from overwork in eliminating these toxins. Grape juice is renowned as an aid in reducing diets. Drink a small glass just prior to a meal. The rapid build-up of blood sugar diminishes the appetite and one eats less.

The negative aspect is that most grapes have been grown on chemically fertilized soil, and also sprayed with poisonous sprays. Even washing in vinegar water may not remove the danger. So eat them in great moderation and even then, if you have a bad reaction, such as a headache, avoid them. If possible, of course, purchase only organically grown grapes.

GRAPEFRUIT

There are approximately 90 milligrams of vitamin C in an average-size *grapefruit*. They also contain calcium, iron and phosphorus. Grapefruit is most beneficial as a remedy for fever, liver trouble, colds, rheumatism, gall stones, pneumonia, catarrh, kidney trouble and arthritis—dissolving inorganic calcium formations in the cartilage of the joints, due to its salicylic acid content. It is a natural antiseptic when applied to wounds as a poultice.

Choose those that are heavy for their size, with smooth, thick skins. Grapefruit can be kept at room temperature or, if you prefer, refrigerated. The fruit should never be cut until just before serving. The moment the peel is open and the nutrients are exposed to oxygen, the valuable food elements begin deteriorating. If you section the grapefruit before eating, include the membranes and white lining of the skin, if possible, for therein lies the valuable bioflavonoids, so essential for the well-being of the blood vessels, gums, eyes, skin and liver.

If you can find grapefruit naturally grown and free of spray pollutions, then make good use of the rind. Boil the entire fruit, then cut it up into the boiled water. Squeeze the fruit, being sure to extract all the fruit substances— and add honey to taste. This concoction is excellent for colds and coughs.

After eating the fruit or drinking the juice, to remove acids from the teeth rinse the mouth with a glass of water to which baking soda has been added. Also, in addition, swish the mouth with milk of magnesia to further safeguard against teeth erosion. Never brush the teeth immediately after eating citrus fruits without first using the baking soda rinse. Otherwise the acid is brushed deep into the teeth enamel.

LEMON

Dr. Som swore he healed stomach cancer in some of his patients simply by correcting the diet and adding pure lemonade to the diet. He gave the following suggestions:

1. Lemons are a prime source of vitamin C, so essential to our health. There are 25 milligrams of vitamin C in a tablespoon of lemon juice. Lemons also contain the drug *synephrine*, recognized as a dilator and decongestant for symptoms of colds and flu.

2. Lemons are *very* beneficial in all bronchial and asthmatic conditions, and to gargle a sore throat since it cuts loose the phlegm lining the throat area. For a cough or cold, squeeze the juice of a lemon into a glass, fill the glass with water and add honey to taste.

Or boil one lemon slowly for ten minutes in enough water to cover it. Cut the lemon in half and extract the juice with a lemon squeezer. Add two tablespoons of glycerine; stir the glycerine and lemon juice well and pour into an eight ounce drinking glass. Fill the drinking glass with honey. Take a teaspoonful when you have a coughing spell. Stir before drinking.

Another throat remedy: gargle with warm lemon water to which sea salt has been added. Another cough remedy: add to a lemon enough water to cover it and boil for ten minutes. Then cut up the lemon into the water and allow it to steep until cool. Strain and add honey to taste. Sip throughout the day. This lemonade will quickly dry up the outpouring phlegm and cause a great deal more to be loosened so that it may pass out of the body. But rinse the mouth with water containing baking soda after each use of lemon juice to avoid erosion of the teeth.

3. Lemons are an excellent aid to digestion and kidney and liver trouble. They are nature's greatest stimulant for the liver, increasing its potential to produce the needed enzymes for digestion. They produce an alkaline ash in the body.

4. The lemon, with its potassium salts, is a blood purifier. It stimulates the circulatory system, removes acid from the body, and helps to overcome conditions of diabetes and gangrene.

5. To heal a boil or exterior ulcer or tumor, roast a lemon in an oven until it begins to crack or shrivel. Then cut off a portion large enough to cover the sore area. Apply the lemon directly and bind it in place as a poultice. Leave for an hour or until the boil breaks. Remove the poultice and clean the area with boiled or distilled warm water diluted with lemon juice. Continue bathing with the diluted lemon water for several days.

6. Lemon juice relieves the itch of insect bites, bee stings and poison ivy.

7. The juice of half a lemon in a quart of warm water may be used effectively as a vaginal douche to maintain the desired acid state in the vagina—unless the membranes of the vagina are inflamed. In this case, avoid this procedure because of the painful after effects.

8. The juice of the lemon is excellent for kidney stones since lemons gradually dissolve the stones. Much shall be explained when writing about the kidneys later.

9. Lemons are natural skin beautifiers: use the juice of the fruit, or slices, or, holding 1/2 an opened lemon, apply directly to the skin to heal blemishes such as pimples, acne, eczema, blackheads, enlarged pores and to avoid wrinkles. Let the juice dry and

remain a few minutes. Then rinse off with warm water and apply moisturizer. Apply both morning and night. Lemon juice contains *Isopimpinellin,* a chemical which produces thickening and toughening of the skin if the lemon juice is allowed to remain on too long, or if the skin is over-exposed to sunlight.

10. The juice of the lemon applied directly to cuts or open wounds is a natural antiseptic, destroying infecting bacteria—or it may be cut up and used as a poultice, as already explained. Continual applications bring rapid healing, even to the most stubborn cases of external infections.

11. For aching feet or for colds, soak the feet in comfortably hot water to which lemon juice has been added. Or massage with lemon juice directly without soaking. To remove a corn, cover with a slice of lemon and tie a gauze cloth to hold overnight. Repeat until the corn dissolves.

As with all citrus foods, use in moderation. For some, the citric acid of lemons is far too potent to be taken with any regularity. Many find great relief from arthritis, for instance, by taking warm lemon water on first arising (eight ounces of water with the juice of one lemon). Others find such regularity causes stomach distress and other complaints. Three times a week may be sufficient for these patients. Each must find what seems best for himself.

It should be stated, however, that often the fruit is blamed as harmful when actually the harm lies in the chemical fertilizer in which it is grown, and especially the deadly sprays with which the rind is polluted. So do try for organically grown lemons, and wash them in vinegar water before using.

Never drink tea with lemon in a polystyrene cup. The acids in the lemon dissolve the cup, saturating the tea with chemical substances from the polystyrene. Consuming such tea habitually is extremely hazardous. Tests with polystyrene report that cancer was caused when polystyrene was implanted beneath the skin of test animals. So use caution. If you *must* drink tea from a polystyrene cup, don't add lemon.

When purchasing lemons, avoid those with light yellow or greenish-yellow skins. They are too tart. Select those that are heavy for their size, with smooth thin skins. Lemons can be kept at room temperature, or, if you prefer, refrigerated.

MANGOES

Mangoes should be eaten only when the skin has turned a beautiful orange. Mangoes are unusually high in iron, calcium and phosphorus. They also contain vitamins A, B and C. Eat the ripe mango as an aid to liver problems and inflammation of the kidneys. They combine well with raw milk, making a good protein and sugar balance. A fast on mangoes and milk is excellent. They are useful in gaining weight, improving eyesight, correcting constipation, indigestion, sexual weakness, and relieving respiratory ailments. They should be part of the diet if one has any type of cyst in the body.

MELONS

Melons in general—the cantaloupe, honeydew, casaba and watermelon—are reportedly better eaten alone. Eaten with other foods may cause digestive problems. Eaten alone, they heal digestive problems. They are also purifiers, glandular stimulators, skin cleansers and as a general tonic for the entire system.

Watermelon is beneficial for epilepsy and yellow fever. It usually should be eaten in moderation because of the sugar content. It contains organic salt and real grape sugar.

Watermelon is excellent for inflammation or infection of the kidneys, bladder and urinary tract. To heal these afflictions, one should immediately revert to a watermelon diet for several days. A famous method of flushing the kidneys or purifying the entire system is to cut watermelon into bite-size cubes and eat a cube every few minutes during the day for an entire day, eating nothing else. This watermelon purge completely cleans out the urinary tract, the bladder and stimulates the kidneys to discharge the congested poisons and toxins. More about this when writing about the kidneys.

When watermelons are out of season, drink watermelon seed tea frequently to purify the kidneys. The seeds, a rich source of linoleic acid and silicon, lubricates the joints and synovial membranes, so it is well to eat them coarsely ground—or, swallowed whole, they act as a perfect roughage to flush the congested colon and small intestines. When purchasing watermelons, select those that have some yellow color on one side. Those that are white on one side are not ripe.

Choose *honeydews* that are creamy or yellowish in color with a smooth texture. Avoid those that are whitish-green. They are not ripe. Honeydews contain about 90 milligrams of vitamin C per melon. Like the watermelon, they are extremely effective in flushing the kidneys. They are also an excellent food for the arthritic.

Choose *cantaloupes* with streaks of yellow or yellow-green. Cantaloupes contain 50 milligrams of vitamin C per melon. Those who need a source of vitamin C but cannot eat citrus fruits, should choose the cantaloupe. It contains a comparable degree of vitamin C without the citric acids. They also contain vitamin A and are high in inositol, an important B vitamin. They aid in problems of high blood pressure, arthritis and inflammation of the kidneys and bladder. If eaten alone, their bland texture aids in healing ulcers and relieving excessive gas. They contain important minerals, such as calcium, phosphorus, iron and copper.

If you are allergic to watermelon, you should also be cautious about eating cantaloupe, pumpkin, cucumber and all squashes. Melons should all be ripened on the vine. As they ripen under sun rays, the natural sugar content increases, as do all the valuable digestive enzymes and vitamins. If such fruit isn't available, then allow that which is purchased to be exposed under sun rays until ready to eat.

ORANGES

Oranges contain essential phosphorus and calcium—in the pulp, not the juice. The fresh fruit or juice, taken daily, not only supplies much of our needed daily requirement of vitamin C but aids in preventing colds, bleeding gums, pyorrhea, loose teeth, sinus problems, mineral deficiency and cataracts. Oranges also aid in keeping the walls of the blood vessels in good repair, preventing such problems as hemorrhoids and varicose veins. A medium size orange contains 50 milligrams of vitamin C.

As well as an effective source of vitamin C, oranges should be in the diet of every arthritic. The citric acid of the orange dissolves the deposits of inorganic calcified calcium in the joints. Such may be painful for awhile but, taken with persistence, the joints will again become flexible. The same is true when the skin erupts after eating oranges. It is the effort of the fruit substances to drive toxins from the body. If the therapy is continued, the eruptions will cease and the system will be free of embedded toxins. Oranges are also effective in cases of pneumonia, asthma, bronchitis, colds, tuberculosis—all respiratory ailments. Also in relieving high blood pressure.

Try to avoid commercial orange juice. It is processed by the removal of all the water content—the liquid containing most of the essential nutrients. What is left is concentrated pulp, devoid of most food elements. Before serving, tap water is added to restore the product to a resemblance of the original—tap water containing chlorine and other undesirable pollutants. So restaurant orange juice, or the carton purchased at a supermarket, is far removed from the fresh.

Never drink over four ounces of orange juice at a time. It contains too much citric acid to be beneficial. Many find it best to drink even this portion only three times a week, limiting the intake. Otherwise, an overdose of citric acid and potassium is possible, which tends to displace calcium and reduce the supply of hydrochloric acid in the stomach.

Fresh orange juice may safely be given to infants, whether breast fed or not. If tolerated, it could supply nutrients to prevent many complaints, especially if the child is *not* breast fed.

Adults should eat the fruit instead of the juice when possible, so that they may include the segments of the pulp and the white lining of the skin. As with grapefruit, these contain the essential bioflavonoids, without which Vitamin C is incomplete. So instead of juicing an orange, eat the entire fruit, except the outer skin.

The greatest harm from oranges usually is not the citric acid, but reaction to the deadly dyes permeating their skins. Government regulations require that the fruit be dyed. The process is appalling. The fruit is often picked when the skins are still green. So it must first be "bleached" to remove the green chlorophyl from the rind. This is done in the "coloring" room—an air-tight chamber filled with poisonous, inflammable ethylene gas—where the fruit is placed for several days. This process leaves the fruit bleached a sickly pale beige.

Now that it has been thoroughly "de-greened," the fruit is washed, then sprayed or run through a vat of hot orange dye and steam heat simultaneously. Now that the fruit is again orange, it is ready for the commercial market.

An unsuspecting public, purchasing such fruit, suffers from gastritis, sore tongues, sore gums, digestive problems, itching anus, and a host of other complaints. The orange is blamed when the culprit is actually the processing. So do try to buy oranges directly from an organic grower—those found in road-side stands or the true farmers' markets.

When purchasing, avoid those unnaturally orange colored. Choose the smaller "uglier" fruit. It will have more juice and be less likely to be dyed. Many people cease to eat oranges, thinking themselves allergic to the fruit, when actually they are reacting to the dye. (If you are allergic to oranges, you should also check reactions to lemons, grapefruit, lime and tangerines.) Wash the fruit in vinegar water before eating.

Never store orange juice in aluminum containers. It will leach out approximately 37 parts per million of the aluminum in the container—and the deadly aluminum accumulates in your digestive system. Nor should orange juice, lemonade or other citrus juices ever be stored in galvanized containers. They are zinc coated and, again, the citric acids will dissolve enough zinc to upset the system if continued. Store citrus juices only in glass containers if it must be stored. But it preferably should be drunk only when fresh.

Because of such leaching power in all citrus fruits, it is well to rinse the mouth thoroughly immediately after consuming to avoid erosion of the teeth enamel. The citric acid must be removed. The rinsing water may contain a small amount of baking soda, which will neutralize the acids and prevent enamel damage. Or the mouth may be rinsed with milk of magnesia, an alkalizer.

Egg yolks are rich in iron, but it is a form the body cannot easily assimilate. Combine them with fresh orange juice and its vitamin C content will transform the iron into a form the body can absorb. A glass of orange juice with egg yolk increases the iron intake four to five times.

When purchasing, avoid oranges withered or with soft areas on the skin. Choose those that are heavy for their size, with smooth thin skins. They are riper and juicier. Oranges may be kept at room temperature, or if you prefer, refrigerated.

PAPAYA

Papaya is rich in vitamins A, C, D, E, K and B, especially niacin. Also in protein, phosphorus, iron—and extremely so in calcium.

If possible, a slice of papaya should accompany the noon and evening meal, and also for breakfast if the meal is heavy. It contains an enzyme known as *papain* which aids digestion. It also possesses great healing powers for irritated intestines. Papain enzyme tablets have been known to heal serious hemorrhoid problems, proving enzymes are effective in reducing inflammation.

If it is not possible to add papaya to the meal, then drink papaya juice before or with the meal for its digestive properties—the malic, tartaric and citric acids. Or mash ripe papaya and add orange juice, enough to create a liquid. This tonic, rich in digestive enzymes and innumerable other nutrients, may be drunk with a meal or early in the morning as a digestive purifier. Papaya juice is recognized as beneficial in the treatment of eczema, warts, intestinal worms and ulcers.

Tenderizers derived from powdered papaya are often sprinkled over meat to make them more tender—or slices of papaya rubbed over meat accomplishes the same, proving its effectiveness as a digestive aid. Papaya is renowned as an aid in healing infections in the intestines and the colon, in cases of diverticulitis, ulcers and colitis. A poultice of papaya leaves, applied to ulcerated wounds and abcesses, will break down pus and mucus, draining and healing the afflictions.

Papain injections are currently being used to relieve the stress of slipped discs. Discs act as shock absorbers to the vertabrae along the spine. When a disc slips, it means the cushion is removed and the vertabrae are pressing against each other and against sensitive spinal nerves, causing torturous results.

The injection, called *cymo-papain*, enters the nucleus of the disc, dissolving the nucleus and almost immediately relieving the painful friction and pressure. This procedure has saved many a patient from painful and too often unsuccessful back surgery. We will pursue this research in our writing concerning backache and spinal problems.

Papaya is also a beautifier. After the meat of the fruit has been scooped out, do not discard the skin. Instead, massage it over the face and throat to feed the cells natural vitamins, minerals and oil. Do use papaya toothpowder, mixed with baking soda, to brush teeth. More about this later.

PEACHES

Peaches contain three important fruit acids—malic, tartaric and citric. They contain essential phosphorus and calcium, and are rich in vitamins A and C. They also contain phosphorus, potassium and a small amount of iron.

Peaches are alkalizers of the blood and should be eaten to aid acidosis, tapeworms, autointoxication and constipation. They aid in afflictions of the lungs—bronchitis, asthma, tuberculosis, and in all types of inflammation, such as gastritis (stomach), and nephritis (kidneys). They are valuable for anemia, high blood pressure and digestive problems. Like the apple, a peach a day may also keep the doctor away. A pound of fresh unpeeled apples supply 242 calories and only 16 milligrams of vitamin C—while a pound of peaches provide 150 calories and 29 milligrams of vitamin C plus 5,250 units of vitamin A.

When purchasing, choose those with no green color and are firm, not bruised. If not obtainable tree-ripened, peaches should be ripened at room temperature, then refrigerated. After washing in vinegar water, the skin of the peach should be eaten along with the rest, since most of the vitamin content is found just under the skin.

PEARS

Pears are rich in phosphorus and calcium. They also contain vitamins A, B and C.

Never eaten until ripe, pears are excellent for constipation and digestion. As with apples, pears cleanse the mouth, removing fermenting particles of food from the teeth. Pears also contain nutrients which aid in health for the gum tissues. Pectin is found in generous supply, aiding in constipation and in reducing cholesterol in the blood. They are most recognized as an aid to digestion, having often been used for patients who could eat nothing else. They are effective for high blood pressure, inflammation of the kidneys and of the colon.

When purchasing, select those that are slightly soft at the stem end, which indicates ripeness. Pears are usually harvested before ripening, however, so they may need to be ripened at home at room temperature, then refrigerated.

PERSIMMONS

Persimmons are high in vitamin C, calcium, phosphorus, and potassium. They are extremely valuable in healing intestinal disorders, such as ulcers, colitis, hemorrhoids and diverticulitis. Because of their bland texture, they can be eaten without fear of irritation to inflamed mucous membranes.

PINEAPPLES

The *pineapple* is a vegetable, not a fruit. But since it is generally considered a fruit, it shall be so classified in these writings.

Pineapples contain 38 milligrams of vitamin C in 2/3 of a cup. They also contain vitamin A, E, several of the B vitamins and the minerals calcium, iron, phosphorus, and potassium.

Pineapple has been called a "miracle" food—probably because of its excellence as an aid to digestion. It contains an incomparable enzyme called *bromelain*. Slices of pineapple should be on every plate at breakfast, lunch or dinner (perhaps alternate with papaya). Or a small glass of pineapple juice should accompany every meal—or be drunk just prior to eating, to provide its own source of the bromelain enzyme and to stimulate the enzyme-producing organs, such as the liver, gall bladder and pancreas.

Bromelain aids in maintaining an acid-alkaline balance in the body fluids, and stimulates the flow of waste debris. Bromelain also stimulates all the endocrine glands to produce their hormones. It is effective in reducing goiters, in cases of high blood pressure, arthritis, tumors, cysts, inflammation and secretions of the mucous membranes, such as bronchitis, catarrh, colitis—and in destroying and expelling intestinal worms.

With their chlorine contents, pineapples are helpful in flushing waste from the kidneys. They are also an aid to an irritated throat. They are excellent blood purifiers. They are also an energizing food, employed many times in the case of disease. They contain organic pepsin which is excellent in most dyspeptic disorders. They should be used freely in the diet, except by those with conditions such as an ulcer. They have been found to lower the cholesterol content in the blood.

Pineapples should be ripened at room temperature, then refrigerated. When purchasing, choose those that are heavy, dark yellow in color, with a fragrant aroma, and with eyes that are flat.

PRUNES

Prunes are dried plums. Avoid those

that have been dried with sulphur and choose those that are sun dried, usually available only at health stores. Prunes create an acid reaction in the body. They are rich in vitamin A and some of the B vitamins, such as niacin, pantothenic acid, thiamin and riboflavin. They also contain iron, and considerable calcium and phosphorus. They stimulate the blood circulation and, because of their iron content, are excellent for anemia.

Prunes contain important bioflavonoids. They should be soaked overnight and eaten the following morning along with the soaking liquid. Chronic constipation has often been corrected with a combination of yogurt and prune whip—or just a glass of pure prune juice daily on an empty stomach. It will stimulate a natural bowel movement.

Prune whip is made by soaking one cup of prunes in distilled water overnight. Then, discarding the pits, pour the prunes and the soaking water into a blender. Add 1/4 cup of chopped pine nuts (pignolias) and beat into a mixture. Add honey to taste. Substitute almonds instead of pine nuts if you wish. Add the yogurt for a delicious and healthful food.

PLUMS

Plums contain a generous amount of phosphorus and calcium. They are also rich in bioflavonoids, the companion of vitamin C. They aid problems with bronchitis, indigestion and liver congestion. Plums should be ripened at room temperature, then refrigerated. If you are allergic to plums, you should also check your reaction to peaches, apricots, nectarines and cherries.

STRAWBERRIES

Strawberries contain 50 milligrams of vitamin C in a half cup. They also contain vitamins A and B, and are high in iron, calcium, phosphorus and potassium.

They are known principally as blood purifiers. In addition, they aid problems with arthritis, gout and rheumatism. They stimulate functions of the liver. They reduce high blood pressure. Even though they often cause skin rash and eruptions in those allergic to them, still they are renowned as skin cleansers and in healing skin cancer and ringworm. Massaging the teeth and gums with the juice of the berry is said to remove tartar and heal the gums. A strawberry poultice should be used for sore and inflamed eyes.

They should be eaten without sugar. If sweetening is desired, use raw honey. When purchasing, avoid stained containers, not only for strawberries, but for all berries. It indicates overripe and leaky berries. Strawberries should be refrigerated. If you are allergic to strawberries, also check your reaction to blackberries, raspberries and loganberries.

CHAPTER 6
THE THREE DEADLY WHITES

One of the first steps toward a program of purification and good health is to toss out the *white sugar*, *white flour* and *white salt*—called the three deadly whites. Next, out go all products containing hydrogenated or hardened fats, such as margarine and lard. Even if you proceeded no further than this, you will have gone a long way toward improving health.

In restocking your kitchen it is well to keep the following rules in mind:
1. Choose food as close to natural as possible, little altered by the hand of man.
2. Choose that which is grown on healthy soil, that is, organically grown.
3. Discard the three deadly whites—white sugar, white flour and refined white salt—as I have just suggested.
4. Be aware that products list ingredients in the order of their predominance. Note that sugar is often leading the list or near the lead. If you must eat food containing sugar, at least avoid those whose labels list sugar as a leading ingredient.

Let's consider for a moment the vast breakfast cereal movement. Scan the supermarket shelves. What do you see? Dead food, dead food—food with every semblance of nutrition removed. Not only that, but white sugar added as an insult, so that the millions of Americans—especially children—who are eating this "food" for breakfast are not only receiving no nutritional value but are actually harming the system. Even the much-touted granola is often found to contain 22 to 31 percent sugar.

And what of the vast ingathering of prepared cake mixes, pies, cookies—all made with white flour, white sugar and hydrogenated fats? And all those soft loaves of white bread with an enlarged label saying "enriched." It's a deadly food with the germ of the wheat berry completely removed, the vitamins, minerals and protein all lost, the flour bleached and softened with chemicals, loaded with mined white salt—yet it is "enriched" by the addition of a few synthetic vitamins and a trace of iron which the body cannot assimilate.

Into that loaf of white bread has gone the required four ingredients—flour, salt, water and yeast—but over a hundred other ingredients are now added, including flavoring, coloring, sweeteners, dough conditioners, mold inhibitors, chemical monoglycerides (to create a softer loaf), and propionates to retard spoilage and give the bread a longer shelf life—all components of chemicals.

And what about the packaged puddings and pies, the hot breakfast cereals, the gelatin desserts, the jams and jellies loaded with white sugar, artificial colorings and preservatives, the peanut butter notorious for its rat hairs, rat droppings, and human filth?

All up and down the shelves of the supermarkets are to be found foods concocted in laboratories, enriched with chemicals, preserved with additives, colored with poisonous artificial coloring. How can these compare with foods produced by the sun, the soil, the rain and the hand of nature. You can't beat nature, So why not join her?

WHITE SUGAR

White sugar has been so refined and chemicalized, it can only be classified as deadly poison in the human system. It is probably the greatest offender of any one popular food. Sugar has been called a greater threat to health than alcohol, tobacco or drugs. It is directly related to heart disease, obesity, high blood pressure, diabetes and hypoglycemia.

Sugar cane—perfected by nature with minerals, vitamins and enzymes—is completely desecrated in the sugar mills. The cane is cut into small pieces which are fed into giant rollers. The rollers separate the juice from the cane, collecting the juice into enormous vats for filtering. The filtered juice flows into vacuum pans where it is heated to high temperatures to evaporate excess liquids. The remaining juice crystallizes or thickens into *blackstrap molasses*. The crystals are bleached with lye (phosphate of lime). To the granules are then added sulphur dioxide, carbon dioxide, bone-black and other special chemicals, designed to bleach it and give it the "sparkle" consumers find so attractive. The resulting sparkling white sugar crystals are the denatured refined chemicalized sugars that find their way into the sugar bowls of the world. No amount of "improving" can truly improve the product.

Can you even begin to conceive of the tons of white sugar consumed by Americans daily? Is it any wonder we are one of the most unhealthy of all peoples on earth? In the days of our great grandparents, the sugar bin was filled with natural raw brown sugar. During the last 50 years, the sugar industry has embarked on an unending campaign to convince the American housewife that raw brown sugar contains "impurities" in its dark brown color. Instead, consumers are encouraged and even brainwashed to buy the "new improved and purified" sparkling white product.

The truth is, the rich brown color represented the minerals placed there by nature. This promotional campaign—to discredit raw sugar in the eyes of the housewife—was sponsored by the white sugar refineries. Their purpose was to break the monopoly held by the sugar plantations, forcing the planters to sell only to the refineries. Even our army has been sold the idea that a bar of chocolate candy will quickly give needed energy to the soldier. True, it creates a momentary false energy because it raises the blood sugar level—but it is followed shortly afterward with a plunge in energy due to a drop in the blood sugar level.

And what of the vending machines so prominent in our schools, colleges and universities? They are stocked with "junk food" and soft drinks, colas, and cigarettes. According to Consumer Goods and Service Industries, soft drink consumption has jumped from 23 gallons to 34 gallons per year per person in the past ten years. Hidden therein is the "waiting peril"—the diabetes, the ulcers, the imbalanced pancreas resulting in hypoglycemia, the diseased liver, the coronary heart disease, the problem of obesity, the high blood pressure, tooth decay, acne and serious skin diseases, arteriosclerosis. We are trading the health of future generations for a "mess of porridge." Between 1900 and 1970 world sugar production leaped from eight million to seventy million tons.

Even the pharmaceutical companies add to the national sugar intake by making medicines sweet. Every updated study reveals more decayed teeth and more gum inflammation in children who received liquid medicines over a six month period.

Sugar is in every hot dog and cold cut. And the canned fruits and vegetables lining the supermarket shelves are rampant with white sugar— especially baby food. Any word ending with "ose" is a sugar. Refined sugars include sucrose, fructose, maltose, dextrose. Then there is saccharin, brown sugar, kleen-raw, confectionary— and even sugar "substitutes" often contain sugar. So many common food items contain alarming amounts of sugar the consumer does not suspect. The list of human ailments resulting from consumption of denatured chemicalized white sugar could well fill the remainder of this writing. To consider a few already mentioned:

1. It is the chief cause of *hypoglycemia*—low blood sugar—causing more fluctuation in the blood sugar level than most other products.

A rough estimate indicates anywhere from 20 to 80 percent of the U.S. population is afflicted with this malady, the majority totally unaware they are victims. If you suspect you are, don't accept a doctor's verdict that your headaches are just tension and you must "learn to live with them." *Do* insist on a glucose tolerance test. Or just change your diet—which usually corrects the problem. You may need to snack frequently to maintain a normal blood sugar level. And you may need to hold honey, fruit and fruit juices to a minimum in the beginning of your changeover. And do ask your doctor about the B vitamins—folic acid, B-15, B-13, and B-17, found to be helpful in overcoming hypoglycemia.

Especially must you avoid refined white sugar and its products. An excess of white sugar is the first cause of hypoglycemia. The sugar creates a sharp rise in the natural blood sugar level, resulting in a false excitation, tension, hurry, a peak of false energy—followed by a sudden drop in blood sugar.

The result is all the symptoms connected with hypoglycemia—nervous fatigue, sudden unexplainable crying spells, mental confusion, irritable reactions, low energy, mental disturbances, dizziness, depression, rapid beating of the heart, migraines, arthritis, indigestion and even polio. The victims of polio are usually those whose diet abounds in products causing low blood sugar.

In 1940 Dr. Benjamin P. Sandler of the Lee Foundation in Milwaukee released a report of his investigations linking polio with low blood sugar. He injected laboratory rabbits with insulin to produce lowered blood sugar. Then he innoculated them with polio virus. All the animals contracted polio. Carrying his investigative work still further, Dr. Sandler published a diet preventing low blood sugar, suggesting that this diet would reduce the cases of polio in America.

He released his report in Ashville, North Carolina, and in that city he succeeded in cutting the cases of polio to one-tenth of that in the rest of the country. He named as the principal offenders: commercialized ice cream, soft drink beverages, white flour and white sugar, because his researchers discovered that the victims of polio invariably included a high intake of these foods. His indictment of these products, however, caused such a reaction among the soft drinks, ice cream, white flour and white sugar industries that radio stations refused to cooperate in further hearings and publications.

Dr. Sandler also noted the effect of sugar on the heart. He concluded that heart attacks are caused by *an oxygen deficiency in the tissues—which is caused by low blood sugar—which is caused by overconsumption of sugar and starches.*

2. Cavities in the teeth increase enormously, since white sugar seems to draw the natural calcium from the teeth.

There is probably no dentist in America who does not decry the overabundance of sugar in the diet of the American youngster, and the problem increases daily. Throughout the schools of America can be found beverage and food machines dispensing candies, gums and sweetened beverages by the ton, all containing the deadly white sugar. Is it any wonder that the teeth of American children are in a deplorable condition, to say nothing of their colds, congestions, influenza and all the other ailments attributable to childhood. If it is deleterious to the health of the youngster, what can be said for the rest of us?—the millions of arthritics, heart patients and on and on. This is not to say that white sugar alone is the culprit, but it certainly must share in the overall gloomy picture of American health today.

3. Arthritis develops because the white sugar, again, draws the natural calcium and synovial fluids from the bones and joints. In the human body, it is important that a relationship of calcium to phosphorous be established and nature has established the ratio at 2 1/2 to 1. But the intake of refined white sugar raises the calcium level temporarily, then causes a sudden drop. This perpetual imbalance contributes greatly toward the degenerative diseases of rheumatism and arthritis. The crystals form deposits in the joints and muscles.

During natural digestion, almost all

foods are converted to sugars and starches in the system. The liver stores these sugars in the form of glycogen and, under normal circumstances, releases a sufficient supply into the blood stream as the body requires them. The liver is unable to store excessive intakes of refined white sugar as glycogen. That which it cannot store floats freely in the blood stream, settling as crystals in your joints, bones and muscles. That which is stored is not released correctly by the liver, causing an imbalance in the sugar level.

4. All manner of physical and mental ailments develop due to a lack of vitamin B in the system. Refined white sugar has been completely stripped of all food value. All the B vitamins—the thiamin, riboflavin, niacin, pyridoxine and biotin—have been completely destroyed in the refining. So have the minerals calcium, iron, zinc, chromium and manganese. Only faint traces of phosphorus, sodium and potassium remain. Zinc deficiencies result in prostate afflictions, loss of hair, depression, schizophrenia, insomnia. Chromium is needed to maintain blood sugar levels, proper insulin production and control of excessive cholesterol.

The blood, greatly in need of these necessary B vitamins, leaches them from various parts of the body—the heart, liver, muscles, stomach, kidneys and nerves, thus depriving them of their needed supply.

A continued intake of white sugar, thus robbing the body, creates a condition of stress, depression, fatigue, loss of appetite, digestive upsets, anemia, skin eruptions, muscle weakness, heart problems, insomnia, anxiety, crying spells, sweating, headaches, dizziness, tremors, muscle pain, backache, blurred vision, nervousness, neurosis and even psychotic tendencies.

Could it be that the teenagers of the world, consuming white sugar products by the ton, are reacting to a deficient vitamin B supply when they turn to violence, crime, rape, muggings, murder, drugs and all sorts of psychotic tendencies?

5. Consumption of refined carbohydrates—especially white sugar— is significantly related to skin disorders such as acne, boils, eczema and psoriasis. Laboratory research discloses that the level of sugar in the skin parallels the level of sugar in the blood. When the blood sugar suddenly rises—after eating a chocolate candy bar, for instance—the skin sugar level also rises.

In laboratory tests, microbiologists use sugar as the medium in which to grow bacteria, because bacteria "breeds well if sugar is present." Thus blackheads and other skin blemishes flourish when the skin sugar level is high. The rise in skin sugar provides an excellent incubation medium for their growth. Simple blackheads blossom into pimples and skin eruptions only when the level of sugar in the skin increases significantly. Sugar isn't the only cause of acne, but it is a principal factor.

The glucose content of the sugar is the direct cause of the deleterious effect on health. All carbohydrates, both refined and unrefined, are eventually converted into glucose (blood sugar), which is a necessary fuel for the body. Unrefined carbohydrates—fruits, whole grain breads, cereals, potatoes, lima beans, corn, dried beans and peas, honey and vegetables—are converted slowly in a series of natural digestive steps and require several hours to enter the blood stream, maintaining the blood sugar at a normal level until the next meal. The natural sugar in a piece of fresh fruit (fructose), breaks down gradually and enters the blood stream slowly.

On the other hand, refined white table sugar —including the so-called raw, turbinado, brown and confectioner's—is a pure chemical composed of two molecules, glucose and fructose, that combine to form sucrose which is broken down in only one step. It enters the blood stream almost immediately, sending the blood sugar level zooming, and dropping it very soon to a dangerous low. Such a sudden drop could even cause a hypoglycemic to enter a coma.

When the blood sugar level rises rapidly, the ability of white blood cells to destroy bacteria is almost completely paralyzed, creating skin problems, even infections. When a cola drink is consumed, for instance, the action of the white cells drops to almost total immobility for from two to five hours. Constant intake of such sugar products is unmistakably related to infectious skin problems because the natural ability of the blood stream to fight infection is significantly impaired—not only skin infections, but anywhere in the system.

6. Tests carried out by a leading nutritionist in London indicated it was not fat in the diet that led to heart problems—it was the sugar.

ARTIFICIAL SWEETENERS

Also dangerous are artificial sweeteners such as saccharin, sucaryl and innumerable other substitutes. They are the products of coal tar which should never be taken into the human system. Some have now been banned, having been proven to cause cancer, and others long since should have been. Saccharin is thought to be responsible for bladder cancer. Glucose is also to be avoided, which means that all items carrying a label including glucose should be avoided, such as corn sugar, corn syrup and cornstarch. Cornstarch is produced by treating corn with sulfuric or hydocholoric acid, after which it is neutralized and bleached with other chemicals. It is often found in canned juices, canned fruits and innumerable other processed products.

Many health-minded people have turned to brown or raw sugar, thinking they are avoiding the culprit, refined white sugar, but this is not true. "Raw brown sugar" is no longer the raw brown sugar of earlier days. It is 96% sucrose. Turbinado is a Spanish word meaning "to spin" or "to whirl," and it refers to the spinning process employed to separate the natural dark molasses containing the important minerals and nutrients from the white sugar crystals remaining.

With such dire warnings concerning white sugar and most sugar substitutes, what is the housewife to do?

Here is a list of suggested sugar substitutes:

1. *Carob powder*—pure and unsweetened, found in health stores. Carob contains a natural sugar and can

be used successfully in many recipes and over cereals and fruits as an excellent substitute for white sugar. In addition to natural sugars, carob contains minerals and vitamins A and B. To satisfy your sweet tooth also shop at health stores for carob candy. Much of it has sunflower seeds and nuts. Carob is very low in fat. It also has a low calorie count. It is an excellent food in every way.

2. *Frozen undiluted fruit juices*—such as apple or grape juice.

3. *Fructose*—also known as fruit sugar or levulose. It is available usually from health stores, as a white powder similar to white sugar, as a liquid, or as a tablet. Pure fructose is derived from fruits and berries.

Diabetics can safely take *pure* fruit fructose in moderation. Taken in excessive amounts, the diabetic is in danger of eye hemorrhages, and damage to the nerve and blood vessels. So whereas it is safer than white sugar, excessive intake could create sorbital, a hidden sugar by-product. The same danger exists for the hypoglycemic. It is safe only in moderate amounts.

Care should be taken in purchasing fructose. Read the label. Pure fructose is fruit sugar, taken from fruits. Other packaged and liquid fructose is derived from corn sugar and chemicals, possibly refined with acid or alkali preservatives. Also, alarming as it seems, many products labeled "fructose" are nothing more than sucrose or sugar treated with a special enzyme—an extremely dangerous item, because the user *thinks* he is avoiding sugar. So read fructose labels carefully. The label should state the source. Search for pure *berry* or *fruit* fructose.

4. *Maple sugar* or *maple syrup*—many brands listed as "pure" maple syrup are a mixture of corn or sugar syrup and maple syrup. Again, read the label.

5. *Barley malt*—is extremely sweet and may not be a safe product for diabetics and hypoglycemics. But scant measurements may be tried in baked goods and over cereals by those whose system is healthy. As with all sweeteners, it should be used with great moderation.

6. *Date sugar*—is often available in health stores. Although it is a processed food it seems safer than most sugar substitutes.

7. *Unrefined sugar cane syrup*

8. *Blackstrap Molasses*

9. *Sorghum Molasses*

10. *Pure vanilla extract* and *cinnamon*—also add a type of sweetening. Also *clover* and *mint*.

11. *Honey*—is by far the best and safest substitute—unheated, unprocessed raw natural honey, rich in vitamins, minerals and natural sugar. (Carob is a close second.) Honey increases the hemoglobin count of the blood because of its content of iron, copper and manganese. It produces quick and long-lasting energy. An upsurge in energy may be detected within 10 minutes after eating. Honey should be used in moderation, of course, since it is a highly concentrated sugar food. But eaten in moderation, it can sustain a high-energy level throughout the day, is easily digested and assimilated, does not cause flatulence and is an excellent food for the heart. The honeycomb should be favored rather than regular honey, when

possible.

These suggestions will aid you in selecting a suitable sugar substitute. The Federal Trade Commission even looks askance at the sugar industry's claims that sugar has nutritional value. The FTC, disputing the claim that sugar-processed cereals do not increase tooth decay, declare that frequent nibbling between meals on such food contributes significantly to tooth decay. The sugar industry claims there is no more sugar in an ounce of sweetened breakfast cereal than in an apple or banana, but the FTC says that many cereals contain far more than 30%. Again, disputing the claim that sugar consumption has remained unchanged for the last 50 years, the FTC figures show a 13% increase just since 1960. Their report states that "sugar contributes nothing to human nutrition besides calories—no vitamins, no minerals, no proteins—." With the FTC stepping into the sugar controversy, perhaps several companies will be compelled to change their advertising and may even eventually be required to state that sugar products "may be hazardous to your health."

RECIPES FOR THE SWEET TOOTH AND BOUNDLESS ENERGY
(From Dr. Som's Kitchen)

Soak a handful of dried apricots several hours. Then chop or grind them together with pitted dates, dried figs, seedless raisins, almonds and peanuts. Add raw honey to taste. Press into a dish oiled with sesame oil or raw sweet butter. Cut into small bars and roll each in grated coconut.

Health Candy

Out of Bernarr Macfadden's health books comes the following recipe for health candy:

Soak equal amount of dried prunes and apricots overnight. Then grind them together and mix with shredded coconut. Knead it and shape it into small bars or patties, then roll it in more coconut. This candy is not only delicious but acts as a mild laxative.

WHITE FLOUR

What is the history of white flour as a part of our diet? Since it obviously is so depleted of the natural nutrients, how did it come to be so prominent in our diet and so much to be desired over the natural whole grain product?

White flour was first used in Europe as a cosmetic, a powder. When wigs became fashionable, even for men, white flour powder found a ready use. It was dusted over wigs to give them their white luster. This cosmetic could only be afforded by the affluent, since it was obtainable only through the labor of servants, sieving the coarse part of the flour. Thus it came to be a status symbol.

A natural consequence was using it for baking in bread and pastries, the product also representing a status symbol of the wealthy, and the darker, coarser bread the natural fare of the peasant.

Today white flour is the result of extensive processing. The original wheat value would be most difficult to find. First, the wheat itself is usually grown with chemical fertilizers, thus lowering the protein content of the wheat considerably. Next, in the refining process, the wheat germ and the bran are carefully removed. The remaining product, questionably called flour, is further insulted by bleaching with chlorine gas. To keep the loaf soft, spongy and preserved for long shelf life, further chemicals are added, so that it can be labeled "enriched" and "improved." The factories thoughtfully add a few synthetic vitamins and a little iron, which the human system finds impossible to digest.

Is this the true staff of life? Whose life? Perhaps the life—or livelihood—of the bread factories and the ad writers but certainly not yours or mine. Time was when bread was truly the staff of life.

> *Behind the loaf is the flour,*
>   *Behind the flour is the mill,*
> *Behind the mill is the wind and the shower.*
>   *And the sun and the Father's will.*

Behind the white loaf of bread is the white flour, denatured, thoroughly processed, refined and chemicalized. Behind the flour is the mill, which has carefully removed the germ and the bran. Behind the mill is the manufacturer, who has hired the finest ad writers to convince you this empty, unwholesome product is the result of "the Father's will."

It certainly isn't a product any farmer would feed to his livestock who are the fortunate recipients of the valuable germ and bran. If it isn't a food worthy of fine stock animals, how is it that humans are supposed to thrive on it?

In the human system, it becomes indigestable lumps of paste. Denatured cereals are said to be no more nutritious than wall paper paste. Actually there are very few bread loaves on the market today advisable for human consumption. Better would it be to bake your own corn tortillas or whole wheat chapatti, as is done in Hunza and in countries "south of the border." They are free of oil which, heated, is injurious to the system.

Many whole wheat breads, containing wheat germ and oil, have chemicals added to preserve the highly perishable germ and to prevent rancidity of the oil. Read the label carefully.

When you choose bread, for instance, choose 100% whole grain bread. "Whole grain" means that the little covering of the wheat grain is left intact, and it is this covering that contains the mineral salts the body so needs. These mineral salts are necessary to supply elements to your teeth, bones and hair.

In refined white bread, only the starch remains. All the valuable elements and mineral salts are gone. If you love your pet dog, avoid feeding it white flour products. Most are allergic to white flour and will react violently, usually with persistent itching and loss of hair, followed by skin sores, then, possibly, death.

About the only good use for white bread—borrowed from a neighbor, of course—is to rub chunks of it over spots on window shades. The spots disappear.

With the approach of wholistic healing and a new age consciousness, there is a tremendous swing back to the natural coarse whole grain bread of our forefathers, and with it we shall see an upswing in the health of the nations, including a drop in dental problems.

SALT

Refined white table salt is reputedly the cause of many human ailments, such as heart disease, high blood pressure, edema, arteriosclerosis, obesity, insomnia, tension, arthritis, dandruff, and even loss of hair. It is today's "new and improved" variety to which we object. It has been so processed that all the natural contents have been removed.

Once salt was not so refined. In its original crude form, it contained calcium and magnesium. Today salt manufacturers have removed these "impurities." They foist on the public a "pure" sodium chloride composite, completely devoid of minerals—to which they have added deadly chemicals to bleach it a sparkling white and enable it to pour more easily. This "pure, new and improved" product can in no way compare to the products from the health store called vegetable salt or sea salt.

Sea salt contains a rich variety of minerals, natural iodine and trace elements directly from the sea. Sea salt is what is left when sea water has completely evaporated. So if you must reach for the salt, consider sea salt or vegetable salt. Even then, if you are experiencing a health problem associated with an overabundance of salt, it is well to blend it with ground herbs such as basil, rosemary, sage, thyme or any other herbs you find flavorable. Or choose *kelp*, a salty seaweed, an excellent salt substitute.

All salt is inorganic except that which comes from fruits and vegetables. But sea salt or kelp are much more easily assimilated by the body than ordinary refined table salt. The latter, like uric acid urates, is deposited in the joints, particularly the knees, elbows, ankles, wrists, and fingers. It cannot be absorbed by the human system any more than sand could be absorbed into the mechanism of your automobile. It recrystallizes, irritates, and slowly destroys.

Refined salt absorbs all the synovial fluids in the joints. If your joints crack when you bend, it is a warning that salt deposits are absorbing all the synovial fluids which act as a natural lubricant in those regions. The numerous glasses of water usually prescribed for good health are necessary to help eliminate salt deposits. But the intake of liquid can in no sense eliminate *all* the salt intake. That which is not eliminated recrystallizes and settles wherever it can be conveniently deposited—in the joints and muscles.

Our wonderful bodies have a self-oiling mechanism, but only if we provide the proper food out of which the oil may be manufactured. It is true that we must have salt in our blood stream but, to repeat, a great deal of natural salt is found in fruits and vegetables. So vegetable salt may be sufficient for your taste buds. All fruits and vegetables contain enough mineral salts to make the taste palatable once one has learned to enjoy food without adding it.

One argument *for* salt usually focuses on the apparent need for animals who seek salt licks a couple of times a year. The salt licks are natural rock salt while our common table salt is charged with chloroform gas. The elk and deer seek the natural salt lick once or twice a year because they must guard against beasts of prey, such as bears and mountain lions.

The natural instinct of the animal leads him to avoid coughing. Its natural diet is grass, which creates strong membranes in the throat. Once or twice a year the throat of the elk and deer find the membrane of the throat undergoing a natural renewing process. When these membranes are loosened they cause throat tickles resulting in the necessity to cough. The cough, in turn, can be dangerous to the animal. Thus the animal's instinct sends him to the salt lick. The salt breaks up the membranes in the throat so that the loosening substance causing the cough will be discharged at once. Instinct tells the animal that salt will help discharge the loosening membranes. Once the membrane is discharged, the animal neither desires nor requires more salt. The natural rock salt formation sought by the animals can in no way compare to our mined and chloroformed gassy table salt.

It should be stressed that salt (sodium), is absolutely necessary for successful digestion and absorption. Salt is required to stimulate the enzymes necessary to disgest food, the first being the salivary *amylase*, released with saliva in the mouth. As food passes into the stomach, salt aids in generating the flow of hydrochloric acids from the intestinal walls. Without some sodium, digestion is impossible. Again it must be noted, avoid refined table salt, but *do* use—in moderation—sea salt or vegetable salt unless your doctor absolutely forbids. If possible, secure "pink" salt, which is the coarse product remaining after sea water has evaporated from sea salt. The "pink" salt is the purest of all sea salt. It is usually discarded as "waste" by sea salt manufacturers, who separate the white from the pink and return the pink to the sea. But research has discovered the discarded pink to contain far more minerals than the treasured white—and a few manufacturers now make it available. Seek for it in health stores.

And then there are ice salt crystals. A friend writes that, left under a pyramid for twenty-four hours, ice cream salt seems to absorb much healing power. A few small crystals in a gallon of water will reportedly charge the water. Ground fine, it may be used as table salt, in moderation. When traveling, add a few crystals to purify a glass of drinking water. A teaspoon of the salt dissolved in a pint of water makes an excellent mouthwash. A drop in the eyes is a soothing eye wash. A cup of the charged salt crystals added to a tub of water is relaxing to muscles and joints, and energizing to the body.

Salt derivatives to be studiously avoided are: monosodium glutamate, disodium phosphate, sodium alginate, sodium benzoate, sodium hydroxide, sodium propionate, sodium sulfide, sodium saccharin and sodium bicarbonate. Read labels. Be especially wary of monosodium glutamate, used to flavor many commercial foods, especially Chinese food in Chinese restaurants.

Pause when considering the use of salt tablets during times of perspiration in warm weather. The body, already lacking in body water, loses even more when salt tablets are taken. The salt draws even more fluids from an already dehydrated body, causing a shock to the nerves, intense irritation, and cell tissue erosion. Instead of salt, drink much water to reestablish the cells' fluid content.

Salt can be extremely useful in the kitchen, other than in cooking. Instead of water to extinguish flaming oils on the stove, toss on a handful of salt. Broiler fires, too. Pour a handful of salt down the drain once a week to prevent odors. To remove burned food in pots and pans, cover with a cup of salt and let it sit overnight. Next morning add enough water to cover the burn and bring it to a boil over a low flame. Boil for five minutes. Then let it cool. The burn should be easily cleaned away. Copper bottomed pots can be restored by rubbing with half a lemon dipped in salt. Add salt to a damp cloth to remove dark stains from china or egg stains from silver cutlery. When cleaning non-stick pans, use salt instead of cleaning powder. It is less abrasive.

When rinsing your food with vinegar water, if some is unusually dirty or sandy, add sea salt to the water. The dirt will be more readily dislodged and will settle to the bottom of the pan.

Some salt substitutes are as dangerous as sugar substitutes. One is potassium chloride, described in a food dictionary as being a "colorless, crystalline odorless powder with a salty taste. Small intestinal ulcers may occur with oral administration. Large doses ingested can cause gastrointestinal irritation, weakness and circulatory collapse." This description appears in the "Consumers' Dictionary of Food Additives." Potassium chloride often contains monosodium glutamate, silicon dioxide and tartaric acid. It is often found on the label of low-salt canned foods, such as soup and dietetic foods. Avoid such foods.

Popcorn lovers who deplore the need for salt to obtain flavor should try 1/4 to 1/2 teaspoon of chili powder per eight cups of popped corn (1/3 cup corn, unpopped).

Epsom salts (two cups) added to a tub soak draws uric acid from the system. Use it often.

CHAPTER 7
COFFEE, KELP AND FIBER

COFFEE

Most seekers on a purification path give up coffee altogether. Some take only an occasional cup. If a weak heart, irregular heartbeat, or any kind of heart problem is indicated, it would be wise to give up coffee altogether—also tea, cola drinks, cocoa and chocolate, because they produce the same disastrous results.

The stimulation results from the intake of an alkaloid. In coffee it is known as *caffeine*. In tea it is known as *theine*. And in chocolate and cocoa as *theobromine*. All three substances are closely related chemically.

Caffeine and theine are narcotic poisons which, if taken in one large dose, would prove fatal. Taken in small doses, as in coffee and tea, it poisons and kills slowly. Caffeine is an odorless, bitter-tasting white powder found especially in coffee, tea and kola nuts. It is also synthetically produced.

A by-product in both tea and coffee is *tannin*, a substance used in making leather. The astringent action of tannin temporarily paralyzes the digestive system, stopping the flow of all the gastric juices. Thus coffee or tea immediately cause digestive problems and, later, constipation.

People who drink a lot of coffee increase the possibility of a heart attack. Reports from many medical research centers indicate that drinking between one and five cups a day increases the possibility 60%, and six or more cups a day raises the possibility to 120%. In other words, heart failure—the nation's number one killer—is directly linked to drinking coffee.

People who drink much coffee usually exhibit the same health syndromes. They are irritable, depressed and nervous. They are insomniacs. They complain of overactive kidneys and make numerous trips to the bathroom, even during the night. They also complain of irregular heartbeat, convulsions, diarrhea, muscle-twitching, circulatory problems and hand tremors. So not only the heart patient but those suffering high blood pressure, kidney, bladder and liver ailments, and these numerous other ailments are also warned to eliminate it from the diet or restrict it.

Like codeine or opium, the caffeine in coffee is a deadly drug. Many seek to escape this indictment by turning to decaffeinated coffee. If you must drink coffee, it is best to drink pure, fresh coffee—not decaffeinated, unless you have a special reason to avoid caffeine. To decaffeinate coffee, a preservative and bleach is used—also a chemical solvent called *methylene chloride*. Methylene chloride is a chemical similar to that used in drycleaning fluids. It removes the caffeine from coffee but it leaves the coffee bean saturated with a residue of chemical solvent that is dangerous either inside the system or inhaled. The decaffeinated coffee could be as dangerous as pure coffee or more so. You may wish to choose pure coffee, but hold the habit to a bare minimum. If you decide in favor of decaffeinated, Sanka seems less harmful than others—held to a minimum, of course.

A coffee substitute may be chosen, many of which can be found in health stores. Also, Postum is suggested—or, better still, try health teas.

Headlines in the Journal of the American Medical Association (March 23, 1979), carried this information: *Benign Breast Lumps May Regress With Change in Diet.*

The article carried a report by a surgeon, Dr. John Peter Minton, of the Ohio State University College of Medicine. The result of many years of research had proven beyond a doubt that chemicals in coffee, tea, chocolate and cola were responsible for benign breast lumps which disappeared when patients were asked to eliminate these substances from their diet. His research also indicated that coffee, tea, chocolate and cola establish allergic addictions. Women who gave up these substances and experienced a healing of breast lumps reported headaches during the first seven days of their new diet. . . proving they had become allergically addicted, and were experiencing withdrawal symptoms. Many people are addicted to these substances, especially coffee, and do not recognize it.

If you are experiencing breast lumps and living with constant anxiety concerning them, it is well to be aware of this medical report. Eliminate all coffee, tea, cola and chocolate from your diet and discover for yourself the satisfying results. If benign breast tumors can disappear with this change in the diet, so can tumors elsewhere in the body. Possibly, also, potential malignant tumors could enter a state of remission. And also many other ailments.

What are the symptoms of a coffee addict? There is wakening with the feeling that you've never been to bed—headachy, depressed and fatigued. Your hands may tremble or muscles ache in various areas of the body. Then there is the headache if the coffee is missed. What is the solution to get you through another day? A cup of coffee.

Make no mistake about it. . . coffee drinking is an addiction. The caffeine is needed to stimulate the nervous system. Withdrawal symptoms can be quite severe. You reach for a cup of coffee first thing in the morning because it is definitely stimulating, not only to the heart but also to the nervous system.

Not only is caffeine a toxic drug but the tars released by roasting the coffee beans are equally dangerous. The roasting process releases several toxic tars which cannot be neutralized by the liver. These tars are deadly to the entire system and one of the tars is a well known carcinogen, or cancer-producer, in experimental animals. And, from all indications, it produces the same effect on man.

The tars settle like brown mud around the liver, restricting its activity. The brown spots that appear on hands and faces are lightly called "liver spots." Why? Because these persons drink excessive coffee. The brown spots make them appear old before their time. The spots on the hands and face are reflecting the tars deposited around the liver. (Birth control pills also produce these "liver spots," so coffee is not the only culprit).

Coffee contains 29 different undesirable acids in addition to caffeine. The acids produced by coffee add to the strictures around the liver. The acid deposit is an insoluble cellulose—a form of cement. Settling around the liver the acids restrict its activities until they become a veritable dam, restricting the inflow of nutrients and preventing the natural activity of the liver. Since the liver is a filtering organ, selecting wisely all the nutritional elements that enter the bloodstream, it should be operating at total potential. When its activities are restricted, so is the filtering process. Innumerable diseases are the result of overacidity, and coffee is a principal acid-forming food.

Another effect of coffee is one that is seldom recognized—a continuous spasm of muscles surrounding the spine. The effect is that the vertebrae are continuously pulled out of proper alignment. When the spinal vertebrae are not aligned, many ailments result—headaches, backaches, nerve damage, kidney problems and muscle spasms. Caffeine also alters blood sugar levels, releasing sugar into the blood stream. The pancreas responds with an excessive release of insulin. Thus the heavy coffee drinker is eventually headed for hypoglycemia or diabetes. Heavy coffee drinkers could also become victims of tremors such as Parkinson's disease, severe anxiety, serious depressions.

Recent research indicates that without doubt caffeine has a detrimental effect upon chromosomes. They break apart in the cell nucleus and the resulting toxins cause a rearrangement of the genes. The result is disastrous—deformed babies. According to media reports, over ten percent of births in this country are mentally deficient. More than this have congenital defects or physical abnormalities. A study just released by the Food and Drug Administration has found caffeine to be a major cause of such birth defects. They do not plan to ban caffeine—simply to consider placing warning labels on caffeine-containing products.

We have warned against drinking tea with lemon in polystyrene cups. To repeat, the polystyrene is plastic and the foam cups are attacked by a substance in lemon rind called *limonene*. Acting as a solvent, limonene penetrates the plastic, dissolving some of its substances into the tea. The same is true of hot coffee and hot milk. The heated caffeine releases dangerous substances from the plastic into the liquids. So drink these liquids from a proper cup, not plastic.

I realize that even after these warnings, most of my readers will continue to drink coffee or Sanka. Its enjoyment is psychologically important to mental well-being. If such is true for you, then drink it with total and complete enjoyment and a positive attitude, forgetting this "enlightening" information—in extreme moderation, of course. I myself drink an occasional half-cup of coffee—and enjoy it thoroughly. Just be aware—and again, hold the "enjoyment" to a bare minimum.

Popular beverages such as "soft drinks" are also potent with caffeine. Coco-Cola is the worst offender. It contains the highest caffeine portion— 64 milligrams (mg) per 12 ounce can. Dr. Pepper contains 6 mg; Mountain Dew 54; Tab 49; Pepsi-Cola 43; RC Cola 33; Diet RC 33; and Diet Rite 31. These figures were released by the Natural Food and Farming publication in August, 1980.

In addition to the caffeine, soft drinks also contain phosphoric acid, which is renowned for destroying white blood cells. These are the "policemen" of the blood stream, rushing to the site of infection anywhere in the body. These white corpuscles of the blood surround and sweep from the body all the toxic substances found poisoning the blood. Their destruction opens the body to infection, loss of energy and toxemia. Soft drinks also contain artificial flavors and sweeteners, deadly white sugar, dyes and carbonated water—all destructive to well-being.

KELP, THE HEAVENLY GRASS

According to Dr. Som, when a physician discovers a patient to have a heart problem, his first prescription should be *kelp* tablets, at least one with each meal. Kelp tablets should also be prescribed for patients suffering from bone fractures that will not heal, or to reduce the healing time. They should also be prescribed for a sluggish thyroid or leg cramps.

Kelp feeds needed iodine into the body which is the usual function of the thyroid gland. Our modern diet is not conducive to maintaining the thyroid's excellent performance, and it often needs the help of kelp tablets, kelp powder sprinkled over food, or seaweed cooked like spinach.

You may prefer to sprinkle kelp on your salads. I always do. And you should use seaweed in cooking whenever possible. Add it to beans while cooking. Also soups. Mix in blender drinks and juices.

In case you object to kelp because it contains so much salt, be aware it also contains twice as much potassium as salt, which balances and renders safe the salt intake. Nor is seaweed or kelp excessive in iodine when eaten in natural form. Iodine is only toxic when taken in excessive doses in an isolated drug form.

Kelp or seaweed contains an important substance called *sodium alginate* or *algin*, which has a chelating effect on many of the heavy metals that enter the body through our polluted environment—*strontium 90* to name one. This dangerous toxin remains in the body throughout life, emitting radioactive rays like x-rays. Medical science believes that strontium 90 causes leukemia, anemia, bone cancer, and perhaps other kinds of cancer. The sodium alginate found in kelp is a nontoxic substance that has proven to be effective in chelating (attracting and holding) and removing strontium 90 from the body. It also removes lead and other dangerous metals, attaching itself to the metals and carrying them out as the kelp leaves the body. Dr. Som believed kelp should be taken daily—a half teaspoon once or twice a day, or from one to six tablets a day.

In addition to algin, kelp contains potassium, nickel, titanium, copper, silver, tin, zirconium, magnesium, silicon which is indispensable to skin elasticity, nitrogen, potash, barium, phosphorus, calcium, boron, chromium which is essential to glucose utilization, zinc for collagen strength and healthy skin, chlorine, sulphur, cobalt, iron, manganese and agnesium. It is especially rich in iodine, a mineral essential not only to thyroid activities, as we have said, but which stimulates vitamin E utilization, metabolic efficiency, and resistance to bacterial infection. Iodine deficiency results in lethargy, susceptibility to illness due to sluggish blood, inability to metabolize foods efficiently, weight gain and goiter. Iodine aids in producing *thyroxin*, a thyroid gland hormone which helps balance estrogen levels in the body. Iodine—and kelp—can be effective in maintaining proper body weight, since thyroid function is directly related to obesity.

Kelp thus is indirectly effective in controlling obesity and neutralizing a high intake of fats. Because of its high magnesium content it is especially effective in preventing heart attacks. Its chlorine content aids the production of hydrochloric acid in the stomach.

In addition to the incredible array of needed minerals we have just listed, kelp also supplies important vitamins— vitamin A, C, E, D, K and B-complex, including the evasive B-12, so needed in vegetarian diets. Not only this, but kelp contains twenty amino acids, making it an excellent protein food. It also contains carbohydrates and sugars— the "good" kind called *mannitol*, which does not upset blood glucose, making it acceptable for the diabetic.

Because of its mucilage content it acts as a mild laxative, a soothing lubricant to irritated intestines, and an absorbing field for undesirable toxins as well as metals.

Because it stimulates the entire endocrine glandular system, it improves the function of the reproductive organs of both sexes, aids digestion, improves skin tone and color, aids heart activities, improves the quality and purity of the blood, absorbs and removes uric acid, thus aiding arthritics. It stimulates kidney and liver functions. It kills germs, increases energy, encourages sleep, relieves fatigue, tension and stress, increases ability to think clearly, to make quick decisions and to remember better. It promotes tranquility.

Perhaps this is why seaweeds were known, in ancient times, as "heavenly grass."

FIBER, THE FABULOUS FOOD

Few foods are as controversial as *fiber*. It has burst suddenly on the nutritional scene and is still in its infancy—that is, to some, it has not yet proven either good or bad for the human system. To Dr. Som, eaten in moderation, it was a great boon, especially for the vegetarian. He believed the benefits far outweighed the problems occasionally created in some weakened digestive systems.

Fiber foods include carrots, cabbage, spinach, broccoli, squash, blueberries, oranges, melons, berries, potatoes, nuts, beans, seeds, bran, peas, whole grains, leafy greens, apples. Whole grain cereals are probably the best source of dietary fiber, including bran, wheat germ and whole meal flour. Vegetables are a close second, including the entire family of leafy vegetables. Fruits are the third best choice.

The proponents of a high fiber diet—including Dr. Som—list several major diseases believed to be related to a deficiency in fibrous foods: coronary heart disease, diverticular or stomach diseases, appendicitis, cancer of the colon, high blood pressure, hiatal hernia, varicose veins, hemorrhoids, diabetes, obesity, and constipation.

Many medical scientists are part of the on-going research concerning this opinion. They believe we should eat 1 1/2 ounces of bran daily—bran being the most effective of the fiber foods. Modern milling methods have destroyed the needed fiber in our grains today. The cereals offered provide no roughage whatever in the intestinal tract as do the natural fiber foods. Sufficient research has been accomplished to prove that fiber in the diet controls fat in the blood. A diet lacking in fiber leaves the heart open to attack by fat congesting in the arteries. But fruits, vegetables, nuts, seeds and legumes are also needed for roughage and for fiber. Many who cannot tolerate the roughage of bran and grains must depend on these foods for their needed fiber. *Too few are aware that a large green salad daily would provide all the needed fiber.*

The diseases listed above are practically unknown in those parts of the world where fiber is part of the daily diet. Research found that substituting a highly refined diet for the usual roughage quickly resulted in the symptoms of constipation, diabetes, hemorrhoids, heart problems, colitis and all the other diseases with which we are so familiar. On a bland diet lacking fiber, fatty substances that cause many of our health problems— cholesterol and triglycerides—quickly develop. These are the two culprits known to be associated with many problems, including circulation and heart attacks. Adding fiber to meals has shown significant improvements in digestion and elimination, rapidly correcting such problems as constipation, chronic diarrhea, diverticulitis, and numerous other disorders of the digestive and eliminative tract.

Here are some of the results of experimental cases:

1. *Diabetes*

Diabetics have found that after including high fiber foods in their diet, they reduced their insulin requirements considerably. In some cases it has been safely eliminated. Dr. Som suspected that lack of fiber in the diet may have been the cause of the diabetes in the first place.

A syndicated column written by Dr. Lawrence Power describes an experiment in which ten diabetics participated. They were placed on diets extremely high in carbohydrates and fiber. Breakfast included bran buns, toast or muffins of whole wheat. Lunch consisted of bean soup, whole grain bread, hash brown potatoes, stewed tomatoes and fruit. Dinner included meat, three vegetables, salad, fruit, and whole grain bread or muffins. This was a diet with 60-70% starch.

On the diet there was an immediate lessening in the need for insulin. Blood sugars fell gradually and, at the end of the test, seven of the ten volunteers discontinued insulin altogether. Fats in the blood decreased and cholesterol levels dropped steadily. An unexpected bonus was that all the patients lost weight except two—who considered their weight to be normal when the test began. Some of the volunteers lost as much as 30 pounds. None ever experienced hunger or the need for snacks between meals.

Dr. Power concluded that whole foods satisfy with fewer calories, and that refined foods result in hunger soon after eating, which leads rapidly to overeating and overweight. He also concluded that our diets must include more vegetables, fruits, whole grains and foods such as beans, peas, soy beans, nuts and seeds. These are all fibrous foods. His tests seem to indicate that adding fiber to the diet could overcome hypoglycemia, diabetes and high levels of unnatural fatty substances in the blood which lead directly to circulatory problems and heart attacks.

2. *Heart Problems*

Fiber has been shown effective in reducing fats in the blood. The intake of fiber foods sees an almost immediate reduction in fats throughout the entire system. With heart disease our number one killer, it is good to know that raw vegetables, bran, pectin, alfalfa and other fiber foods are making an impact on this health problem. For some years now, we have known the effect of fibers on the intestinal tract. We are now beginning to be aware of their benefits on the heart. All fiber foods have been found to reduce blood clots which block the flow of oxygen to the heart. Pectin, found in fruit, greatly improves circulation and prevents the build-up of cholesterol.

Alfalfa has been shown to be especially effective in removing cholesterol deposits in the arteries, even though the diet continues to contain such foods as eggs and other high cholesterol foods. Sprouted alfalfa seeds are especially effective—topping salads and sandwiches. If such seeds aren't available, alfalfa tablets are an excellent substitute. Alfalfa is now being processed first into juice and then into a new leafy food, rich in protein. As our animal-protein source becomes increasingly scarce, and more and more expensive, alfalfa "meat" may soon appear on many tables—palatable, too, according to researchers.

3. *Obesity*

Fiber is used to great advantage in reducing diets. Experimental tests conclude that obesity is almost always connected with a diet low in fiber. Fiber foods encourage chewing and mixing with saliva before ingestion. This action decreases the absorption of calories, aiding in weight reduction. Fiber-rich food satisfies hunger more quickly than "dead" processed foods. It forms a bulk which moves through the intestines so quickly that calories are not readily absorbed.

Obesity is prevented on a high fiber diet because it is so satisfying and so filling. The blood sugar stays at a balanced level for long periods, preventing the necessity to snack to satisfy hunger. Stools become soft and easily expelled, thus preventing hemorrhoids, which result from constipation. A fiber-deficient diet results in small hard stools which lead to constipation. Pressure is created in the veins around the anus, weakening their walls, resulting in the formation of hemorrhoids.

When white flour products such as white bread, pies, cakes, cookies, donuts, etc., arrived on the nutritional scene, the human family began to lose its powers of digestion, to experience obesity, diabetes, spastic colon, diverticulosis, ulcers, and to enter a health decline. There is now a swing back to whole grain products and a decline in the consumption of white flour products and cereals. If this trend continues, "healthians" will begin to include fiber foods as a natural part of the diet, automatically reducing the intake of calories, and automatically ingesting fibrous foods that purify the intestinal tract, reduce obesity, and provide excellent nourishment at the same time. No doubt an upward trend in better health will automatically follow.

4. *High Blood Pressure*

Tests have proved a lowering of high blood pressure when fiber is added to the diet—that a diet high in fiber considerably lessens the chance of strokes, heart problems and circulatory difficulties because the fiber diet reduces fatty substances implicated in these diseases—usually beginning with high blood pressure.

5. *Gallstones*

High fiber foods are also believed to reduce the incidence of gallstones. Animals fed diets low in fiber rapidly suffered gallstones made of cholesterol. Adding fiber to the diet corrected the problem. Fiber in the diet causes the excretion of excessive cholesterol, reducing the likelihood of cholesterol-rich gallstones. Gall bladder problems often arise from eating too much sugar and other refined carbohydrates—foods containing no fiber. Such problems are corrected by adding fiber to the diet and eliminating sugar.

6. *Intestinal Diseases*

Irritated intestines, cancer of the colon, constipation and innumerable other digestive problems are directly related to a diet low in fiber.

Dr. Som was fond of reminding his lecture audiences that, in the days of the pioneers, no one needed to be concerned about fiber in the diet since foods were whole and natural. Nothing was processed and nothing was polluted. Foods went directly to the table as nature supplied them. Thus fiber was as natural a part of the diet as food itself. As processing slowly became part of the nutritional scene, fiber was largely destroyed.

He added that foods moving through the intestinal tract without the aid of fiber became more or less a spongy, pasty substance, much of which clung to the walls of the intestines. Ultimately it hardened into a cement-like substance, blocking the flow of nutrients from the villi of the stomach into the blood stream. Thus the individual might be eating a diet sufficient in every way and still experience malnutrition, because the nutrients in the diet could not reach the blood stream. He was unable to absorb the elements of good from his food.

Before health could be restored, fibrous foods had to be added to the diet. They would slowly dislodge the ingrained masses along the intestinal walls, unblocking the villi once more, and opening these passageways from the stomach into the blood stream. Dr. Som declared that only fiber foods could dislodge these ingrained substances—the whole grains, the leafy green vegetables, the fresh fruits, the legumes such as beans and peas, and the seeds and nuts.

Regeneration must also include cessation of all refined foods, white flour products and white sugar. Only on such a purification program could health be restored once the intestinal tract was impeded with the pastry debris of refined processed foods. On such a diet, chronic constipation was the norm. Unnatural bacteria breeded in the large intestines and bowels, creating the potential for all the dire possibilities of disease.

Dr. Som explained the cure of intestinal diseases through fiber thusly: The colon is composed of "small bladders." Food progresses from one bladder to the next by a series of natural intestinal contractions. The "active" bladder—the one through which the food is presently passing—tightens at both ends and contracts with enough force to propel the food mass forward into the next bladder segment. But when fiber is lacking, more force or pressure is required, resulting in "pouches" or "pockets" which become inflamed and infected, often requiring surgery. When fiber food is added, the problems disappear.

When in recent years it was first announced that fiber should be added to the diet—and the "fiber fad" became fashionable—many swung to the extreme of adding high quantities of bran to a diet still including refined and processed foods. They experienced some intestinal difficulties. Thus, the fiber foods should be added cautiously along with a gradual reduction in refined foods.

The simplest way, of course, is to eat a raw salad daily. Or add small portions of bran to daily meals. Plain unprocessed miller's bran is available at most health stores. It is highly recommended since it is low in fat. It may be sprinkled on salads or in soup, baked in casseroles or meat or vegetarian loaves. Or it may be eaten as whole grain toast. Its magic is that it absorbs many times its own weight in water. And it is this water content that creates large soft stools and stimulates natural bowel action. So when adding bran to your diet, also add a liberal intake of water.

Do be sure to obtain the coarse, unprocessed bran from a health store. The usual processed bran flakes sold as breakfast cereals contain heavy sugar contents and malt, which neutralize the beneficial effect of bran.

Wheat germ is another excellent source of fiber. It contains high quality protein, polyunsaturated oils, vitamin

E, all the B-complex vitamins, and a generous supply of iron, magnesium and zinc. It is highly perishable and should be kept refrigerated. Sprinkle raw or toasted wheat germ on yogurt or applesauce, or add it to blender drinks, over cereals and to baked goods. Although bran will keep for months under refrigeration, oil-rich wheat germ should be used quickly since it turns rancid rapidly, even when refrigerated.

Bran is the coating of the wheat berry. Milling removes the wheat berry when whole wheat is milled into white flour. Wheat germ, the tiny germ in the wheat berry, contains the energy and life germ necessary for growing another wheat plant. A wheat seed will not sprout if the germ is removed. All the vitamins and minerals of the grain are concentrated in the bran and wheat germ. That which remains when these two are removed is mostly empty starch.

Brewer's yeast, another source for fiber, is perfect protein, and contains all B-complex vitamins, and many trace minerals.

Avoid popular cereals like the plague—even those "new improved" brands. They are only grains with every natural goodness removed. With sweetening and milk added, they are probably the very worst "food" available. A few exceptions are All-Bran and Shredded Wheat. If the labels are to be believed, they are plain whole wheat with no sugar or additives added. In the nineteenth century, a movement toward food reform was led by one Silvester Graham, who claimed that indigestion was the result of a diet too refined and concentrated. Determined to put bran back into wheat flour, he became the producer of the *Graham Cracker*, the only cracker recommended by nutritionists.

It should be stated that those suffering from an intestinal tract already inflamed and irritated may not be able to tolerate high amounts of fiber foods. They should be approached cautiously in such cases, but they certainly should be included. If raw fruits and vegetables are not tolerated then they should be cooked slightly and taken in small amounts. A mixture of raw and slightly cooked foods may next be tolerated until the colon is healed and ready to function with a normal diet including moderate degrees of fibrous foods.

In hospitals in England, postoperative patients are immediately placed on a high fiber diet. Death from blood clots following surgery are being reduced to zero because the high fiber diet of whole wheat bread and bran causes easy and rapid elimination of toxic wastes. Constipation can quickly lead to blood clots by interfering with the blood flow. Fiber in the intestines absorbs moisture and makes stools larger and softer which reduces stress on the bowels. It also has a purifying action, diluting and removing potentially harmful chemicals and viruses that often accumulate in the intestines during and following surgery.

Some people refrain from eating seeds and whole grain products because they believe their *phytate* content to be harmful. Phytate is renowned for excreting calcium from the system, and these people do not wish to lose calcium. But whole grain breads which have been leavened by yeast have phytate in a form which has no deleterious effect—in other words, yeast renders the phytate harmless. Sprouting also breaks down the phytates, making them harmless. Thus, when possible, eat sprouted grains and seeds. Or buy sprouted grain breads. Unleavened bread—that which possesses no yeast—can be harmful if eaten to excess. The amount of phytate found in nuts and seeds is so nominal it should be completely discounted. Besides, these wonder foods possess other offsetting ingredients—neutralizing properties. They should not be eaten to excess, however, especially nuts.

Almost all commercial breads contain fat or oil or an emulsifier. The emulsifier used by most commercial bakers is called *monoglyceride* and it is extremely dangerous. It dissolves tissues in the body. Also the oil cooked inside the loaf has been made rancid with the cooking. It is good to eat all bread in moderation. There is now on the market a bread containing no oil and no flour—only sprouted grains. It can be found in health stores.

Don't ever leave home without it!—unprocessed bran, that is. When traveling, it is a must, to insure elimination. Also choose black or dark bread. Unabashedly sprinkle bran over your breakfast cereal, soup or fruit. Or pop a spoonful in your mouth and drink it down with water. The bran is important because in most foreign countries tourists should avoid raw foods such as salads.

If you *must* take along a medical drug to be assured of escaping the proverbial diarrhea that ruins so many vacations, then choose the antibiotic *Doxycycline*. Be aware, however, that it discolors developing teeth, so should be avoided by pregnant women, infants and children under eight years of age.

Much can be said for fruits in connection with fiber foods, especially apples, oranges and grapefruits. Please refer to the section on fruit for details. Suffice to say they are abundant in pectins which act as fiber in the system. Pectins—powerful agencies removing toxic effects from chemicals in the diet—are abundant in apples and grapefruit. Their bulky mass tends to absorb undesirable substances, ushering them out of the body as wastes. Pectin is the substance in apples that causes apple jelly to "jell." Packaged "jell" pectin has been used medically to improve and heal diseased colons and to create bulk which assures easy passage of stools. Certainly any diet, whether one is aware of fibers or not, should include at least one apple a day—and one grapefruit, if possible.

When you begin adding fiber foods to your diet, *also be sure to add supplements of minerals such as calcium and iron, because increased fibers tend to cause less absorption of minerals, thus a daily mineral tablet is required.*

CHAPTER 8
FOOD ADDITIVES, CHEMICALS, PRESERVATIVES AND DYES

I like to think I'm using "gentle persuasion" in pointing you toward vegetarianism. At least I hope the chapter you are now reading may influence you to reduce the flesh foods in your diet. You may not wish to become a total vegetarian but at least be aware of the dangers in your food. Meat is not the only contaminated item, but for a moment let me focus on why you should be cautious concerning meat.

The U.S. Government Accounting Office—GAO for short—releases, free of charge, a report that should increase your awareness. It may even shock you. You can obtain it by writing to U.S. GAO, District Section, Room 1518, 441 G. Street North West, Washington, D.C. 20548. The report states that a high percent of all meat and poultry sold in the United States contains "potentially harmful residues of animal drugs, pesticides, and even environmental contaminants." The substances listed are already known to cause cancer, birth defects, allergies, and toxicities. One hundred and forty-three drugs and pesticides are listed in the report. Forty-two have been proven to cause cancer, twenty are known causes of birth defects.

The report lists some of these contaminants found in meat and poultry—DDT, cadmium, carbontetrachloride and hexachlorobenzene. These are only a few of the many insecticides listed. Drugs used on animals include antibiotics and tranquilizers which obviously find their way into the human system consuming the animal flesh. The report states that tests have shown that 33% of the cattle, 37% of the pigs and 82% of the chickens in a given test were found to have DDT in alarming amounts—but within the government's legal limits.

An unsuspecting public eats these contaminated and poisoned foods—these dangerous chemicals—day after day. Arguments attempting to soothe the public state that the amounts are so minimal as to be without significance, but they do not state that the public eats these "insignificant" amounts day after day after day and that they are cumulative in the system. The consumption of meat is only one source of contamination. Nearly all of America's farm crops contain one or more of the following deadly cumulative poisons: DDT, parathion, lindane, selenium, manganese, toxaphene, malathion, chlordane.

DDT has been loosed all over the world since 1939. There is hardly a living thing—human and animals—whose blood stream, cells and fatty tissues are not saturated with it. It flows unseen and unrecognized in our rivers, bays, streamlets and even our oceans. And it will remain there for an unknown number of years, stretching into our future. It is a known carcinogen and is also linked to liver disease. Fat-soluble, it is stored in the fatty tissues of the body, especially through meat, since the flesh of the animal is heavily polluted. Meat is estimated to contain thirteen times the DDT as fruits, vegetables and grains.

Meat is also permeated with antibiotics in an effort to control animal diseases such as cancer, anthrax, blackleg, hog cholera, bovine tuberculosis, diphtheria. In addition to the yearly standard vaccination shots given feed animals, the antibiotics include terramycin, bacitracin, hygromycin B, oxytetracycline tyosin, neomycin, aureomycin—mixed with their feed also to promote growth. These drugs, consumed with meat, are cumulative in the system, eventually resulting in hazardous conditions, beginning with diarrhea, mysterious vomiting and headaches. Aureomycin, used widely in animal feed, destroys, for instance, favorable bacteria in the intestines upon which we depend for absorbing the nutrients we eat.

Let's just consider Crohn's disease, as an example. It covers a multitude of ailments such as regional enteritis, ileitis, ileocolitis and transmural colitis. All these intestinal inflammations begin with diarrhea and abdominal pain followed by headaches, intermittent fever, loss of appetite, jaundice, skin itching and rash, arthritis with painful and swollen joints.

The disease then destroys the mucosal surface of the small bowel, making it impossible for the perplexed patient to absorb nutrients from the food he eats. Stools contain large portions of protein, resulting in a sudden weight loss and drop in energy. Some patients develop fistulas—abnormal connections between the bowels and skin of the abdominal wall, with subsequent fecal draining.

Medical science declares there's no known cure for Crohn's disease—it's a most mysterious malady. Is it, really? It could be simply the result of constantly consuming contaminated, polluted and medicated meat!

And what about *polychlorinated biphenyl*—known as *PCB?* It, too, can be found interpenetrating the fatty tissues of most living things and it is extremely toxic. PCB has been linked to cancer. In experiments with laboratory animals it caused stillbirths and miscarriages. It is also known to cause—in humans—tumors of the liver, atrophy of the thymus, porphyria (a metabolic disorder), acne and learning disability—plus peculiar behavior patterns.

The breast milk of mothers who eat meat have been found to contain 100 times the amount of PCB normally ingested by the vegetarian mother. The pesticide levels in vegetarian mothers have been found to be as low as one-third the national level. Feeding infants via the bottle is even more dangerous, since animals' milk contains more pesticide chemicals than that in mothers' milk. It would seem that pregnant women and mothers with infants would do well to become vegetarians at least during the breast-feeding period of their infants.

A deadly dye—*Yellow No. 5*—is used as a food coloring in innumerable foods—especially commercial ice cream. It produces extremely toxic and allergic reactions. This dye is so dangerous the FDA is proposing it be listed on labels so that those who are allergic to it may avoid it. But how many of the populace know they are allergic to it? How many with an elusive type of illness think of connecting it to Yellow No. 5?

And then there are the polybrominated biphenyls—chlorine, bromine, iodine and fluorine—a bromine compound used in the manufacture of a fire retardant. It is recognized as PBB.

In 1973 several thousand pounds of PBB were inadvertently poured into livestock feed in Michigan, then sold to unsuspecting farmers throughout the state. The feed was fed to many farm animals, primarily dairy cows. Many of them died. Some did not. Those that did not were sold to the Michigan stockyards to be purchased over the butcher counters. The accident was not detected for almost a year and, by that time, everyone in Michigan, and many far beyond the boundaries of Michigan, had been poisoned.

Mysterious symptoms alerted farmers that something was wrong. Their cattle refused to eat, hair fell out revealing toughened, unnatural hide. Too many calves were born dead or died shortly after birth. The animals acquired bizarre behavior and symptoms which veterinarians were unable to diagnose. Then the bizarre symptoms began to strike the human population—birth defects, weight loss, fatigue, loss of hair, aching joints, and other maladies too numerous to mention here. The details of this incredible happening may be read in a book called *PBB: An American Tragedy*, by Edwin Chen.

Turning to that which may be closer to home, do your children exhibit bizarre behavior patterns—temper tantrums, arthritic pains, crying fits? The medical scientist calls these reactions allergies to "food," but could it not be that they are allergic to chemicals and pollutants *in* the food? Many react to milk, eggs, chocolate, potatoes, fish, corn and wheat. It is necessary to remove these foods from the diets of these "allergic" patients, but the reactions could well be caused by the combination of chemicals in the foods with the chemicals inside a particular human system. It is true that these low level pesticides do not produce immediate death or even diagnosable illnesses, but is it not possible that they may so damage nerve structures, eyesight or glandular productivity, that we easily fall victim to all manner of contaminations, diseases and behavior patterns?

Even though pesticides do not trigger immediate death, they certainly may create devastating injury and long-term effects upon a human system, causing unique and bizarre maladies which cannot be diagnosed and certainly not properly treated. For instance, pesticides are found in many coffee beans being consumed by millions of coffee drinkers, so limit your intake or become victim to a steady input of dangerous chemicals. If you are fortunate enough to find it, do purchase Kona coffee produced in Hawaii and relatively free of pesticides.

Agriculture department officials report that 1.7 percent of the nation's pork liver contains illegal amounts of organic arsenic. This additive is also found in poultry feeds. Arsenic, a recognized poison, is used in animal feed as a growth stimulant. Arsenic compounds include arsenilic acid, sodium arsenilate and hydraxyphenyl arsenic acid. This compound is also used as a "dip" solution on cattle and sheep to dispose of ticks, lice, fleas and other parasites.

One of the most dangerous of chemical preservatives is *BHT*, found in potato chips, crackers, cereals, cake mixes, etc. BHT has caused cancers and tumors in test animals.

Many pears are contaminated with a spray called *BAAM*, an insecticide which is a potential health hazard. Tests indicate it produces tumors in man. Growers in Washington, Oregon, Utah and California were given governmental permission to spray their pears with BAAM. If possible, select pears grown elsewhere.

A chemical called *benzine* is widely used in industry as a solvent, a major ingredient used in plastics, rubber goods, gasoline additives, drugs and pesticides. Millions of workers exposed to benzine are subject to genetic damages. Workers tested for benzine contamination were found to have chromosomal changes in their white blood cells, having ten times the amount of damaged chromosomes as found in normal blood tests. Such findings indicate that benzine poses a significant risk of birth defects, blood disease, and cancer.

Three extremely dangerous chemicals—*sodium nitrate, sodium nitrite,* and *sodium sulphite*—are found in many popular foods. *Nitrates* are used as color fixatives in cured meats and, combining with natural stomach acids and food substances, create cancer-producing agents in the body. They are present in medications, drinking water and in most of our foods.

Both nitrites and nitrates are used as preservatives to retard the putrefaction process to which all meats are subject, but especially are they prevalent in sandwich and luncheon meats such as frankfurters, salami, hamburger, bologna and sausage. These dangerous preservatives are known carcinogens— that is, cancer causing agents.

Sodium sulphite, another suspect, is used to give a "fresh red appearance" to rancid meat that has turned black with decay and to eliminate the powerful odor of putrefaction. The common symptoms after consuming such chemicals are dizziness, irregular breathing, unsteady gait, increased rapidity of heart beat, lowering of blood pressure and body temperatures.

Most insecticides, herbicides and fungicides destroy Vitamin B complex. Nitrates and nitrites are particularly destructive. Nitrogen fertilizer has been prevalent since World War II. Used to increase crop yields, it has resulted in higher levels of nitrates in soil, seeds and water. The best possible security against such devastation is to eliminate refined foods from the diet—the white sugar, white flour, white salt, and processed foods. The intake of raw salads, natural honey, whole grain cereals, wheat germ, whole wheat flour and raw certified milk will do much to aid the liver in converting residual toxins to harmless substances. Also, a daily intake of Vitamin C and Vitamin E aids the body in destroying the ingested poisons and chemicals.

The growth stimulant DES—diethylstilbestrol—has been barred by the government for use in the meat industry. DES has been mixed with feed or implanted as pellets under the skin of animals to fatten them before slaughter. Tests have proven DES causes cancer in humans and animals. The ban does not affect the DES already polluting soils on which animal feed is grown or crops on which it is sprayed. Nor does it affect medicinal uses of DES in small doses in humans, including synthetic estrogen for women. So if you must take estrogen hormones, refuse the synthetic estrogen usually prescribed. There are natural sources (Premarin and homeopathic ovarion tablets).

Although banned from skin implantation, DES continuously sprayed on animal feed still fattens the animal which eats it. If it fattens the animal, what will it do to the human who eats the flesh of the animal? The DES in the animal flesh *could* be fattening to the human who consumes it, couldn't it? Did you ever wonder why the majority of all Americans are consistently overweight? Always and forever dieting—yet never able to maintain a normal weight. Could it be the regular consumption of DES in meat? Vegetarians are not notoriously and consistently overweight. If you *really* want to lose weight, try being a vegetarian a while.

A myriad assortment of chemicals widely used for various purposes include chlorinated hydrocarbons, organic phosphates, systemic insecticides, and inorganic insecticides. They are marketed with three and four lettered brand names: DES, BHC, HCH, DDT, TDE, TEPP. They are sprayed widely on all yielding crops and in the food eaten by food animals—which means that meat, poultry, fish, fruits and vegetables contain these deadly poisons. DDT was banned in 1972, but so massive was its use, it still manifests in our agricultural fields and will persist for many years to come. TEPP is reportedly 250 times as toxic as DDT. It has not yet been banned.

Added to these dangers are the man-made chemicals deliberately used in food production—food processing, additives, food coloring and food preservatives. Much of the fruit found in supermarkets must be washed in vinegar water to, hopefully, remove much of the downpouring pollutions in the atmosphere. Some are directly deliberate, such as apples, citrus fruits and pears deliberately coated with wax containing a fungicide, thiabendazole. Many children eating such fruits—especially apples—have violent reactions and display peculiar behavioral patterns. The same is true of oranges which have been dyed. Wash such fruit in vinegar water to remove some of the wax and dye. There are an estimated 10,000 chemical food additives now in our food supply, compounded by chemical contaminants in air and drinking water, with hundreds of new ones being introduced each year.

Once consumed, these foreign substances in the system must be broken down and made water soluble before the body can excrete them—as is true of natural nutrients. The task of such performance falls upon the liver. A persistently overloaded liver causes the liver cells themselves to deteriorate and weaken. This means the toxic waste remains longer in the body, circulating through the bloodstream into every cell.

When enough of these toxic substances adhere to the DNA cells, the result may be cancer, birth defects, or mutations. On the journey to becoming cancerous, there are the months, perhaps years, of headaches, colds, flu, dizziness, sluggishness, inertia, inflammations—all the symptoms of a body headed for a serious illness.

An additive widely used in foods, skin creams and medications is *propylene glycol*. It is resulting in mysterious skin rashes and painful itches—allergic reactions to the drug. It is replacing glycerin in many products.

Its first symptom is itching, followed by an unnatural redness of the skin. Then strange blemishes resembling pimples occur, or even small blisters. If you are experiencing peculiar skin problems, check the labels on your skin creams and foods. Here is a list of some items containing the additive:

Room spray deodorants
Cake mixes
Lubricating jellies
Eardrops
Skin Creams
Cosmetics
Soft drinks
Frozen cakes
Household cleaning products
Popcorn
Salad dressings
Grated coconut
Whipped topping mixes
French fried onions

And what about nuclear energy? In the 50's the government began announcing "There's no cause for alarm. Nuclear tests show you are perfectly safe." But nuclear reactors emit radiation steadily even when normally operating. There are seven times the incidents of deformity, miscarriages, leukemia and cancer in the vicinity of nuclear reactors than elsewhere.

In foods such as hot dogs and bologna, the USDA now allows up to three percent of ground bone. These could cause violent reactions, certainly headaches, because they carry residues of radiation, since animals grazing where fallout exists store more radiation in bones than in tissues. Kelp, a seaweed derivative, has been found to *decrease* the amount of radioactive strontium that lodges in bones and teeth. So do take kelp tablets or sprinkle powdered kelp over your foods, just as you do salt... or as a salt substitute.

And what of x-rays used so promiscuously in physicians' and dentists' offices? The outcry against them has become so vociferous that x-ray is about to be replaced by sound waves, to take pictures of the inside of the body. At least there is finally a step in the right direction, moving us away from cancer-causing high levels of radiation and toward ultrasound.

X-ray examinations are standard practices in most doctors' offices whether the patient needs x-ray examination or not. Yet it is well known that such radiation is potentially harmful and always cumulative. X-rays are high energy electromagnetic impulses. These impulses radiate not only from the x-ray machine in the offices of physicians and dentists, but from radio, television, radar systems, luminous watch and clock dials, microwaves and nuclear energy generators.

An early warning of adverse reactions to food additives, pollutants or radiation can be a headache. Those exposed directly to x-ray—especially following examinations in the physician's office—should counteract the effect by taking lecithin in the daily diet. It is also suggested that the exposed person should soak for 20 minutes in a hot bath containing a cup of sea salt and a cup of baking soda. This presumably nullifies the effect of radiation. This should be repeated four consecutive days directly following exposure, and once a month thereafter. It is also reported that massaging the body with olive oil shields it from the effects of radiation. This may be applied before such exposure if the patient is aware that exposure is about to happen.

With exposure to all these dangerous contaminants, the marvel is that the human body can survive for 60 to 70 years. The answer is that we are wonderfully made by our Creator. The human body is a walking miracle. But "survival" and "existing" aren't the real answer to man's quest for a good life. We survive and exist—but with such a struggle to maintain health and happiness.

If we lived more naturally, we could possibly *live*—not simply survive—for 100 or 150 good, healthy, happy years. Most humans have some constant pain or problem they endure—surviving and struggling through the busy days, but existing without really experiencing total well-being. What magnificent specimens the human race could be if we could manifest perfect health!

Now that I have shared all the horrendous aspects of food with you, I am sure you are ready to fast the rest of your days. It seems to indicate that eating can be a dismal necessity indeed.

Truly I have not meant to be negative. We cannot go through life with a foremost thought that "living—and eating—can be hazardous to your health." *All* food is contaminated. My reason for even including such a somber section is to point you toward the foods *most* hazardous to your health.

I haven't meant to depress you—and I want to encourage a rapid dismissal of the "enlightening" information herein. If you intend to continue eating meat—and all the other "forbidden" foods—then do so with a positive attitude. Do not think of them as harmful. Just continue to enjoy them.

All I really want is for you to be aware. If and when a health problem approaches, just be aware that it *could* be your diet. So many times doctors, finding a particular affliction, will begin a drug approach to healing, never once considering food. This entire section is included to make you aware that the cause *could* be a simple reaction to a certain food. I'd like to suggest a change in diet in an effort to restore health, *before* the drug routine is started—if possible.

Just awareness—that's all.

CHAPTER 9
THE MYSTERIOUS MAGIC OF THE BEE

My son, eat thou honey because it is good, and the honeycomb which is sweet to thy taste.

Proverbs 24:13

It has been estimated that honeybees have existed on our planet for over forty million years. The questions may well be asked—where did they come from? If they were brought here from some other planet, who brought them?...and how did they become involved in mankind's diet? Many ancient writings from Egypt, India, Persia and China refer to honey as an important adjunct to man's diet, not only for health, but for purification purposes and rejuvenation.

Honey has been part of mankind's Earth life for as long as history has been recorded. Even scriptures recorded prior to our Christian Bible mention honey. It was prominent in many forms in ancient Egypt. The Egyptians and Assyrians covered their dead with beeswax and honey. It has been found in Egyptian pyramids. Greek mystics, including Pythagoras, carried information from Egypt back to Greece and, in establishing their own Mystery Schools, recommended honey as essential in the diet of their disciples.

All the ancient Greek philosophers referred to raw honey—with its pollen, royal jelly and propolis—as "nectar for the gods."

The Greek philosopher, Democritus, recommended daily dosages to prolong life. He made such a fetish of honey that, when he wished to shorten his life, he simply omitted honey from his diet.

Hippocrates, the father of medicine, looked upon honey as a perfect food-medicine for the restoration of health. He prescribed the marvelous sweet substance for those who wished to live long, healthy lives. So, historically, it has a therapeutic value. Ancient civilizations regarded honey as an aphrodisiac, using it in their religious fertility rites to restore generative powers.

If the honeybee and its magical properties have been around for 40,000,000 years, that should be long enough to satisfy even the F.D.A.'s demand for a testing period.

Honey is made from the nectar produced by flowers. The nectar, gathered by bees, is carried back to the hive where the bees transmute it through a process of water evaporation.

That which remains is the thick amber liquid called honey. To protect it in the beehive, the bee seals the honey with the cells of the honeycomb.

Honey contains an astonishing category of vitamins, minerals, hormones and vital enzymes needed for normal healthy physical functioning—all in perfect balance, polarity and quantity. Although the minerals supplied are minute, the body only requires diminutive quantities to maintain mineral balance.

The minerals are: iron, copper, manganese, silica, chlorine, calcium, potassium, sodium, phosphorous, aluminum and magnesium. These elements, diffused through the soil in which the plants grow, are transmitted by the plant to the nectar from which the bees make honey. Thus the mineral content varies according to the sources in the soil.

In addition to the minerals, honey has a high nutritive value—supplying malic, citric, formic, acetic, succinic and amino acids. These acids are of tremendous importance in balancing the polarity of the body.

Also carotin and xanthophyl pigments, albuminoids and invertase, diatase, catalase and inulase enzymes are found in honey. The vitamin B-complex components supplied include: riboflavin, nicotinic acid, thiamine, pyridoxin (B6), folic and pantothenic acid, and biotin. It contains a generous supply of vitamin A.

Naturopaths and physicians attuned to natural healing have long extolled honey's restorative powers, and physicians now entering the wholistic healing field are again turning to honey for many purposes.

In addition to aiding digestion, honey builds blood, perhaps due to its iron content. Iron is often difficult for the human system to assimilate, thus the iron supplied by honey is most excellent since honey, already digested by bees, requires little if any energy to digest.

Honey is one of the greatest healers of infectious bacteria. It is almost impossible for bacteria to live in the presence of honey. Tests have proven that various disease germs, placed in a pure honey medium, die within 48 hours. Germs causing chronic bronchial pneumonia die within four days. Dysentery-producing germs are destroyed in ten hours. Bacteria associated with peritonitis, pleuritis and suppurative abcesses die within a short time. Potassium is credited with this phenomena. It withdraws from bacteria the moisture essential to its existence.

Honey has repeatedly been reported as extremely effective in controlling problems of the respiratory system and in healing allergic reactions. When a sore throat threatens, a spoonful of honey eaten slowly enables one to swallow again. Mixed with lemon juice and warm water and sipped slowly, it drives infectious diseases and the symptoms of the common cold from the body. It is a major source in healing flu and bronchitis. Both asthma and hay fever respond to honey if it contains pollen to which the sufferers are allergic. It creates an in-built antibiotic and immunization effect.

It should be used any time a mild laxative is needed. Chewing the honeycomb is especially effective as a safe natural laxative.

New age physicians realize the value of honey in treating diabetics. This seems incredible, since sugar is one of the antagonists to be studiously avoided. Taken in moderate portions, however, honey aids the pancreas to metabolize insulin, which, in turn, metabolizes the natural sugar of honey. Deficiency in insulin indicates an oversupply of sugar in the blood. A malfunctioning pancreas, unable to supply the insulin, results in diabetes. It is now believed that diabetes is further caused by lack of fiber in the diet, and too much white sugar and white flour products, which drain the body of vital nutrients. These dead foods eventually affect the ability of the pancreas to produce insulin. When the diabetic, or potential diabetic, discards white sugar and substitutes honey in the diet, the pancreas is immediately released from the stress of metabolizing sugar, and the demand for the pancreas to continue pouring out insulin ceases. The diabetic must use honey in great moderation, of course, but it can be a useful tool in controlling blood sugar and insulin.

Ancients used it also as we do today—to produce a sudden need for stamina and energy. Trainers in today's athletic games insist that their major athletes consume two tablespoons of honey thirty minutes prior to games or endurance tests. Entering the blood stream almost immediately, it produces an upsurge of energy and a recovery from and prevention of fatigue. It is taken in more moderate amounts throughout any period requiring sustained energy and stamina. The natural sugar contents (levulose and dextrose) are transmuted into glycogen. This is the stored up substance drawn on by the athletes when facing an endurance test. The body, needing sudden stamina or energy, draws upon this stored supply of natural blood sugar. Many athletes, wishing to avoid muscular fatigue and exhaustion, now take a spoonful of honey instead of reaching for the accustomed candy bar, which is filled with preservatives, white sugar and usually chocolate. The honey provides quick energy because of its rapid absorption into the blood stream. It is also an easy-to-digest alkalizer.

The ancients used honey as a poultice dressing. A soft cloth was saturated with the golden liquid, placed over the exterior affliction and covered with a top cloth for heat and protection. Today we recognize *potassium* as the healing agent in the dressing balm though the ancients may have called it something else. As a poultice, honey is useful in healing burns, skin infections, ulcers, boils and all exterior sores and skin afflictions. If used in conjunction with cod liver oil, a balm is created to heal inflammation of the skin, relieve pain, and aid in balancing the blood sugar.

Dr. Som used the honey poultice similar to the ancients. He poured raw unheated honey on a small piece of gauze or soft cloth and applied to the affliction. He then covered it with a piece of plastic—such as covers clothes from dry cleaners—another slightly heavier soft cloth and taped or bound the poultice.

If the wound was draining, the dressing was changed at least once a day. If it was a small wound, the poultice was left two or three days. The removal of the bandage usually disclosed a complete healing. Som said the potassium content of the poultice prevented a build-up of infectious bacteria. Bacteria simply cannot live in honey, he said. He also applied the poultice to bring about a rapid healing of afflictions such as leg ulcers, chillblains, and small wounds.

Some physicians prefer to add ingredients to a honey poultice—a small measure of vaseline or cod liver oil, for instance, may dilute the honey. Also a few drops of vitamin E may be added, and a teaspoon of powdered ascorbic acid. Others prefer equal parts of honey and baking soda. To heal rashes, applications of one part honey and one part apple cider vinegar are often effective. To this formula, the powder from a capsule of bee pollen adds potency.

Dr. G. N. W. Thomas of Edinburgh, Scotland, testing honey with heart patients, wrote the following in the British medical publication *Lancet*:

"In heart weakness, I have found honey to have a marked effect in reviving the heart action and keeping patients alive. I suggest honey be given for general physical repair and, above all, for heart failure."

More than one physician has cited the value of honey as a heart and muscle stimulant. When one is especially nervous and high-strung, or experiencing heart pains, honey in a bit of warm water soothes the blood. In addition, honey relieves depression. It has been used for hypoglycemics in moderation to stifle cravings for sweet and rich foods. It certainly is a natural to counteract a craving for alcohol. It is now used to prevent and cure anemia, relieve asthma, hay fever, arthritis, sore throat, ulcers.

It has a diuretic effect on the kidneys and bladder. A great many naturopathic doctors stoutly affirm that it is helpful in preventing cancer, strokes and the lameness of arthritis. It is used to heal bee stings. Honey is applied every hour. Not only is pain alleviated, but no reaction develops.

Presumably it sharpens the eyesight. In ancient India, black honey from special sources dropped into the eyes was known to loosen and remove cataracts. Inflamed eyes respond to applications of cotton pads soaked in warm comfrey tea mixed with raw honey.

Bee venom is well-known in the treatment of some types of arthritis, especially in homeopathic (minute) dosages. It is highly effective in the treatment of neuralgia, rheumatism, neuritis and rheumatic fever. It is also effective in treating various skin diseases.

Honey is renowned as a beauty aid. Taken internally, it adds sparkle to the eyes and enhances the possibility of clear skin. Used as a facial or night cream, it nourishes and bleaches the skin. It has an astringent and antiseptic action also.

It is excellent as a hair conditioner for dark hair only. Try the following formula: mix thoroughly in a blender one cup of honey and 1/2 cup of pure cold pressed green olive oil. Just prior to shampooing, massage some of this mixture well into the scalp and hair.

Cover your head with plastic—a tight fitting plastic shower cap will do—then cover this with a terry cloth turban or towel wrung out in hot water. Reheat the turban several times in hot water each time it grows cold.

When insomnia is a problem, a teaspoon of honey in a glass of warm water frequently induces sleep. Or try the following sleeping "potion": add two tablespoons of honey to the juice of a lemon and an orange, and add enough water to fill a glass. Sip it at bedtime.

The renowned Dr. D. C. Jarvis, of "Folk Medicine" fame, made use of honey to induce sleep. He suggested one tablespoon of honey with the evening meal each day. If this were not sufficient, he offered a formula of three teaspoons of apple cider vinegar to a cup of honey. Two teaspoons should be taken while preparing for bed and repeated within half an hour if sleep still evades. He suggested repeating at hour intervals as long as necessary to induce sleep.

Dr. Jarvis suggested the use of honey to stop bed wetting. He claimed it was most effective. The moisture-absorbing ability of honey was its secret power. It attracts and holds the fluids in the child's body during the hours of sleep so that bedwetting is prevented. The child is simply given a teaspoon of honey at bedtime. It acts not only as a sedative to the child, but will attract and hold fluid during the night preventing it from reaching the kidneys.

Honey is a staple at our house. It serves many purposes. We take it almost daily with apple cider vinegar and pure water. It was a favorite remedy of Dr. Som's.

But it was Dr. Jarvis who immortalized the following magical health formula—honey and apple cider vinegar—which seems to perform all manner of wonders. His formula is: 2 teaspoons of raw natural honey and 2 teaspoons of apple cider vinegar in a cup of water. It may be taken regularly first thing in the morning, or three times a day, any time you feel headachy, cold symptoms, any unusual aches and pains, or the need of energy. This natural home remedy has dramatically cured: colds, rheumatism, arthritis, high blood pressure, hay fever, kidney problems, sinus infections, sore throat, constipation, chronic headaches, indigestion, insomnia, and food poisoning. For full information concerning this old home remedy, see Chapter 10.

Dr. Jarvis healed many a cough with a simple nature remedy. He suggested boiling one lemon slowly for ten minutes to soften the fruit, after which the lemon should be cut in half and the juice extracted with a lemon squeezer. Into a drinking glass should be placed the lemon juice and two tablespoons of glycerine. The glass then should be filled with honey. Sipping this remedy should heal the cough. Apple cider vinegar may be used instead of lemon if preferred. A teaspoonful of the remedy should be taken on rising, in the middle of the morning, at noon, in midafternoon, after dinner, and at bedtime. It should be repeated any time a cough occurs during the night.

Dr. Jarvis found honeycomb invaluable in treating respiratory difficulties. As much of the honey as possible should be drained from the comb and it should be chewed. Chewing the honeycomb has been known to heal the common cold, hayfever, congested nasal passages, sinus congestion, and coughs. The remedy is to chew a comfortable mouthful every hour for from four to six hours. Chew each "remedy" for fifteen minutes and discard the remainder.

Chewing the honeycomb has been known to prevent the onslaught of hayfever if begun prior to the usual springtime appearance. Chewing the comb three times a day should prevent or heal attacks of hayfever. If honeycomb is not available, two teaspoonfuls of liquid honey should be consumed at each meal.

Dr. Jarvis declared two teaspoons of honey to be an excellent remedy for twitching eyelids or the corner of the mouth. It should also stop cramps elsewhere in the body, especially in the legs and feet during the night.

If one is subject to liver upsets, honey should be taken in great moderation. Hepatitis cases should test continuously before including honey in the diet at all. If adverse reactions result, it should be avoided until the hepatitis condition clears.

As a fruit sugar, honey has many advantages over cane and beet sugar. Since they are refined, they drain vital mineral elements from bones and body tissue, rather than aid the body in nutrition. Sugar is a whole chemical formula. When it is refined, it means the formula has been disrupted and part of its chemical composition has been removed. That which remains seeks by its nature to be reunited with that which was removed. Thus, when taken into the body, it leaches from the bones, teeth, and other structures, the missing substance to make itself whole again. Thus it robs the body of the very vital mineral elements it is supposed to supply.

Honey, on the other hand, is a natural food and medicine in every way. Only raw unheated honey should be used. The label should read "raw" and not "uncooked." The latter may have been heated which destroys the natural vitamins, minerals and enzymes. The most excellent source is wild flower nectar, preferably taken from healthy soil. That which is extracted from sugar water should be avoided. Dark honeys should be preferred because they have the highest mineral content and are especially high in iron. Honey is not a cure-all, but two teaspoons a day is a powerful deterrent to disease and ill health and should be used as a preventative medicine in every household.

ROYAL JELLY

Inside the beehive, honeybees construct *the honeycomb,* composed of innumerable cells. Some are larger than usual. These larger cells are called the *royal cells*. The queen bee deposits her eggs inside these larger cells for the sole purpose of producing potential queens. The queen's exclusive diet is *royal jelly* from the royal cells.

As opposed to the amber color of honey in general, royal jelly is a pearly white gelatinous mass, containing approximately 45 percent proteins, 13 percent fats, and 20 percent glucose and levulose sugar substances, plus all known amino acids—plus a mysterious x factor not yet amenable to analysis.

Royal jelly is believed to be a natural antibiotic. We have said bacteria cannot long exist in honey, and we have given the hours required for its destruction, once exposed to honey. Royal jelly is 1076 times richer in germ-killing properties than honey. Germs that die in honey in two days, expire in a minute in royal jelly. Taken prior to or during an onslaught of a virus infection, the patient rapidly recovers.

It is also believed to have an incredible effect in blocking the aging process. It seems to possess a moisturizing ability which, applied to the facial skin, aids in reducing wrinkles. Royal jelly is believed to contain a mysterious bee-produced hormone (perhaps the x factor)—plus a rich supply of nucleic acid, biotin, and especially pantothenic acid—which may be the secret of its ability to retard aging and reduce wrinkling.

Because of its abundant pantothenic acid, it is effective in controlling arthritis. It has also proven to be effective in controlling Parkinson's disease, which is a palsy-like affliction affecting the entire nervous system. Patients given therapy with royal jelly found the palsy-like shaking to be considerably reduced, probably due also to the abundance of vitamin B-6 in the product.

Royal jelly has been found to be effective in treating sterility and gonadal deficiencies.

POLLEN

Bees also collect pollen from flowers. Pollen is a dust-like male reproductive element of flowers—the generative force, or sperm, of seed bearing plants, comparable to the spermatic cells in male humans and animals. The principal activity of bees is to carry pollen from one plant to another, which is nature's way of assuring that plants become fertilized. Since plants cannot navigate from one place to another, they must depend on other sources. The bees and the wind assume this task. Bees flock to bright colored flowers from which they gather nectar and pollen. They intuitively select pollen which does not create allergic reactions.

Pollen, carried back to the beehive, is infused with nectar from the bees. The infused pollen falls to the bottom of the hive. It is fed to young working bees that produce royal jelly, which, again, is the sole food of the queen bee. Beekeepers gather the substance from the bottom of the hive and create tablets or granules for human consumption.

Pollen has been declared the most complete food in nature. Analysis reveals that it contains every nutrient needed by man. It contains all twenty-two amino acids needed for health—the structural building blocks of protein. Fifteen percent of pollen is *lecithin*, which is a fat-melting substance. For centuries, pollen has been considered to possess the potential for rejuvenation. Pythagoras and other Greek philosophers attributed to pollen the secret of eternal youth. Could it be because it contains all the known nutrient factors? All the known water-soluble vitamins? All the twenty-two amino acids? And an incredible supply of minerals, including magnesium, zinc and calcium—to say nothing of the enzymes and hormonal substances, especially gonadatrophic hormones? Gonadatropin, a hormone emitted by the pituitary, has a subtle effect upon the sex glands.

Pollen also contains a mysterious prophylactic, giving it generative powers. Probably its stimulating effect upon the gonads, the sex organs, gives it its ability to firm and tonify the skin, especially that of the face. It contains 20% complete protein. The only vitamin lacking in its incredible array is B-12.

Tests upon volunteers have proven pollen to be effective in increasing energy, immunizing against disease and effective in deterring such problems as allergies, respiratory difficulties, asthma and infectious diseases such as cold, flu, pneumonia and bronchitis.

Tests in Sweden proved pollen effective in treating prostate inflammation and advanced cases of hemorrhoids. Other health problems benefited were chronic colitis, high blood pressure, hay fever, and imbalance in the endocrine system. Epileptic attacks diminshed and frequently ceased when treated with pollen injections.

There is also accumulating evidence that bee pollen and *propolis* prolong life. Experiments conducted in the Soviet Union have uncovered surprising but unmistakable evidence that centenarians by the dozen all were beekeepers who declared their principal food to be honey fresh from the hive, abundant with pollen.

It has been tested but not yet admitted that pollen contains an anti-carcinogenic substance—which means it can be used to fight cancer. A report in the National Health Bulletin credits European scientists with healing cancer of the uterus in a group of women who submitted to being test-treated with bee pollen. All were patients with cancer of the uterine cervix. They were given 20 grams of bee pollen—about 3/4 of an ounce—three times daily during the course of their therapy. The report records that the women all recovered. Tests disclosed that the women maintained a higher level of Vitamins C and E in their bodies, were protected against bladder inflammation, nausea, insomnia and general malaise. Cholesterol levels plummetted and red blood cells increased, which means that life-giving oxygen was carried to the cells and the deadly carbon dioxide destroyed, creating a cell rejuvenating effect.

Thus, this ancient "ambrosia of the gods" is rapidly becoming known as the new age therapy of the coming century.

PROPOLIS

Propolis is a waxy-resinous substance which bees collect from trees in the late summer and fall. The chief source of the substance is the balsam poplar, the wild chestnut, the Gilead, and other conifers. This "sap" is a life-giving force of the trees themselves, updrawn from deep within the earth through the roots of the trees and transformed into a resinous nectar, secreted to aid in the tree's own struggle against infection. Bees gather the substance from the leaves and bark of the tree and carry it to their hive. There they add a glandular secretion of their own. The resinous propolis substance, together with the glandular secretion of the bees, solidifies in the cracks and openings of the beehive, lining it and protecting it against the elements. It acts also as a shield to protect the bees from bacterial infection.

Inside this incredible beehive factory, the bees prepare honey, pollen and royal jelly. Propolis, then, contains all these factors, plus the mysterious factors of propolis itself.

How did propolis come to be recognized as an incredibly important addition to the human diet? The decision to use it resulted from the analysis of propolis. It was found to contain not only honey, pollen and royal jelly, but all the vitamins, minerals, amino acids, flavonoids, ferulic acid and antibacterial substances. It also contains a mysterious "x-factor" which performs seeming healing miracles.

Propolis is called "a miracle of nature." It apparently is a natural antibiotic. Scientists involved in research work with it enthusiastically proclaim its antibacterial actions to surpass that of penicillin and other wonder drugs. It is enthusiastically called "the medicine of tomorrow" although it is in no sense considered to be a "medicine" but a natural food.

Many of our modern ailments respond simply to the taking of propolis capsules. There are seldom any side effects as there are with many of the antibiotic drugs now used extensively by the medical profession. It is a natural product working seemingly in conjunction with the body's own immune system, increasing the body's potential to fight off infectious diseases. It has been declared the new age natural antibiotic, seeming to prevent infections as well as heal them, once they are contracted. Many doctors thoroughly believe that, as propolis becomes more widely used, many dangerous drugs and drug-related chemicals may be abolished.

It is believed that propolis stimulates the activity of the thymus gland, once believed to be atrophied in adults until tests indicated otherwise. The thymus is now declared the source of life energy and its hormones seem to be compatible with bee propolis.

Patients suffering from exposure to radiation are reported to have experienced near-miracle healings by Yugoslavian scientists. The tests were conducted for a period of two months. Patients were fed propolis with other bee-made products daily. A placebo was given to another group of patients with similar problems. The patients receiving propolis recovered with remarkable results while no improvements were noted in the placebo group.

Austrian physicians report remarkable results in treating ulcers. Patients being tested were fed an extract of 5% propolis—a dose of five drops in water before meals three times a day. Pain disappeared within three days in the majority of the ten patients, and six of the ten experienced a healing of the ulcer within ten days.

The results reported by athletes around the world are so incredible as to be beyond belief. Olympian athletes from many foreign countries take propolis as part of their daily diet, and practically all the Olympian winners confess that, after taking propolis, they have experienced "fantastic" results in energy and well-being. They all admit that it significantly improves their performance and none report negative results.

During 1976 a symposium occurred in Hungary called *The Second International Symposium on Propolis*. This gathering of distinguished scientists, all investigating the amazing reports concerning propolis, called it "the hope for total healing." The summation of their reports read like a panacea for human ailments—incredible power to mend broken bones, speed cell growth, improve diseases of the mucous membranes, heal hitherto difficult problems of the skin, lower high blood pressure, increase sexual potency, and improve the health and well-being of all patients. It proved amazingly effective against migraine headaches. Arthritics reportedly experienced total healings. Persons exposed to influenza warded off the contagious influence if they began taking propolis immediately after exposure.

It is suggested that taking propolis should become a daily habit so that the body becomes immune to many diseases, and so that sexual impotence is much improved or totally overcome. Those who do not wish to follow this procedure would do well to begin taking the capsules immediately after exposure to colds, flu, pneumonia and all types of contagious respiratory illnesses.

When beekeepers gather it from the hive in the summer, it must be obtained by scratching it loose from the frame and rolling it into lumps. Before it can be ingested by humans, it must go through a process of cleansing.

Propolis is now added to facial creams to be used especially for those with dermatitis, acne and other skin problems. Propolis in cream or tincture form has been amazingly effective in healing benign skin tumors.

Propolis may be found in capsule, lozenge, cream and liquid form. A product called Propolis-H is proving to be effective in dentistry in treating paradentosis. It is also available as a toothpaste. Propolis-H is also effective in treating thyroid nodules, and in problems of dermatitis, such as acne and herpes.

It would appear that all these incredible bee products may be well on their way to replacing many drugs containing contra-indications. *Dr. Som says it is well to remember to take it— capsules usually—on an empty stomach, at least half an hour before or after a meal.*

Dr. Som suggests the following:

1. For a sore throat, even infected, or for any other infection—open a capsule of propolis powder and dissolve it in a bit of alcohol or brandy. Rub it on the throat. Also use propolis available in liquid form. Saturate half a teaspoon of raw sugar with the liquid and swallow it every two hours. You may be amazed at your rapid recovery— without having to take dangerous antibiotics or other drugs.

Also, empty a propolis capsule into half a cup of raw honey and take a teaspoon of it. Allow it to dissolve slowly in the mouth and coat the throat thoroughly. Repeat every hour until relief is obtained.

2. For any pain anywhere, or on any open wound, again open a capsule of propolis powder and empty it into enough raw honey to cover the affliction. Cover the spot with the honey, cover it with a soft cloth and bind it in place. Go to bed and rest overnight. Remove the poultice the next day. You may experience a total healing. Keep repeating the treatment until the healing is complete. Even large draining ulcers have been healed thusly. And if exterior wounds can be healed, why not interior?—such as ulcers, infections, diverticulitis, tumors, cysts?

3. For facial acne and skin blemishes, apply liquid propolis on the face with a sterilized cotton pat several times a day. Try it also on herpes and even *shingles*.

4. For infected teeth and gums, before deciding to have extractions, try liquid propolis applied with pure cotton pads four or five times daily. Or for any type of tooth problem, empty a propolis capsule or some liquid propolis into a half cup of raw honey and take a teaspoon of it. Allow it to dissolve slowly in the mouth, coating the inflamed gums.

5. For hay fever, sinus, nasal congestion, coughs, flu, bronchitis, pneumonia, even tuberculosis—take 3 capsules of propolis a half hour before or after each meal daily.

Let me tell you our first personal experience with propolis. During the winter of 1979, I experienced an attack of flu. I ignored it for days until suddenly, one day, my body pain made me realize I must submit to bed rest. I asked a friend to visit a health store for food shopping. While there the attendant suggested propolis for my flu, saying it was an excellent natural remedy. She suggested three capsules daily. So amazing was my sudden rapid recovery, I immediately began research on this incredible product.

Seeking always to find ways of helping others, I bought books about propolis and began recommending it to others.

Robert's only health problem is a bout with hay fever every spring. (Robert is my husband.) In the spring of 1980, the attacks were unusually severe. One day when he was experiencing extreme discomfort—the nasal passages draining profusely—I suddenly remembered propolis and that the books all said it would help.

Now Robert is reluctant to take pills in any form, but his problem was acute and he was faced with giving a sermon that day, Sunday, so he took a propolis capsule. To our amazement, the draining stopped almost immediately. The healing was so dramatic, he continued the daily treatment. One day, several weeks later, he decided to cease the capsules, whereupon the hay fever returned overnight. He returned to the daily treatment, and will probably continue it the rest of his life since the propolis seems to add to his overall well-being.

So impressed is Robert, he recommends propolis to practically everybody for practically everything. So do I. And for practically *anything*, it works!

6. For male impotence, for female menstrual and menopausal problems,

for estrogen deficiency, try propolis capsules.

7. For arthritis, for migraine or any other type of headaches, for radiation sickness in attempting a cancer cure, try propolis capsules. Doctors all over the world are reporting incredible results in their research.

8. For any painful injury—a cut, a burn, a scratch, or sunburn—apply the honey-propolis poultice. The pain leaves almost instantly.

9. For gastric or duodenal ulcers, for diverticulitis, use liquid propolis or capsules, available from health stores. Pain will diminish almost immediately and a healing should not be far behind.

10. From Europe comes reports of cancer cures—from taking 15 drops of liquid propolis in a glass of water a half hour before each meal! If you suffer from cancer, do discuss the treatment with your doctor. Propolis in tincture form is now available.

All the above suggestions are not my own. They have come from Dr. Som and as a result of my own research after my healing experience from flu and Robert's from hay fever. I can add this: I credit much of my incredible energy and vigor to the following:

Awakening daily in the early hours of the morning—anywhere from 3:00 to 5:00 a.m.—I take a capsule of propolis, a capsule of ginseng herb and a Gerovital (GH3) procaine tablet. Later in the day, about an hour after breakfast or lunch, I repeat the same formula. If I am experiencing any kind of muscle aches, I use a splash of DMSO—about which I shall write later—on the sore muscle or joint.

My experiment may not be conclusive—yet I work incredible hours seven days a week, writing and teaching without tiring. At my seminars—teaching and healing—I spend long hours on the platform, if the initiation-healing program requires it. If I am traveling, this performance is repeated over a period of several days. I am astonished that I seldom experience fatigue during these taxing seminar programs. Whereas my attendants during long healing services must all seek occasional rest periods for recuperating, I have never found it necessary.

My abundant energy may exemplify that these products *are* effective—together with meditation, a vegetarian diet, acupuncture, and a link-up with the Unseen Forces that overshadow my spiritual efforts. I certainly have noticed an upsurge of well-being since I have added bee products to my program. My only reason for referring to my personal program is to encourage you to embrace any or all the above suggestions in your own ongoing journey through this time-space we call life on Earth.

CHAPTER 10
THE FAMOUS HONEY—APPLE CIDER VINEGAR COCKTAIL

What was the forbidden fruit in the Garden of Eden? In the story of Adam and Eve, no specific fruit was ever mentioned in scriptures...yet the fruit most commonly accepted as the forbidden fruit was the apple. How did the apple come upon such a fate?

It is commonly believed that eating the forbidden apple brought about the recognition of the sexual act between Adam and Eve. Is there some mysterious factor about the apple that mankind has not yet discovered?...some fertility factor?...some mysterious connection to the function of sex and fertility?

Or could it be that it is connected with the uplifting of the sexual energies to the higher chakras? Could it be that the apple has some transforming quality—some transmuting ability not yet recognized? Certainly health benefits of the apple are much applauded. And its derivative—vinegar—is without equal as a purifier, an energizer, and as a total adjunct to man's well being. The list is almost endless.

It was Dr. D. C. Jarvis, writing in *Folk Medicine*, who made apple cider vinegar respectable, even among his peers. It was he who first made popular the honey-apple cider vinegar remedy now so renowned among naturopaths and many who seek home remedies for ailments rather than allopathic drugs.

It was Dr. Jarvis who firmly established the importance of the acid-alkaline urine test, proving beyond a doubt that an over-alkaline urine was an indication of an on-coming health problem—a cold, flu, hay fever, asthma, and many other symptoms.

He believed that a lack of energy or any degree of ill health could indicate an over-alkaline system. He suggested that a urine test be taken first thing in the morning to determine whether or not the desired acid blood condition existed. To conduct the test at home, he advised purchasing a package of *nitrazine* paper at a health or drug store—sometimes called *litmus* paper. He explained that the color scale on the nitrazine package was called the PH scale, and its range was from 0 to 12. He suggested holding a small strip of the paper under early morning urine, then comparing the resulting color change against the acid-alkaline gauge—the PH scale—on the package of the nitrazine paper. The color would range from yellow to deep, brownish purple.

7.0 was neutral on the PH scale. If the stomach acidity and the blood acid were normal, the urine coloring would register from 5.5 PH to 6.0. All points below 7.0 indicated over-acidity; all points above 7.0 indicated over-alkalinity. An over-alkalinity reading meant the stomach was too alkaline and one should begin the vinegar-honey remedy, which would quickly neutralize stomach alkalinity within a few hours, or certainly within a few days.

His remedy was to add two teaspoons of apple cider vinegar and two teaspoons of raw honey to a glass of water. This cocktail was to be drunk first thing on rising if the PH test indicated an alkaline urine. Or a glass should be drunk with each meal if the ailment was more severe. Or, omitting the honey, one or two teaspoons of vinegar added to a glass of water and drunk once or twice a day became firmly established as a home remedy for numerous ailments.

Clearly established, too, was the connection between an over-alkaline urine and health problems. The alkaline urine test gave warning to the approach of a problem. Taking the vinegar-honey cocktail usually stopped the symptoms, or the disease manifested only mildly. Doubtless the potassium in the apple cider vinegar was of supreme importance in recovering from or preventing disease.

If the morning urine test indicated low energy (a purple or blue coloring), Dr. Jarvis often recommended a "sponge" bath of apple cider vinegar and water. He suggested adding one teaspoon of apple cider vinegar to a half glass of warm water. The amount approximating a teaspoon was poured into the palm of the hand and little by little rubbed over the body until the solution evaporated into the skin. This, he said, would bring the entire body back into proper acidity. Any itching of the skin required, he believed, a hand rubbing of the vinegar-water solution—even an itching scalp.

He very seriously suggested testing soap with the nitrozine paper. If it turned blue or purple, the soap should be discarded. He believed we should only use soap that tested acid. If an alkaline soap was preferred, its use should be followed with the suggested hand rub of apple cider vinegar and water so that the skin would be brought back to its normal acidity.

He declared that migraine headaches became less severe or disappeared altogether if, after testing the urine and finding it alkaline, one began taking the honey-vinegar cocktail. He applied the same therapy to high blood pressure. Honey in water taken at each meal attracted excessive fluid from the blood and lowered blood pressure. Dizziness was treated successfully with the honey-vinegar cocktail. Dizziness, he claimed, was an alkaline reaction of the urine.

Dr. Som taught me many of these things long before I heard of Dr. Jarvis. Once when I had a sore throat, Dr. Som prescribed the following: four ounces of apple cider vinegar mixed with four ounces of water. Add one teaspoon of sea salt. Take one mouthful of the solution and gargle repeatedly, then swallow the gargling solution. This remedy of one mouthful of the remedy was repeated every two hours. The entire glassful should last a day or so. Swallowing the gargle was effective in reaching the lower throat. When the soreness was alleviated, time intervals were extended to once every three hours. Taken too often could irritate the throat. He claimed even a streptococcic throat could be healed in twenty-four hours.

It was Dr. Jarvis who establshed that apple cider vinegar was perfect medicine for an upset stomach—diarrhea and vomiting. One teaspoon of the vinegar added to a glass of water was fed to the patient—a teaspoonful every five minutes. He stipulated that an upset stomach would not accept a whole glass at once, but, fed in small amounts every few minutes, it would ultimately settle down the digestive tract and return the body to normal. He often used vinegar in a glass of water to correct kidney-bladder infections and inflammations. The dosage was sometimes one teaspoonful in a glass of water, sometimes two, depending upon the individual's taste and acceptance of it. He used the same methodology in curing chronic fatigue, chronic headache (including migraine), high blood pressure, dizziness, heart trouble and overweight.

For insomnia, he offered the following: 3 teaspoons of apple cider vinegar to a cup of honey, placing the mixture in a wide mouthed bottle or jar so that it could be stirred with a teaspoon. The jar was to be kept by the bedside, two teaspoons of the mixture was to be taken when preparing for bed, which enabled one to fall asleep immediately. But if sleep was evasive at the end of an hour, two more teaspoons were to be taken. It might require several such dosages if awakening during the night, but with each awakening, the dosage was to be repeated. He called this nature's own infallible treatment for insomnia. He claimed honey taken by itself was a natural sedative, but combining it with apple cider vinegar was more effective.

The vinegar-honey cocktail flushes many poisons from the system, purifies the blood stream and destroys many disease bacteria and germs. The vinegar acts as a natural virus antibiotic and the honey destroys bacteria. It should be taken first thing in the morning and nothing else eaten for at least half an hour, to allow the ingredients to perform their magic.

How does this miracle food perform such amazing miracles? First of all, apple cider vinegar is only a fermentation of the apple, and everyone is familiar with the old adage that "an apple a day keeps the doctor away." This has certainly been tried and proven. The apple, rich in many vital minerals, is further improved with fermentation, resulting in apple cider vinegar. The vinegar is rich in potassium, phosphorus, magnesium, calcium, sulphur, iron, fluorine, chlorine, sodium and silicon. In addition to retaining all these important nutrients and vital minerals, the vinegar possesses the power to kill bacteria and germs, destroying them in the system and reducing the phlegm congesting the lungs, bronchial areas and digestive tract.

Especially important is its potassium content. Symptoms of potassium deficiency are a constantly dripping nose, or a post-nasal drip, insomnia, aching soreness and inflammation in the body joints, chronic fatigue, susceptibility to colds and coughs, and dry, itchy skin.

Raw honey, rich in minerals we have already mentioned, also contains natural vitamin C and many of the B vitamins. Since it directly and immediately is absorbed into the blood stream, it supplies quick energy. Recognized as a gentle, natural laxative, it also produces a mild natural sedative to the nerves. It has been used for centuries as a healing lotion to the throat, acting as a cough suppressant and destroying bacteria and germs in infected throats and bronchial tubes. Many infections yield to its application, especially coughs, bronchitis and respiratory ailments. The vinegar-honey cocktail is most effective in relieving the pain of arthritis and rheumatism, swollen joints, and aching muscles.

Here are a few more honey-vinegar benefits, as suggested by Dr. Jarvis or Dr. Som:

1. Vinegar as a hair rinse to cut the soap from the hair.

2. Vinegar applied to skin red with sunburn. It not only draws out the fire, but prevents the skin from peeling and results in a beautiful tan.

3. As a poultice to be applied to burns. A cloth soaked in apple cider vinegar should be applied directly to the burn and covered with a dry cloth.

4. As a poultice applied to sprained wrists and bruises. Wrap a swollen sprained ankle with a cloth dipped in vinegar and cover it with a cloth dipped in iced water. Keep changing the iced cloth so that it stays cold. The swelling will disappear like magic. Or if only one cloth is desired, mix the vinegar with the iced water. Wet the cloth and apply.

5. For a sore throat, dip a soft cloth in apple cider vinegar, wrap it around the throat, then cover with dry cloth, preferably cotton flannel, to hold in the heat of the body.

6. For thyroid deficiency, add one drop of iodine solution once or twice a week to the daily intake of apple cider vinegar.

7. To alleviate lameness and rheumatic pains, add one tablespoon of turpentine and one tablespoon of apple cider vinegar to a beaten egg yolk. Rub this mixture into the aching area.

8. To alleviate the itching and burning of *shingles*, and as an aid in the cure, rub apple cider vinegar directly on the skin area of the shingles. The application should be applied four times during the day, and at least three times during the night if the patient is wakeful.

9. Apple cider vinegar should be applied directly to varicose veins, both morning and night, and thoroughly massaged into the skin. The varicose vein treatment will be benefited by also taking two teaspoons of vinegar in a glass of water twice a day.

10. Add vinegar full strength to toenails just before cutting. They are softened.

11. Add vinegar to water when soaking burnt-on foods in pans, or boiling to soften encrustation. It aids in the loosening action.

12. Elsewhere we have described the use of 1/2 cup vinegar to a gallon of water in which to rinse all vegetables and fruits to aid in removing fall-out pollutions and sprays.

13. Apple cider vinegar should never be used as a vaginal douche. It causes a fungus growth. Always use white vinegar for this purpose.

14. Any heart patient would do well to add the vinegar-honey cocktail to his diet, for its effectiveness in revitalizing damaged heart tissue.

15. An alcoholic is a person with a health problem—a potassium deficiency. If the vinegar-honey cocktail is added to his diet it may evidence an amazing turn-around. If he still desires liquor, it means he needs even more honey or a potassium supplement to compensate for the potassium deficiency in the body. Both honey and vinegar, rich in potassium, will counteract the craving for alcohol.

CHAPTER 11
THE MAN WHO GREW YOUNG AT SEVENTY

Some type of bodily exercise is absolutely necessary if one expects to live, not only long, but in good health—if the body is to remain in a purified condition, receptive to the downpouring spiritual impulse.

Stretching, walking, yoga, tai chi, aikido, do-in, any of these techniques stimulate and activate the blood stream, flushing out accumulated poisons. They also begin the flow of *prana* throughout the body, energizing and stimulating every gland, cell, muscle and tissue. Alternately exercising, *then* relaxing, enables muscles, organs, and tissues to discharge their accumulated toxins and acids, releasing them into the blood stream which throws them out of the body through the usual waste channels. This purification opens all areas of the body to absorb pure prana, thereby developing a physical instrument vibrant with energy.

Disciplined exercise, in a surprisingly short time, can actually streamline the body, reduce flabbiness, change the contours, and reshape the form into one of dynamic controlled power, poise, grace and beauty. Even if you are weak or bedridden with a temporary debilitating illness, you can begin some form of exercise. Start with deep breathing. Next, begin stretching, twisting and turning while lying in bed. Soon you will be able to sit up in bed. There, do arm stretch exercises with deep breathing. Next try to sit on the side of the bed and perform leg and other exercises. Soon you will be able to stand and walk a few steps. As soon as possible, begin taking those steps outdoors, increasing your stride and the time of your walking daily until you can walk vigorously around the block with deep rhythmic breathing. Next, try for a mile a day.

If you do not care for yoga or any of the martial arts, then at least walk, swim, bicycle, play tennis, trampoline jog, or just tense, stretch and relax the muscles. When walking, be sure to inhale deeply to a specific count of three, four, five, or six, whatever is your capacity.

Hold to the count of three or more, then exhale gradually to whatever count is comfortable. Hold the breath out as long as comfortable.

To derive the best curative and regenerative effect from physical exercises, your mind and your will must focus fully upon the activities. Systematic exercise—with mind power directing the flow of pranic energy—enables you constantly to stir and remove poisonous accumulations in your body. It increases the blood and lymphatic circulation. It stimulates activity of the glandular system. It enables your lungs to expand to their fullest capacity. Such an expansion will increase the inhalation of oxygen and prana, both of which are rich sources of abundant energy for purification of the blood stream.

Elimination of waste matter will again become a normal functioning through bowels, kidneys, skin and respiratory tract. Elimination of poisonous substances must be daily and habitual for the physical form to manifest as a channel of purified nerve energy and life force. The body must be kept free from pathological conditions, the organs functioning to their full capacity so that they may be instruments of the inflowing life stream. They must carry this impulse to the interpreting centers in the brain, via the nervous system. It is the nerve energy which gives function to all of the organs.

The main "cable" of the nervous system is the spinal cord. From this cord emanate the numerous nerves leading to every organ of the body, distributing the life force throughout every cell and atom. If destructive pressure is applied to a nerve, injury to its motor and sensory function may occur, causing a cessation of normal activity. It is abnormal pressure on the nerve points which causes blockages in the form, thus creating an abnormal imbalance. Proper exercise removes pressure on nerves, releasing such blockages so that pranic life force can flow freely, restoring the body to a positive-negative balance.

EXERCISE ELIMINATES TENSION

Tense? Nervous? Don't take that tranquilizer! At last, medical records affirm what mystics have long taught. Gerontology researchers—seeking the whys and wherefores of old age—have finally concluded that as little as 15 minutes of exercise daily can alleviate short-term nervous tensions. And exercise has been found to be more positively tranquilizing than pills or alcohol. Doctors in gerontology centers are convinced that in experiments with tense and nervous elderly patients, better results are obtained with exercise than with tranquilizers. Unlike drugs, exercise has no side effects. Tranquilizers cause the entire body to slow down, not only the brain but all the muscles, often proving to be hazardous to health. On the other hand, exercise improves the muscles, the blood stream, and the thinking capacity.

OLD AGE—
ITS CAUSE AND PREVENTION

Even though I regained my health with yoga (and walking) as my chosen exercise, I am fully aware that many do not care for the stretching, bending, time and effort involved in yoga. As I began my preparations for writing this book, during my meditations I prayed I might, through some manner, receive instructions about exercises or yogic techniques applicable by seekers of any age, and easily practiced by even the senior citizen—exercises not only easily accomplished, but dynamically effective.

No sooner had I completed this prayer then there arrived a box of books from a devoted Astarian who offered them as a donation to Astara's expanding mystical library. Among the books was one called *Old Age—It's Cause and Prevention* by Sanford Bennett. This book was the answer to my prayer. I am thoroughly convinced it came into my hands through unseen teachers who are as anxious as I to present to Light seekers everywhere techniques to regenerate and rejuvenate the physical form so that it may become a better instrument of Holy Spirit.

This amazing book was written and copyrighted in 1912 and the author had much to say about how and why he wrote the book. Since I truly believe the book came as an answer to prayer, I am offering much of the author's teachings directly, and the photographs which demonstrate his techniques will be of the author himself. His teachings will be interspersed with mine, based on my own years of yogic training.

THE LAZY MAN'S REJUVENATION

The techniques presented are called *The Lazy Man's Method of Rejuvenation* because it is possible to perform them all while lying in bed, usually very comfortably under the covers. But do not let the title persuade you that they are ineffective. The alternate muscular contractions and relaxations are highly effective and, if followed persistently, bring about very definite benefits, completely rejuvenating the entire body and restoring health.

First of all, circulation is vastly improved and the glands are stimulated, to say nothing of muscular restoration. The advantage of these exercises is that one is never too old to begin them; nor are they too strenuous to perform. Even those in a weakened physical condition will realize tremendous benefits if persistent.

It is my firm conviction that these exercises will enable many to throw away their pills and medicines, and allow nature full control in restoring the physical form to complete health. The exercises require no mechanical devices and, since they are nature's method of restoration, no financial expenditure is involved.

It is the concensus of opinion among many nature lovers and naturopaths that old age is a disease, and that it is therefore progressive. It begins with sedimentary deposits in the arterial structures, and spreads throughout the physical form. As these deposits increase and become more solidified, the elasticity of youth begins to disappear. The result of these deposits is called arteriosclerosis—hardening of the arteries—which is nothing more than the clogging of the arteries by chalky deposits. A person is truly only as old as his arteries.

To repeat, old age is actually nothing more than the progressive disease of clogged arteries caused by these chalky deposits. Arteries become obstructed with these deposits much as calcareous incrustations form in boiler pipes. As these incrustations thicken, the supply of blood to the brain is restricted, affecting the memory and all the mental operations which require vitalized brain cells to function optimally. The brain, increasingly denied its supply of all-important blood, degenerates into general senility, too often characteristic of old age.

What applies to the brain also applies to the entire muscular and organic structure. As the arteries become increasingly obstructed with chalky deposits, the blood supply to the various muscles and organs becomes restricted. As a consequence, deterioration begins and, if elasticity of the arteries is not restored, if sediments are not removed, old age frailty is the natural consequence.

It would seem to be obvious that the diet, including the character of the water we drink, has much to do with arteriosclerosis. It must be realized that exercise alone can never restore and maintain the vitality of youth. Along with exercise, a change of diet *must* be considered. However, it must be equally realized that diet alone cannot restore elasticity to the muscles, nor can diet alone entirely cleanse the arteries of the obstructing debris which causes arteriosclerosis.

Regeneration also requires the toning action of muscle contraction and relaxation, methodically and persistently practiced. To avoid a recurrence of hardening of the arteries, a change in diet is most assuredly advisable. The great yogis of the world are able to demonstrate longevity through practicing three steps.

1. Daily yogic asanas (postures) and mudras (symbols or symbolic gestures), which keep the body in a state of regeneration through muscular contraction and relaxation, performed slowly and deliberately.

2. These are combined with intense concentration of the mind and will during the practice.

3. Both are enhanced by the proper purifying diet.

The yogic exercises presented in the following writings—the tensing and relaxing—are those which can easily be practiced by the "lazy man," or any person who is unable to perform the exotic asanas and postures popularly known as yoga. These are a completely different type of yoga, but they most assuredly will help restore the physical form to a healthful condition.

Since many of my readers will already have begun to experience the effects of middle and perhaps even "senior" age, they may feel it futile to attempt a rejuvenation. Having known those who have proved this method, I can only make this promise—that contracting and relaxing body muscles is nature's surest method of cleansing arteries of chalky deposits and debris. It is also a sure and certain method of restoring elasticity to the body. The continued use of these exercises will break up these deposits and, if methodically and faithfully executed, will restore a great degree of youthfulness to the body regardless of the age they are begun.

Certainly we cannot avoid the approach of the latter years, but we can defy "old age" and render it ineffective. There must be a cause for growing old. To understand it, we need to investigate human anatomy. First we need to understand that the human body is composed of millions of minute microscopic bodies which medical science terms cells. These cells are sustained through the air we breathe, the liquid we drink, the food we eat, and the miraculous process of digestion and assimilation. Through this process, the air, the liquid and the food are converted into cellular tissue.

These cells are forever coming into birth and dying. Having died, they become waste matter in the system and must be eliminated. Failure to eliminate dead cells adds to the impediment in the arteries, and the body slowly degenerates into old age.

With such impediments the muscles cannot receive proper nourishment, thus they shrink and become flabby. The brain is denied its supply of blood and the person becomes "senile." Old age must assuredly result. No medicines, no serums, can restore the body to a youthful state. Only nature can provide the answer. Through the yogic method of alternate contraction and relaxation of the muscles, nature itself dissolves the impediments and debris obstructing the arteries, and the body becomes rejuvenated. Through this yogic system, the body discards waste matter which is deposited in the veins and glandular systems, and it is then eliminated through the process of bodily excretions.

Having received the book with these particular exercises through unique circumstances, as mentioned, I'm happy to recommend and teach them because they are easily accomplished even by those who are weakened with illness. The remainder of this Chapter, then, is the first part of a continuing excerpt presented directly from the book *Old Age—its Cause and Prevention* by Sanford Bennett.

THE MAN WHO GREW YOUNG AT SEVENTY

All statements in this book are based upon my successful, personal experience in the art of physical rejuvenation in advanced years, and this success is a result of long and persistent investigation of the causes of physical old age and the practice of nature's methods for its prevention. These investigations, combined with 25 years of experiments upon my own body, have taught me how to postpone that unpleasant condition.

I am not theorizing or writing the experiences of someone else, but verify the truth of my own statements by my own youthful physical condition at 72. If my case was simply one of physical preservation in advanced years, other instances would be cited equally unusual, but mine is not a case of physical acquisition or acquiring the elasticity, strength and health characteristic of youth at three score and ten—an age when such an improvement has hitherto been supposed to be impossible.

At 50 I was physically an old man. Many years of a too active business career had resulted in a general breakdown. I was then wrinkled, partially bald, cheeks sunken, face drawn and haggard, muscles atrophied, and thirty years of chronic dyspepsia (indigestion) finally resulted in catarrh of the stomach—with acid rheumatism periodically adding its agonies. I was an old man and looked it. It was the desperation of my case which induced me to undertake the experiments.

I have made many mistakes which it has required time to rectify, but the desire to live has impelled me to struggle on and finally I have succeeded. But the road to that success has not been easy, as, lacking experienced guides, I had to pioneer my own way over a road that proved to be long and difficult. Another great obstacle was that the customs of my shortlived family could not be readily abandoned. If any of us were sick, we promptly "took something for it," something we bought at a drugstore.

In my many sicknesses as a child, I have had an intimate acquaintance with apparently most alleged medicinal remedies—anything my anxious relatives could think of or an allopathic family physician advised. It is a depressing list to look back upon. It ranges from "Adams Calomel pills" to "Zeehandlers—World Renowned Fever and Ague Cure." But I think I have sampled them all. Naturally I grew up with a firm belief that in medicine lay the only curative process, and I regarded drug stores as lifesaving stations. I maintained this belief until I reached the age of 50, and—broke down.

The enumeration of my physical woes at that age is a truthful statement of the conditions then existing. And now in my 72nd year I present the healthy condition of an athlete in training and the appearance of a man of little more than half my years. Under these conditions my success is too obvious to be overlooked. The fact is—unacceptable as it may be to the vast number of the medical profession and also to the industries connected with it—I succeeded only after I had discontinued all medicines. Health cannot be found in drugstore prescriptions, nor can life be materially prolonged by any medical preparations. The solution of the problem lies only in nature's principal methods of inducing health—sunlight, pure air, pure water, nourishing food, cleanliness and exercise. Given these most important factors and an observation of what we know as the general laws of hygiene, health and a long life are possible and usually very probable. But without these conditions they are not obtainable and a long category of medicinal remedies with which the world has been afflicted will not replace such conditions.

What I have accomplished is possible to almost everyone who is not organically so wrong as to be hopeless. But to the average man or woman whose condition is simply that of general physical deterioration termed "old age," I extend this message of hope: Follow my example and success will be yours. I have been an old man and now, at over three score and ten, I am a young man and look it. Really, I am now a younger man physically than I was in the best period of my early manhood, say at 35. In some respects, I seem to have accomplished the fabled miracle of Faust as, to a considerable extent, I have transformed an old body into a young one and this without the aid of Faust's friend or any supplies obtained from his extremely popular medical departments.

Sanford Bennett at 50 years of age.
San Francisco, Cal., June 8, 1889.

Sanford Bennett at 72 years of age.
San Francisco, Cal., January 4, 1912.

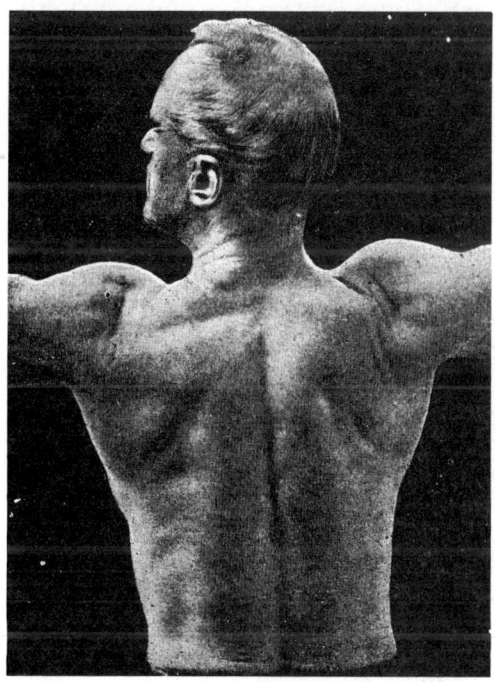

Development of the shoulders and
muscles of the back.

Development of the shoulders and
biceps at age 72.

As I have said, I have been compelled to find the right path alone and, although I've read extensively upon the matter on which I write, I have never found a satisfactory guidebook to the goal I sought—that is, one based upon the author's authenticated personal experiences. I have found many well-authenticated cases of persons who have lived nearly to the limit of human life, that is, 100 years. I have found several who have reached that period, but no authenticated instance of any human being who, in advanced years, had regained to any considerable degree the physical conditions and appearance of youth. Counterfeit, yes, but like all counterfeits, detection finally resulted. But when you become young by the methods I practiced, you will pass muster under the most searching investigation. My trouble now is that all who see me agree that, while I look but little more than half my age, they express doubt that I am in my 72nd year.

I came into this life January 4, 1841, a sickly little nervous shred of a child, whom no one ever expected to live through childhood and to whom reaching maturity seemed an impossibility. But "there is a divinity that shapes our ends, rough hew them as we will." And now at 72, I realize that my mission in this life is to show others nature's simple methods of health and how, by their observance, our stay here may be prolonged, and lost physical youth may be regained. This at an age when such improvement has heretofore been supposed to be impossible.

These were the unfavorable conditions of my feeble childhood, and throughout my boyhood the haunting spector of consumption was ever-present. At the age of 50, worried and worn out with the financial cares of a great mercantile industry, suffering from lack of exercise, hurried meals and a "no time to spare" life, I collapsed. The brink of the precipice had been reached. A month's enforced rest gave me ample time to think over the discouraging situation. Then I woke up to the realization that I was almost a subject for Osler's chloroform treatment. I decided to turn over a new leaf. What is the method by which I have transformed an old worn-out body to an elastic, healthy, and, to all appearances, a young one?

That is the subject of the subsequent writings which are a record of my own personal experience in the art of physical rejuvenation, with a clear account of the methods by which, at the age of 72, I have thrown off the conditions of age and have become physically a young man again. And this has been accomplished without the use of medicinal preparations of any nature. What has been possible in my case is most probably just as possible in yours. The muscular contractions and alternate relaxations of every muscle of the body which are the basis of this system are all performed while lying in bed. The methods I describe will, if persistently and methodically practiced, result in improved circulation, healthy glandular activity, and will materially prolong your life.

From babyhood to the age of 50, I was never a well man until I ceased the habit of "taking something for it" when I was the least indisposed. Now I am mad all over when I think of that long, distressing experience. Nature does not cure that way and a long healthy life is not possible by the practice of such antiquated methods. Those who have had the same experience will agree with me. You will find my views on this matter expressed again and again throughout these writings which is a plea for nature's methods of cure, therefore a protest against the alleged medicinal "remedies" which so nearly ended my existence. I repeat—a long and healthy life is not possible by such methods, and I never was a healthy man until I realized that fact. My success in regaining at 72 the health and elasticity of a body characteristic of the condition of healthful youth has been so remarkable that I am convinced the annals of medicine cannot show any case in which, by the use of medicine alone, such results have been obtained and, I will add, they never will. I realize that my mission here must be to show others the path which has led to my success.

In the almost unceasing activity of childhood and early youth we see the manifestation of nature's method of removing dead matter from our bodies. The restless action of a caged animal is but another instance of the same method. In all ages, man has vainly endeavored to restore to the aged human body, by medicinal means, the elasticity and vitality characteristic of youth. This was the disappointed dream of the early alchemists. It is even now the faint, half-hearted hope of science. But as years roll on, bearing with them the precedent of countless millions of failures and not one authenticated success, that hope is becoming dim. Still we struggle upon the same misleading, beaten track—but before the end of this century, I predict that the simple but effectual methods for the prevention of age and prolongation of life which I practice will very largely take the place of medicinal methods in the treatment of aged persons, and that physical culture methods generally will be considered of the first importance in the science of gerontology.

The cells of your body are nourished by the air you breathe, the liquid you drink, and the food you eat. They live their brief life and then they die. Having become dead matter, they must be eliminated from the system to avoid impeding its function. If not, the muscles, not being properly nourished, shrink and signs of age appear. If the clogging waste matter can be eliminated, the conditions of youth will return. But this can never be accomplished by medicinal means. Nature alone provides the method.

It lies in the alternate contraction and relaxation of the muscles. In this way you force out of the body any waste matter which may have deposited in the venous and glandular systems, and it is then carried out by the ordinary bodily excretions. Any muscle or set of muscles so exercised will increase in size, strength and elasticity and finally will be practically rejuvenated. This being true of one muscle, it is true of all, and as all parts of the body are in sympathy with each other, any agitant gland or organ will be benefited. Therefore, if all parts of the structure are so exercised, a general rejuvenation results.

My system is simply using a systematic series of contractions and alternate relaxations of every large muscle or set of muscles of the body. These exercises I practice while lying in bed, comfortably ensconced under the bed clothes. By this means, and the other simple methods I describe, I have accomplished my rejuvenation. These movements might be described as a kind of muscle-pumping process, as that is what exercise really is. This system is especially adapted for those in advanced years, or of sedentary modes of life, and is equally beneficial and advisable for either sex.

But in considering the causes of old age, there is another and a very important factor to be taken into consideration, and that is the condition of the glandular functions. In old age, there is usually inactivity in this direction, defective assimilation being therefore a marked characteristic of advanced years. With that condition, there is a loss in flesh and, while it exists, it is impossible to build up the body. The remedy lies in general muscular activity. This, if practiced with all of the muscles of the body, will mechanically stimulate all glandular action and, whether that function is of the nature of secretion or excretion, greater activity will follow. The result will be improved assimilation and, as that function is the basis of life, it is evident that health will therefore be improved. The secret of healthy, glandular action lies in the mechanical process of agitant muscular activity.

One of the problems that once badly puzzled me was that I found very thin people often gained flesh by these exercises, while those suffering from a surplus of adipose tissue lost that unwelcome superfluity. In the former case, the explanation is found in the stimulation of the glandular action as described. Therefore, improved assimilation brings an increase in flesh and more healthful conditions while, with the stout persons, muscular activity works off the unwholesome superfluous fat. There seems to be a certain physical standard or outline which is ours at birth and by heritage, and the nearer we approach that outline, the healthier we will be. Health is really the condition of equilibrium between assimilation and elimination and, if reached, the result is perfect health.

Nature's plan is that we should all reach and maintain that condition. Why so few of us do is our own fault. If assimilation and elimination are in perfect equilibrium, and the mind is as healthfully active as the body, then you have reached the condition nature intended and will warrant the expectation of your living to the full limit of the term fixed for your stay here, which is 100 years. But to accomplish this, your mental attitude must also be considered, and this is a very important matter, for, undoubtedly, a positive mental activity and a hopeful, cheerful disposition are great factors in the prolongation of life and, just as certainly, the contrary attitude will shorten it. If your general impression is that "fate has it in for you," that you "never had a chance," then of course you will lose courage and, without the will to spur you on to effort, you will not succeed either in your business or in prolonging your life.

That pessimistic state of mind retards your digestion and has a bad effect upon your liver. Such despondent people are usually unhealthy, and therefore unhappy. Feeling that "there is nothing to live for," they usually age more rapidly than optimistic people. The remedy lies in both physical and mental activity, for the same law applies to the mental organization as the rest of your body, so that if you would keep young mentally, you must exercise your brain.

The list of old men, thinkers, writers, statesmen and orators who have achieved their greatest successes in advanced years is too long to recite, but the secret of their success in every case was that they kept busy. There is an old German proverb:

> If you rest, you rust.

It is true, and if you would be hoping for longer life, don't get into a rusty condition, either mentally or physically. If you do, then, like any other piece of machinery, your term of usefulness being passed, you will be relegated to the junk pile and your stay here will be shortened. There is a close sympathy between the mind and body, and if either deteriorates, the other will speedily share in its deterioration. Therefore, keep active mentally as well as physically, and the easiest and most effective method for keeping your body active and therefore healthy will be found fully in these writings.

But as to exercising your brain, that is a matter which depends largely upon our tastes, habits, environment and natural ability. Have an interest in human affairs. Become a member of some religious organization and go to church. I have a high respect for church and church people, for I have realized after many years of experience as a choir singer in many churches, that there I found the best people. And such people will be of value to you and make life more pleasant.

But don't join any church where the "terrors of the Lord" and the awful fate which befall those who don't agree with such ideas are preached. If you do, your dyspepsia will be worse and you will be worse and you won't be happy. I speak from experience. My people were Presbyterian of the ultra-puritan type and I was brought up on the "shorter cathechism," "infant damnation" and the "fires of hell." This spiritual Sunday diet, in combination with cold mince pie and fried donuts, laid the foundation of the digestive disorders which troubled me for many years afterwards. Moral: if you have any tendencies to dyspepsia or suicidal melancholy, don't join that kind of church, but hunt up something modern and progressive—where you will meet cheerful people who have made their church popular by the social amusements possible to such a congregation. And if the leader of that congregation, whether clergyman, priest or rabbi, is a believer in sunshine, fresh air, out-of-door pleasures, that is the church to belong to, for there you will find the kind of society which will assist you in maintaining a cheerful disposition, an aid to health and one of the factors in deferring old age.

THE WILL IN EXERCISING

The effect of the will upon the body is very marked in these exercises. Each set of muscles being exercised by itself, there is a concentration of thought or determination of will force to that point, and it would seem that the speedy and very remarkable muscular development often resulting from the practice of this muscle-tensing system is due as much to the will force concentrated upon the muscles placed in action, as by the exercises.

On first thought, this statement may not find favor with the average reader but when you consider some of the phenomena which are undoubtedly caused by the action of the will, this theory of the cause of rapid muscular growth is not illogical. By force of will, the beating of the heart may become slower or quicker, or may even cease under the stress of emotions such as anger or fear. A very great fright may even cause death. Concentrated attention—that is, attention concentrated on any portion of our body—produces manifest changes there.

Thus, redness or paleness may be induced in the face, or swellings on different parts of the body. Certain monks are known to have induced the red marks of stigmatism or the signs of Christ's sufferings upon their bodies. And it is an established fact that, by fixing the attention upon any part of the body, positive pains may be produced. Rage affects the salivary glands. Fear disturbs the functions of the heart and anxiety the digestive organs. The will has much to do with the determination of our lives and our physical conformation, impressing our character and modes of thought upon our features. And in exercise, especially in these muscle-tensing exercises, it is a very important factor in muscular development.

The will also has a law in common with the muscular system, that is, it grows in strength when exercised. If things were always as hard to do when tried for the first time we would never progress. But the way becomes easier as we continue our efforts and exercise the will, so that those who practice these exercises will find the desire to execute them grows. The difficulties first encountered disappear, and finally that which was distasteful becomes an attractive habit.

Mentality has much to do with our health and the duration of our lives. A fixed determination to live will prolong life just as certainly as the feeling that we are growing old lessens our courage and hastens the end. If we lose faith in our strength, it leaves us. If we believe that age is beginning to weigh heavily upon us, we take to sedentary habits and little by little we lapse into sluggish lives. Our blood stagnates and lowered vitality invites diseases which we know as the signs of age. We lose faith and courage in ourselves and then truly become old.

It is a worn but truthful adage that "you are as old as you think yourself to be." If you think yourself aging, surely you will hasten that condition, and marks of physical decay appear which your years may not warrant.

Remember this, when you think young and act young, people think you are a good deal younger than you are and finally you will come to believe it yourself. When you have reached that stage you will have the courage of your convictions and the battle is half won.

The same is true of these exercises. If you can understand that with every muscular contraction and its alternate relaxation, you are expelling the worn-out and dead tissue which is the real cause of physical age, you will be encouraged to go on, and as you do so and you find your physical condition and health improving, confidence in yourself, faith in the system I describe will come to you and success in your efforts will surely be yours. To concentrate attention upon the muscles you are endeavoring to develop, count the movements and try to remember the position as shown in the illustration of the exercise you are practicing.

EXERCISING IN BED

You may be under the impression that to obtain the benefit of exercise, you must join a gymnasium or perform a variety of violent motions at unpleasant hours and possibly with inconvenient surroundings. Also you may think you need a physical culture instructor. Ordinarily, yes—but in this system you will need no teacher other than the instructions here presented. The exercises described and illustrated are all performed while lying in bed, and as each set of exercises is very simple you will have no difficulty in learning them. Each set of muscles is brought into activity by itself and, as all of the movements are executed slowly, the bed clothes need not be disarranged, while if your movements are deliberate, neither will the pulse be unduly accelerated. This last is very important. As in gymnasium work, over-exertion greatly accelerates the pulse and a consequent strain upon the heart often results. This is very injurious as enlargement of the heart is a serious matter.

The running path, bars, punching bag and the various other appliances of a well-appointed gymnasium cannot be too highly recommended, as they form an excellent road to health—for an athlete. Also, a good method of obtaining strength and elasticity of body. An athlete, preparing for an athletic event demanding great exertion, needs such adjuncts and regular training to get into regular condition. But I write simply for those advanced in years or sedentary people whose only aim is health, and such people should confine themselves to the few movements I advise for each set of muscles.

Don't try to learn and practice them all at once. Go slow and learn each set by itself before you take up the next. There is still another advantage to my system as compared with gymnasium practice. In the gym, one is very likely to develop one set of muscles and neglect others that are equally important. The body therefore gets out of balance and, like any other badly balanced machinery, is not capable of the efficiency nature has intended that it should have. But in the system I am describing, all of the muscles are brought into activity and a general, even development results.

In my case, I am evenly developed all over—a fact that has always been specially commented upon by those surgeons who have examined me. I practice these exercises at a time when I am absolutely idle. I habitually wake at about 5:30 a.m. I do not rise but leisurely commence the movements one after the other and, during the next half hour or more, I practice them all.

By that time I have systematically brought into action every muscle of my body. A healthy glow and a wide awake feeling have resulted. The windows are wide open, the air is pure, the bed is warm and comfortable and the sun is probably streaming in with its life-giving rays. I exercise continuously but slowly for over half an hour. My heart beat is steady. Then I get up, shave, take a quick tepid shower and, being perfectly healthy, I realize the job of living to the full.

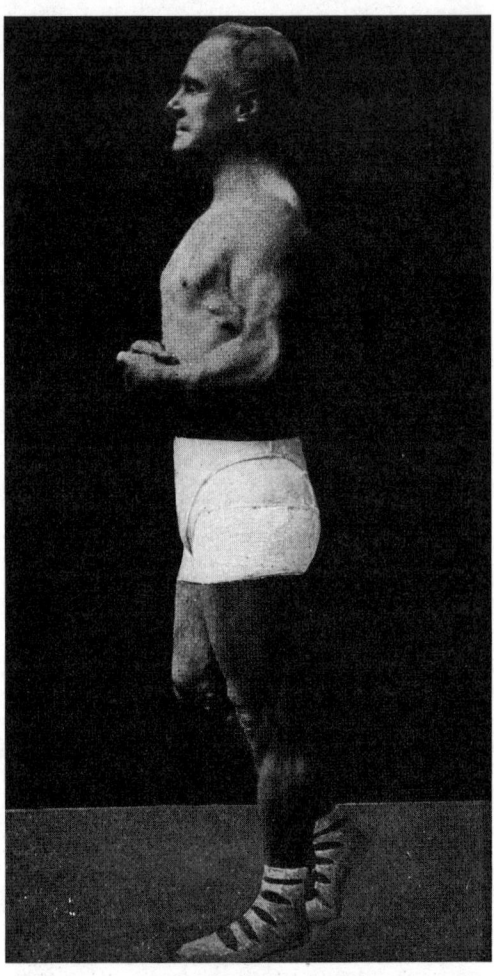

General Development at age 72.

THINGS TO BE REMEMBERED

Commence the exercises as soon as you are awake, performing them under the bed covers. Count the movements—this concentrates your attention and growth is then more rapid.

During these exercises, frequently take deep breaths.

A glass of water before beginning is beneficial, especially a glass about 15 minutes before breakfast as a remedy for constipation.

Eat slowly and masticate your food thoroughly. Digestion is retarded and digestive organs impaired if you hurry.

Keep your windows open.

Take a tepid shower or bath every morning after exercises.

Do not try to master too many at once. Learn each one before taking up the next.

The changes in position may not seem absolutely necessary, but I have found that even a very slight change of position will often bring into action an entirely new set of muscles; sometimes of muscles which do not seem to be a part of that action. Therefore, if you desire general muscular activity which is the keynote of this system, do not omit these slight changes in position and do not execute the movements too quickly. Nothing is gained by rapid action. The object is to tense, hold and relax muscles slowly—which stimulates circulation and healthy glandular activity. A steady, deliberate rate of action—stretch, tense, hold, relax—will be found far more beneficial.

Do not flounce around in bed as you practice the movements. You will only disarrange the bedclothes. That is not necessary and, if the movements are performed with deliberation, it will not happen. My experience has been that most people commence this or any other system of physical culture by going too fast. As a consequence, they soon become sore, strain muscles, become discouraged, and give up. Don't fall into that error. Learn this system just as you would learn typewriting or the piano. That is, one thing at a time. And when you can execute a number of these movements without getting confused, you will be surprised to find how easy it all is and how rapidly you improve in health.

CHAPTER 12
THE LAZY MAN'S METHOD OF REGENERATION

Here are the exercises perfected by Sanford Bennett:

EXERCISE ONE

FOR STRENGTHENING THE LOWER ABDOMINAL MUSCLES

In the human being the lower abdominal muscles, which cover that part of the abdomen lying between the hips and the lower portion of the pelvic bones, are subject to continual strain, as they support the heavy viscera within. If they become weakened through inaction they will relax, and that unsightly condition known as "pot belly" may result. A far greater danger is also ever present: the possibility or probability of rupture from any sudden strain. A brief description of these muscles will enable you to understand more clearly the following exercises, many of which will automatically strengthen these muscles.

The external, or descending oblique muscles, are situated on the side and forepart of the abdomen. They are the largest and most superficial of the broad, thin, flat muscles that brace and support the lower part of the abdomen. They are firmly attached to the external surface and lower borders of the inferior, or lower, ribs. From these cartilaginous attachments, other smaller muscles proceed in various directions. They lap, overlap, and interlace, and thus form a muscular webbing designed to support and protect the underlying bowels and organs. These external muscles are again braced by a system of deep-seated internal muscles, the whole forming a wonderfully ingenious structure designed to support and protect the underlying organs.

At this part of the body great muscular strength is requisite to sustain the pressure of the viscera within. If these muscles become weakened, serious results may follow. The importance of especially exercising and strengthening these supporting muscles is therefore evident. This is very difficult to accomplish while standing erect, but can be readily effected in a recumbent position, as follows:

1. Lying on your back, bend one knee upwards and inwards. As you do so, draw up the hip of that side. You will find this action tenses all of the lower abdominal muscles. Hold to the count of six, relax, then repeat several times.

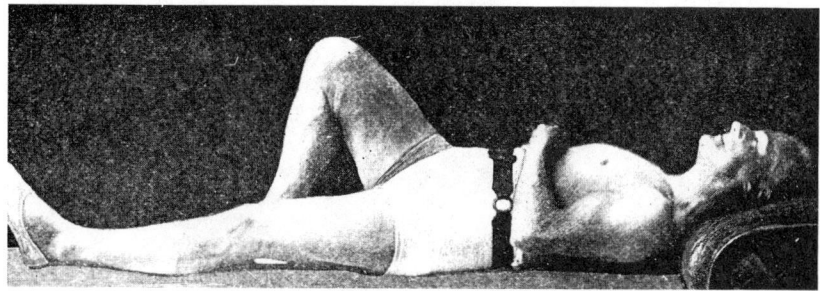

2. Drop that leg back to its original position and, bending the knee, draw up the hip of the other side. Hold, relax, then repeat.

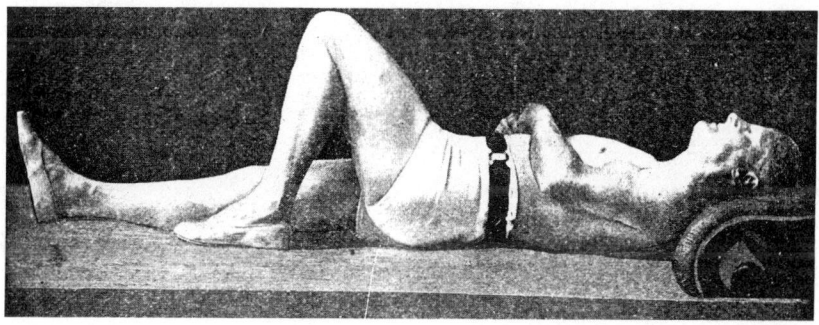

3. Alternate in the exercising, first upon the right side and then the left. Commence with three movements upon each side, increasing to twenty-five as your physical condition improves. This exercise is valuable in cases of constipation; and when the muscles described are toned up and strengthened, rupture is very remote.

EXERCISE TWO

FOR STRENGTHENING THE LOINS

In that system of military drill familiarly known as the "setting-up drill," there is an exercise especially designed for the development of the loins and side muscles. Standing erect with the hands on the hips, the trainees bend the upper part of the body as far to one side as possible, then reverse, bending to the other side, thus alternately tensing and relaxing the muscles of the loins. It is an excellent method for strengthening the body at this point, as well as a remedy for constipation.

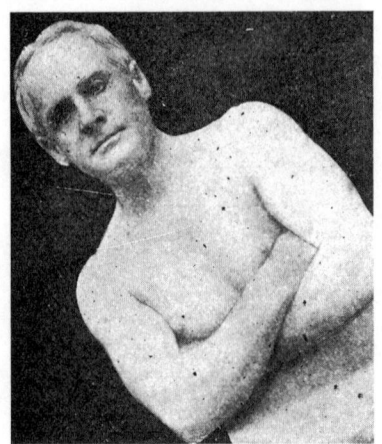

This exercise can be easily performed while lying in bed. Resting upon your back, with your arms folded across the chest, raise the head and shoulders slightly so as to clear the pillow. Commence with 10 movements—that is, 5 upon each side. As your physical condition improves, increase to 25. This action will tense the abdominal muscles and place a moderate tension upon the loin muscles, the weight of the head and shoulders being an excellent substitute for the mechanical appliances sometimes used. Every muscle of the loins and sides will be brought into healthy action.

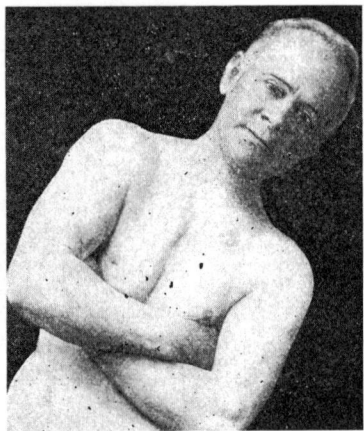

EXERCISE THREE

FOR STRENGTHENING THE ABDOMINAL MUSCLES AND AIDING DIGESTION

Many people are afflicted with some digestive disorder. It is not alone what you eat but also how you eat it. If your food is not thoroughly chewed and, in that process, thoroughly insalivated, it will be digested with difficulty when it reaches the stomach. And if this habit of swallowing the food hastily and without proper mastication is persisted in, indigestion with its various complications will surely result. There is no exception. Nature is a stern creditor, resenting any infraction of her laws. If you violate them you will certainly suffer for it, and the severest penalties she inflicts are for trespassing the laws of digestion.

To preserve the human body in a state of wholeness, or to restore it after it has undergone some deterioration cannot be done when serious digestive disorders exist. Until they are remedied, improvement will be slow, because the trouble is usually caused by hurried eating and consequently insufficient mastication. The logical remedy is to take more time at meals, and chew the food thoroughly. This change in habit alone will most probably improve the digestive conditions in a short time. The next step is to strengthen the muscles of the stomach, for the digestion of food depends largely upon the strength of those muscles.

The remedy lies with one's self, and, if the following brief directions are followed faithfully and persistently, anyone will succeed. Chew your food slowly, that it may be thoroughly insalivated and digested readily. To repeat, it is also necessary to strengthen the muscles of the stomach. This can be accomplished by following this simple exercise:

1. Lie on your back and bend the head well forward. This will contract and tense the abdominal muscles.

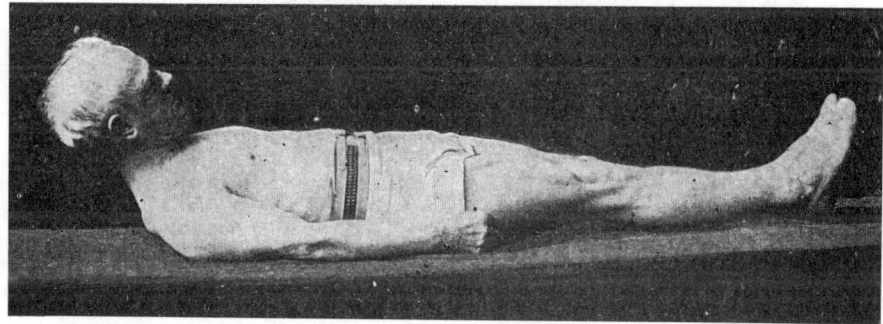

2. Drop the head back to the horizontal position. This will relax the abdominal muscles. These alternate contraction and relaxation exercises will, of themselves, materially strengthen the abdominal muscles, but percussion will greatly aid in producing that result.

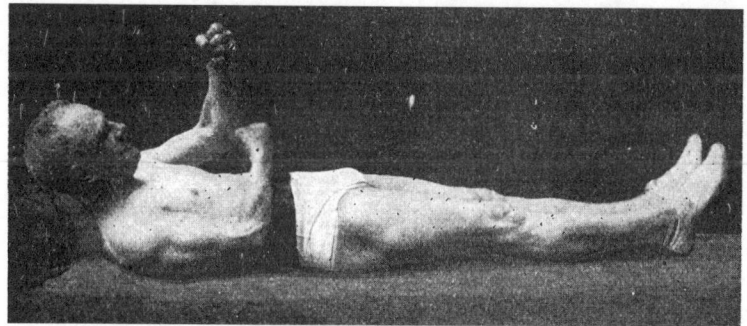

3. As you alternately raise and lower the head, and thus contract and relax the muscles, strike the abdomen rapidly with your clenched fists. At first lightly, but afterwards increasing the force of the blow, as the muscles become stronger. Commence with twenty-five quick strokes. Increase as your physical condition will warrant to one hundred or more.

The percussion should be light and rapid. Continue the percussion, both in the tensed and relaxed positions of the abdominal muscles—as produced in the foregoing exercise—the tension and relaxation being caused by alternately raising and lowering the head. If you find you are impeded by the bedclothes, bend the knees, which will raise the covering clear of the abdomen. This exercise will direct the blood to that part, will produce a healthy circulation and strengthen the digestive organ. This is an excellent exercise and has a very beneficial effect upon all the digestive organs.

During intervals of rest, if it is desired to reduce the abdominal fat, massage and rub the fatty deposit as directed below.

REDUCING AN OBESE ABDOMEN

Fat has been termed the packing of the body and, while it is necessary to have sufficient packing to fill up the interstices of the muscles, thus presenting the roundness of the body characteristic of health and youth, an excess is undesirable and frequently becomes a very serious affliction.

When there is a tendency to "take on fat," it is usually deposited in greater quantities on the abdomen than upon any other part of the body, for the reason that the fat, being inert tissue, naturally gravitates to the point of least activity. The legs, arms and back, being constantly exercised in the normal habits of life, do not offer such a favorable resting place for fat as the abdomen, upon which the deposits will first appear. Consequently, in persons of sedentary habits, we frequently find attenuated limbs, in marked contrast to an obese abdomen. To remedy this unsatisfactory condition, various methods of diet are practiced. In addition, the exercise I describe is effective and not troublesome.

It is not definitely known what fat really is or what is its cause. A carbohydrate diet—that is, such as contains starch or sugar in some form—usually produces the trouble. But when the system has a well defined tendency to form fat in excess of its normal condition, a course of dieting and attendent self-denial may not always be successful. We frequently hear people complain that everything they eat turns to fat, which in a great measure often appears to be true. Fat would seem to be undeveloped tissue, formed in the ordinary process of digestion and assimilation, but, upon reaching a certain stage, is arrested in its further development and, instead of becoming living cellular tissue, changes to this inert substance known to physiologists as adipose tissue, or fat. When for some unknown cause, an abnormal tendency has developed, causing an oversupply of this form of tissue, it is doubtful if the remedy lies alone in the diet.

Muscular activity and agitation of the

point of excessive deposit is probably the most direct, surest, easiest and safest method of elimination. This activity has the same effect on such deposits as it has on worn out and clogging dead tissue, which, I have explained, can be forced from the point of lodgement by the alternate contraction and relaxing of the muscles. In short, by this exercise fatty tissue, when thus dislodged, will be carried off by the ordinary process of excretion. And my experience has been that, under no circumstances, is it possible to convert it into muscular tissue.

Obesity is evidently caused by local inactivity and, that being the case, the only logical and successful remedy would seem to be muscular activity or agitation, where the fatty deposit is situated. Walking is highly recommended and is undoubtedly beneficial. But it is only an indirect means of attacking the trouble, the motion of the legs not especially bringing into action the muscles of the abdomen which are covered with fatty deposit. Therefore some more direct means of forcing into activity and thereby dislodging this accumulation of inert adipose tissue would be more effective. It is a logical deduction that, if the fat is accumulated by reason of sluggish surroundings, then any method which changes that condition to one of activity will remedy the trouble. The method I have found most effectual is massage while the abdominal muscles are tense. The process will be more readily comprehended by the full instructions which follow.

Fat is really carbon, and the phenomena of spontaneous combustion—the cause of many mysterious fires—is a familiar illustration of the method by which fat is consumed in the system. And exercise of the muscles, or friction of the fatty deposit, will remove it. When the muscles are exercised—that is, alternately contracted and relaxed, or vigorously rubbed—there is an increased flow of blood to that point, and therefore an increase of oxygen, as the red corpuscles, of which the blood is composed, consists largely of oxygen. These, coming in contact with the carbon, or fatty deposit, burn it up.

This is the simple explanation of the phenomena. The pumping action of the muscles in their alternate contraction and relaxation expels the ashes, or debris, resulting from this combustion, into the venous and glandular systems, and it is then carried off by the ordinary excretions of the body. Briefly, the remedy for fat is muscular activity. And the exercise described is a safe, easy and effectual cure for it.

1. As previously directed, tense the muscles of the abdomen by lying on your back and raising the head. Then lowering the head to relax the muscles. Apply the blows of percussion as described. Then proceed to:

2. Place the palms of the hands upon the tensed abdomen, with the head raised.

3. Press down firmly and rub the accumulations of fat back and forth, not permitting the hands to slip. Otherwise the skin will only be rubbed, and no benefit results. Massage and rub much in the way a washboard is used.

4. Vary this process by striking the

abdomen rapidly with your clenched fist, alternately contracting and relaxing the abdominal muscles. Contract by raising the head, relax by lowering the head. If you find you are impeded by the bedclothes, bend the knees, which will raise the covering clear of the abdomen.

These excercises are very effective methods of attacking the objectionable deposit and, if systematically and persistently practiced, will certainly achieve satisfactory results. Both of these exercises can be performed most easily and effectively in a recumbent position in bed. They are harmless, inexpensive, and far more effective than the most widely advertised and most lauded indigestion cure.

THE LIVER

When the liver is wrong, everything seems wrong, for the health of the body depends largely upon its condition and activity. If it secretes bile normally and performs its other functions healthfully, then the whole body has the benefit of its good work. But if, on the other hand, it is lazy or congested, trouble commences—a torpid or fractious liver being a very serious affliction. The list of trouble resultant from this condition is a long one.

The liver is really a filter through which the blood must pass to be purified, and if this process of purification is improperly performed, the blood is poisoned, and any or all of the organs may be affected more or less seriously. When the liver is sluggish, there is usually a dull aching pain in the right side and often under the right shoulder blade, Then, too, there are pains in the forehead (more rarely in the back of the head). There is also a furred tongue, an unpleasant taste in the mouth at morning, a dingy yellow color in the whites of the eyes, loss of appetite, often dizzyness, drowsiness after meals, and a generally pessimistic view of life. These are some of the disagreeable conditions that result in varying degrees of intensity, and there are others more serious that may follow if this, one of the most important organs of the human system, is not kept up to its normal activity.

Without going into the physiological details and functions of the liver, think of it simply as a filter through which the blood must pass to be free of its impurities. And remember that it must be kept in an active state to properly perform its duties. To accomplish this, it must be exercised as must every other organ of the body. The simplest and most effective method is rhythmical agitation, or massage, performed in bed, preferably in the early morning when the stomach is empty. It is best to first acquaint yourself with the position, size, and general characteristics of the liver, before commencing the exercises that follow.

The liver is a gland, or rather a multitude of glands bound together in one conglomerate body. In an adult, it usually weighs 4 pounds and is nearly one foot in length in its longest dimension. It is situated upon the right side of the body. It occupies a large space in the abdomen, just under the diaphram, and is partially covered by the lower ribs. The most accessible point for its exercise, or agitation, is immediately above the angle of the right hip bone, and under the lower ribs. It is held firmly in place by five strong ligaments, and nothing but great abuse, such as tight girdles, unnatural pressures, or accidental injury to the region, can displace it. Hence there is no possibility that these exercises will injure the organ. Benefit alone will result, and that under the most comfortable conditions, and without medication or expense. The practice of the exercises which follow will relieve you of any liver complaint and indigestion problems.

EXERCISE FOUR

FOR AGITATING THE LIVER

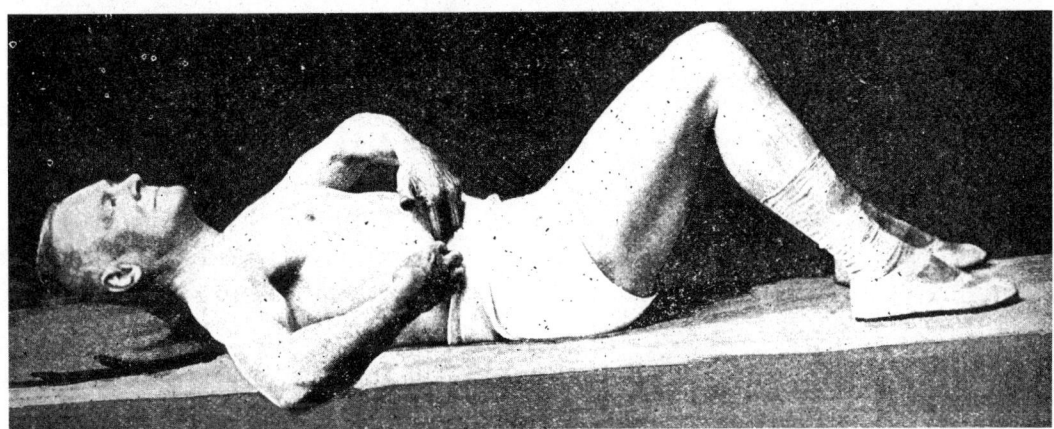

Lying on your back, place the ends of the fingers of both hands over that region of the liver at the right side of the abdomen, above the angle of the right hip bone, and below the edge of the lower rib. Then press the fingers upward and well under the rib. The abdominal muscles, being in a relaxed condition in this position, will readily yield to the pressure, and the liver can easily be moved or agitated. Press under and upward, then relax the pressure.

Commence with 20 movements, and increase up to 100 when your condition warrants. The effect of this agitation of the organ is the same as that obtained in riding a trotting horse, an exercise universally recommended by physicians when the liver is sluggish.

(Trampoline jogging may help if you do not have a weak bladder—Dr. Earlyne.)

WALKING IN BED

As you lie in bed in the morning with the windows open, combine deep breathing with the same movement as in walking, while lying on the back.

Like a chain which is only as strong as its weakest link, this, the weakest part of the body, suffers. If you would be healthy, develop the body evenly.

And if these exercises for the lungs are practiced as described, you need not fear pulmonary diseases. I speak from experience, for my father died of consumption at the age of 42. I inherited weak lungs, and a tendency to that dread disease. By these lung strengthening exercises I have increased the expansion of my chest from 2 1/2 inches to 5 1/2 inches, and am absolutely free from coughs, colds, or any lung weakness. I strongly urge the adoption of these breathing exercises in this or any other system of training or physical culture.

Insertion by Dr. Earlyne: Sanford Bennett has mentioned walking in bed but failed to give details. I have evolved my own procedure which I share with you:

(1) Lying on your back, exhale vigorously through opened lips.

(2) Inhale and hold the breath.

(3) Stretch the heels downward, one leg at a time, with the toes pointing toward the head. This will tense the leg muscles.

(4) Continue the procedure as long as the breath is retained comfortably, stretching each leg alternately downward. Then exhale, relax, inhale and stretch again. Do not hold each leg stretched down indefinitely since muscles could cramp. Keep alternating.

(5) Perform for three inhaled breaths. Exhale vigorously and totally relax.

This stationary walking-stretching is excellent for bringing the spine into alignment, especially the pelvic area. It also aids the sciatic nerves, the muscles of the thighs and calves, the ankle bone structure and the arches. The alternate tensing and relaxing of the leg muscles will also release uric acids in the muscles and joints.

EXERCISE FIVE

FOR BROADENING THE SHOULDERS

This is given only for those who wish to broaden the shoulders. Lying on your back, grasp the left elbow with the right hand, and the right elbow with the left hand. As pressure is exerted, you will feel an outward or lateral strain upon both shoulders. The upper arms, under this cross pull, act as levers forcing them apart. The pressure from the right hand upon the left elbow acts upon the shoulder muscles of the left side, while a corresponding effect takes place on the opposite shoulder. In this position, practice that motion familiarly known as shrugging the shoulders. The lateral strain and tensed condition of

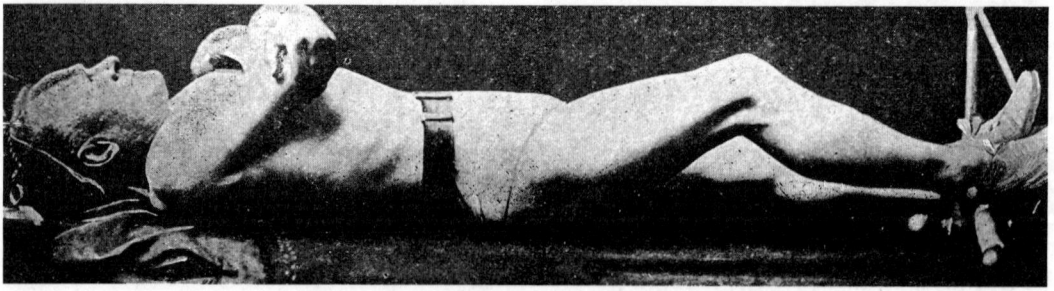

the muscles, combined with the up and down movement of the shoulders, is a most effective method of developing that part of the body. The tension should be upward and forward as far as possible.

Commence with 5 movements on each side. In a short time all feelings of soreness which may result from the first attempts will disappear. The movements can then be increased without fatigue and with very satisfactory results, to ten times the original number. This movement will bring into action the large muscle attached to and covering the shoulder blades. It is an excellent exercise for ladies who may be deficient at this point, improvement being certain if these directions are faithfully followed. If your shoulders were ever well developed and symmetrical, that condition can certainly be restored by persistent practice of this exercise.

EXERCISE SIX

FOR THE MUSCLES WHICH COVER THE SHOULDER BLADES

Lying upon your back, as shown in the illustration, strike with your elbow across the chest. This movement will bring into action and develop the muscles covering the shoulder blades. Five movements for each arm will be sufficient to commence with. This exercise is valuable when there is any indication of acid rheumatism in the muscles described. I speak from personal experience.

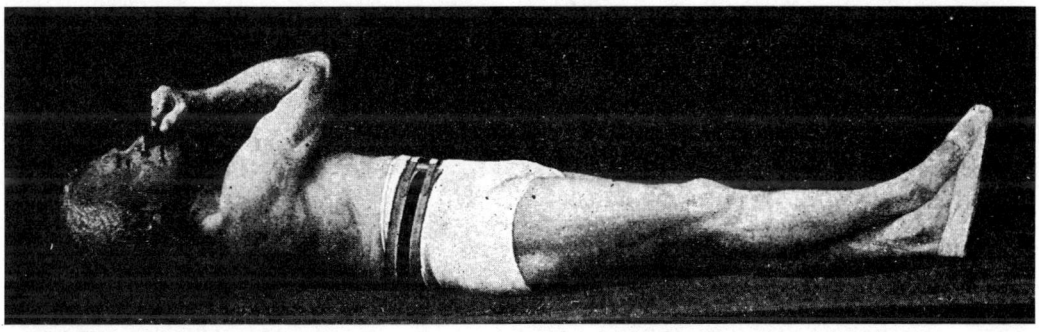

RHEUMATISM

To those who have a tendency to acid rheumatism, the methods I have described of eliminating the worn out or dead matter from the system are of great benefit. By this process of systematically exercising all of the muscles of the body—by alternate contractions and relaxation—the uric acid which is the basic cause of the trouble, and which the kidneys have failed to eliminate, finds no place of permanent lodgement. It is compelled by the persistent agitation to move on, and is expelled by the natural excretions of the body before it has found time and place to settle and form into the minute crystals which, like so many splinters, are the cause of the acute pain characteristic of the disease.

Rheumatism has been termed "the disease of age." This is not altogether true, for, while it must be admitted that as we advance in years it is ever to be dreaded, to think that it is the inevitable disease of age is an error. It should be termed rather, the disease of inaction, and consequently disordered digestion. The remedy is systematic muscular activity. In this way, it is possible to eliminate from the system the cause of the disease.

The simplest, most effective and easiest method is the system of tensing and relaxing every muscle of the body. This will surely prevent this most painful ailment, and, when it is not too far advanced, will effect a cure which may not be possible by the drug method.

EXERCISE SEVEN

FOR THE NECK AND SHOULDERS

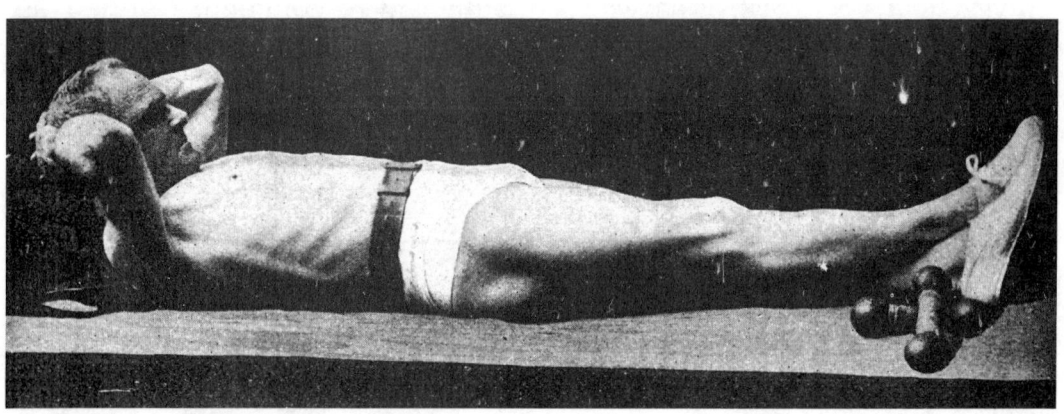

Still lying on your back, raise the head clear of the bed and clasp the back of the head firmly between your hands. Then press the head backward, tensing every muscle, while at the same time applying pressure with the hands to prevent the head from lowering. Hold the tension to the count of six. Tense both the arms and neck muscles as you count, then relax. Commence with 5 movements and increase to 25, but never perform over 25, since the exercise may make the neck muscles too powerful and thickened for symmetry and beauty.

EXERCISE EIGHT

FOR A BEAUTIFUL THROAT AND NECK

Lie on your back with a pillow under your shoulders so that your head is tipped backward with the chin up. Now very slowly raise the head, tensing every muscle of the throat, neck, chin and jaws. Lower the head, continuing the tension. As your head touches the bed, relax completely. Repeat alternately raising and lowering the head while tensing and relaxing the muscles.

Perform only 5 movements to begin, increasing up to 100 as the muscles grow stronger. This exercise not only strengthens the muscles of the throat and face, but also those of the abdomen, reducing obesity.

Remove the pillow for the next exercise.

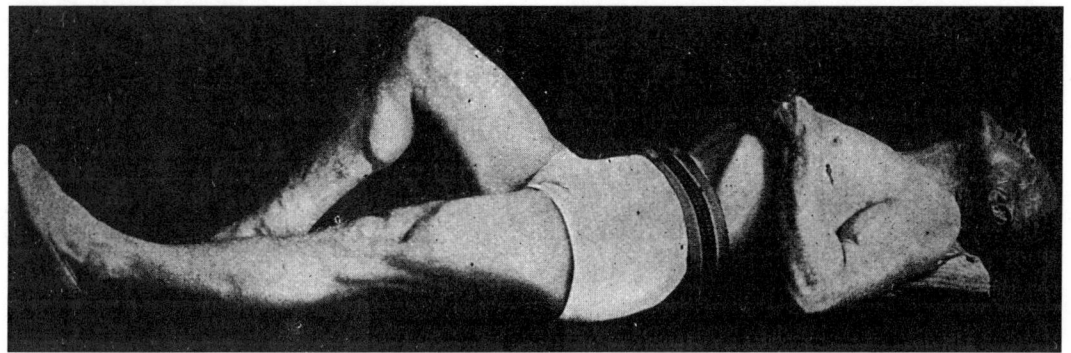

EXERCISE NINE

ARM EXERCISE WITH OR WITHOUT DUMBELLS

Step One

If you have dumbbells weighing from 2 to 4 pounds, grasp them in your hands. If not, clench your fists. Raise both arms simultaneously toward the ceiling, tensing the muscles of the arms and hands vigorously as you slowly push them upward. Hold the tension, pretending you are pushing the ceiling higher. Now slowly lower the clenched

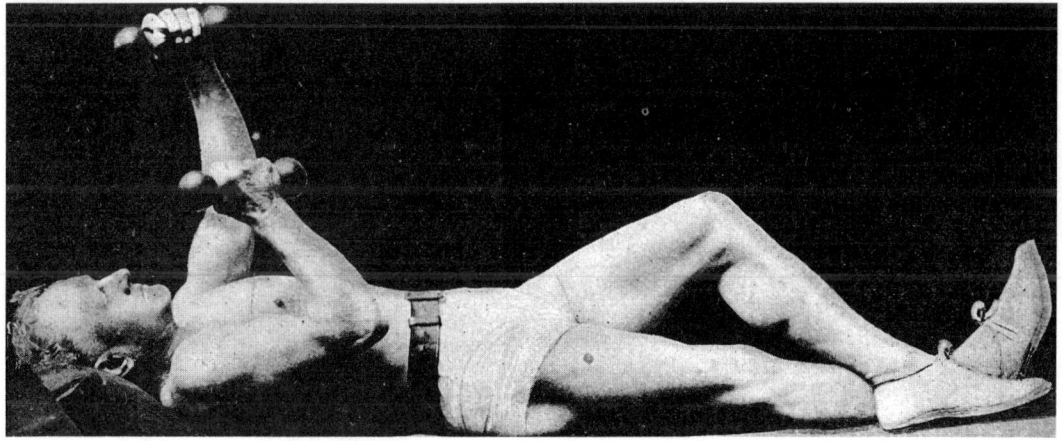

fists back to the chest, still tensing every muscle. Pretend you are drawing a resisting object toward you. When your fists reach your chest, relax completely. Repeat 3 to 5 times.

I strongly advocate the use of light dumbbells. The pair I use weigh four pounds, but half that weight will be sufficient. I have experimented, as I lay in bed, with all sizes up to forty pounds, but I have found moderately quick action with weights of from two to four pounds the most effective. There is always a danger of over-exercise with heavy dumbbells. The continuous strain may affect the heart. And it certainly has a tendency to bring on that condition known in athletes as muscle bound.

Step Two

Raise only the tensed right arm with the fist clenched. Now grasp the tensed right arm with the left hand between the shoulder and elbow and massage it. Lower it slowly, still tensing and massaging. When the fist is lowered to the chest, relax completely. Now raise the tensed left fist and arm, grasping it with the right hand and massaging it. Lower the tensed arm slowly to the chest. Relax. Repeat only 3 times for each arm. The daily practice of this entire exercise should be sufficient to keep the arms strong and flexible.

Step Three

Now extend both arms straight out from your sides. Alternately turn or twist your wrists back and forth so that the arms will partially revolve in their shoulder sockets. If there is a tendency to rheumatic pain at this point where deposits of uric acid frequently occur, this movement will be beneficial, as it will dislodge such deposits. Commence with 5 movements and gradually increase to 25, which at all stages will be sufficient.

You have now completed all the exercises to be performed while lying on the back. Now turn on your right side to continue. When completing all the exercises on the right side, turn on the left side and repeat.

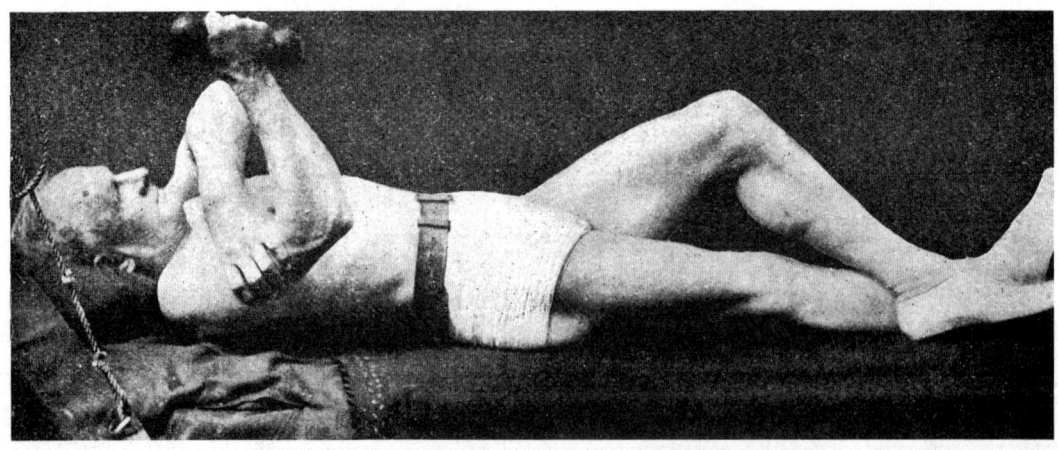

EXERCISE ONE
DEVELOPING THE MUSCLES OF THE THROAT

Throw the head backward. Place the thumb of the right hand under the chin to act as a restraining rod. Bring the head forward until the chin touches the chest, resisting the movement with the thumb. Tense every muscle of the throat and jaws. When the chin touches the chest, relax the tension. Then, tensing again, move the head backward, still using the thumb. When the head is tilted backward again, relax. Alternately contract and relax the muscles of the throat as you move the head backward and forward. Begin with 10 movements, increasing up to 50 as the muscles strengthen.

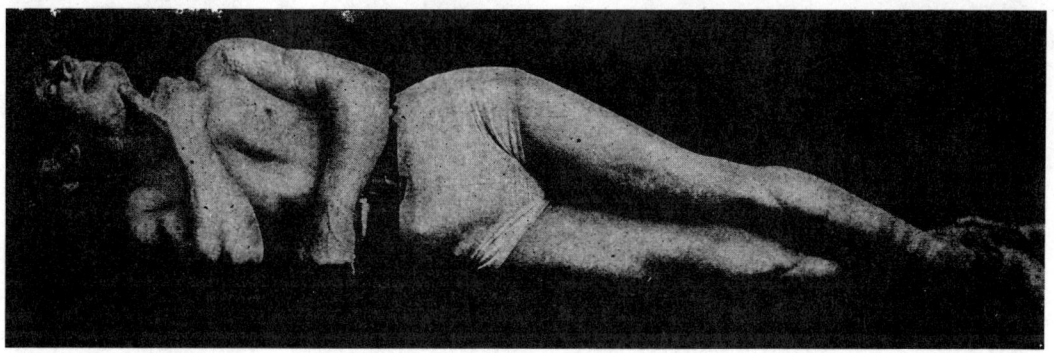

EXERCISE TWO
DEVELOPING THE LEG MUSCLES

Lying on your right side, drop the heel of your left foot downward and turn the toes upward. Stretch the left leg downward, tensing every muscle. Hold the tension to the count of six. Release, briefly relax and stretch again in a kind of kicking downward movement. Pause and repeat. This exercise will develop the calves and firm flabby muscles all along the leg from the thigh to the foot. Begin with five stretches of each leg, increasing as your muscles grow stronger.

EXERCISE THREE
DEVELOPING THE SIDES OF THE NECK

This movement will contract the muscles on the side of the neck and bring into action those muscles of the throat immediately under the chin. Their alternate contraction and relaxation will develop the muscles of the sides of the neck and improve the contour of the throat. Any deep lines which cross and recross the back of the neck will wholly disappear. My appearance at this point is that of a man half my age. Ladies who contemplate practicing this exercise need not fear the appearance of undue muscularity, which this picture exhibits. The effect of exercise on the muscles of women is not the same as in the muscles of men. Their muscles always remain soft, elastic, and more graceful in their roundness than those of men. This exercise will improve and beautify the neck at a time when, in middle life, it is usually very scrawney.

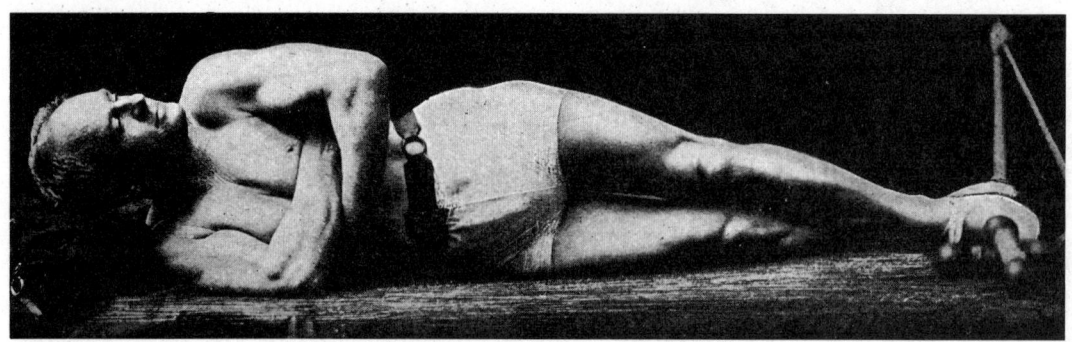

Lying on your side, fold your arms across the chest, as shown in the illustration. Now turn the chin as far as is possible toward the upper shoulder, contracting the muscles on the side of the neck and of the throat, pulling the left-hand corner of the mouth toward the upper shoulder as far as possible. Hold the tension to the count of six. Drop the head back to its original position and relax. Repeat the contractions and relaxation 5 times and increase to 50 as the muscles strengthen.

EXERCISE FOUR

TENSING EXERCISE FOR THE WHOLE BODY

There are many deep-seated minor muscles which are not called into activity by the special exercises previously described. The capillaries which should nourish them, and the microscopic veins, by this inactivity may become clogged, losing their elasticity and efficiency, just as the larger arteries, veins and muscles will deteriorate under like conditions. It is therefore necessary to bring this dormant machinery into action. To effect this:

1). Lie on your side, fold your arms across your chest, grasp your elbows with the hands, throw your head well back, and stretch your body to its full length, as shown in the illustration. In this attitude exert at first but half the strength of your folded arms—the pressure coming upon the elbows, over which your hands are clasped.

2). As you do this, stretch and tense your entire body until it becomes rigid.

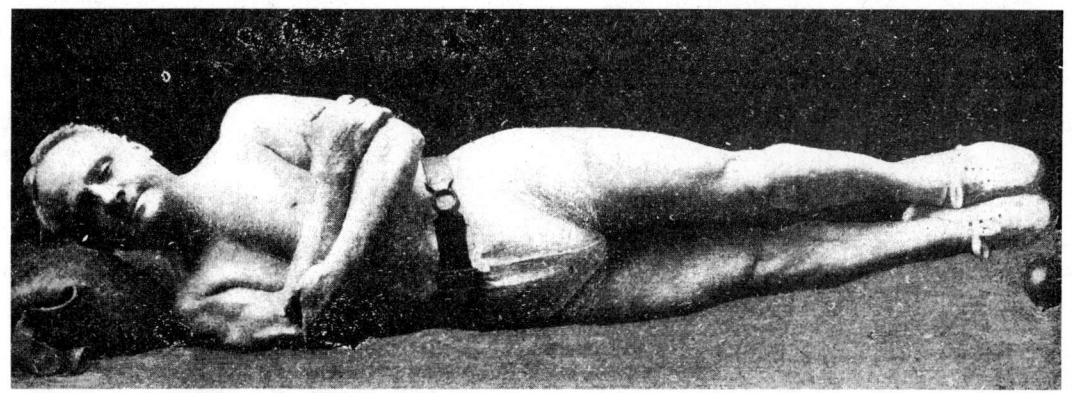

Hold this position but two or three seconds, as the effect is as though you were lifting a heavy weight. Relax for a few seconds, then repeat the effort.

Three or four movements—that is, alternate tensing and relaxing of the muscles as described—are sufficient. This exercise will set the blood tingling in every vein and, most probably, will be followed at first by perspiration. Commence the exercise cautiously. Exert only half your force in the pressure of the folded arms, and gradually increase, as your strength increases. Commence with not more than 3 or 4 movements. Increase slowly until you have reached 10, which will be sufficient.

EXERCISE FIVE

FOR DEVELOPING THE MUSCLES OF THE SIDES AND LOINS

Lying on your right side, fold your arms across the chest with your hands hugging the torso under the arms. Now raise the head and both feet simultaneously, contracting the side muscles of the loins, the muscles immediately below the armpits, the legs and the abdomen. The exercise will also strengthen the muscles of the stomach. Begin with but 3 movements—6 or 7 will probably prove the limit to which you will care to go, as the strain is equivalent to lifting a heavy weight by the muscles described.

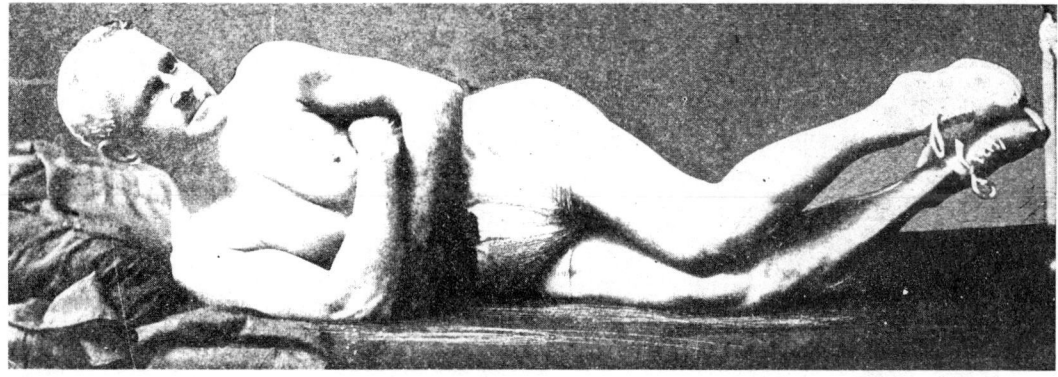

EXERCISE SIX
FOR DEVELOPING MUSCLES OF THE SHOULDERS

Lying on your right side, extend your left arm the full length of the body, folding the right arm so that the right hand rests beneath the left arm. Shrug the left shoulder, the tension being upward and forward as far as possible, and turn the chin upward. Hold the tension to the count of 6, then relax.

Begin with 5 movements of the left arm, increasing as your strength improves. In a short itme all soreness will disappear. This exercise will also benefit those with arthritis and bursitis.

EXERCISE SEVEN
FOR THE HIPS AND LOINS

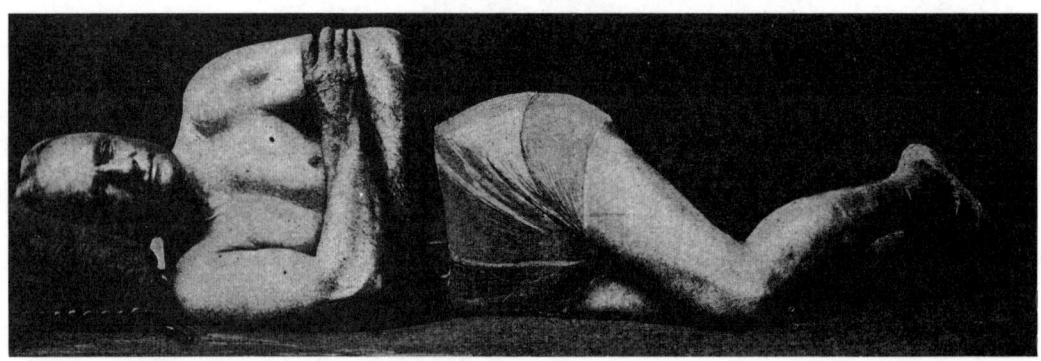

Lying on your right side, throw the left hip forward by holding the right leg straight and bending the left leg, locking the left foot near the ankle of the right leg. Slightly twist the body. Fold your arms across the chest, with each hand hugging the torso.

Now pull backward on the left arm as far as possible while twisting forward with the left hip, tensing the muscles of the loins and of the contracted arm. Allow the chin to turn toward the upper shoulder.

You are adjusting the spinal vertebrae much as does a chiropractor, with the left hip tensed forward and the left arm tensed backward, twisting against each other. Relax and repeat from 3 to 5 times, increasing as your muscles grow stronger.

EXERCISE EIGHT
RESISTANCE EXERCISE FOR DEVELOPING THE FOREARMS

Still lying on your right side, grasp the wrist of your right arm with your left hand. With your left hand, attempt to force your right arm to the ground, resisting with your right arm. Press with your full strength downward to the count of 6. Relax and repeat. Begin with 5 movements and increase to 10 as your muscles improve.

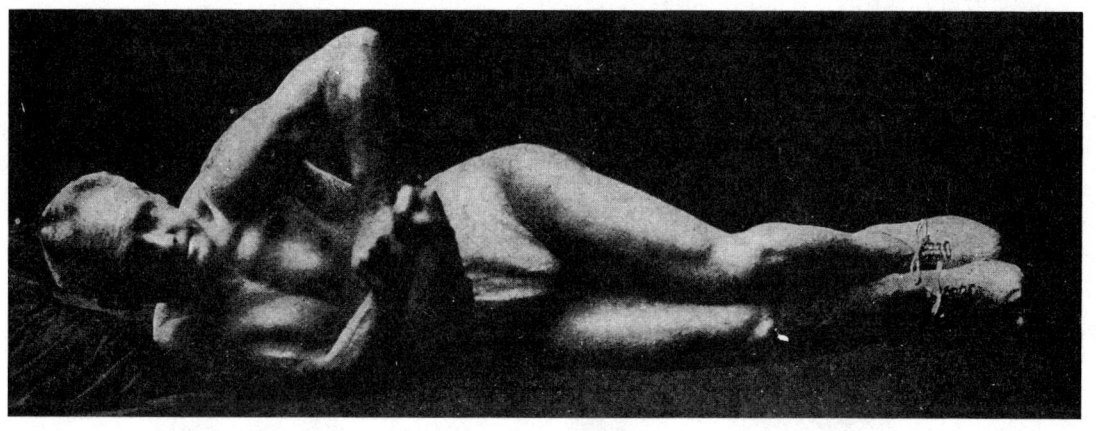

EXERCISE NINE
FOR DEVELOPING THE TRICEPS OR BACK MUSCLES OF THE ARM

Lying on your right side, firmly grasp the upper left arm with your right hand between the elbow and the shoulder. Pull backward with your left arm, at the same time resisting the backward pull by the downward pull of the right hand and arm. Hold the tension to the count of 6, then relax. This will tense both arms.

Begin with 5 movements, alternately pulling and relaxing the tension. Increase to 10 as your muscles improve. I do not know of any gymnasium exercise, aided by mechanical appliances, that will so speedily develop the muscles described. It is safe, simple, and very effective.

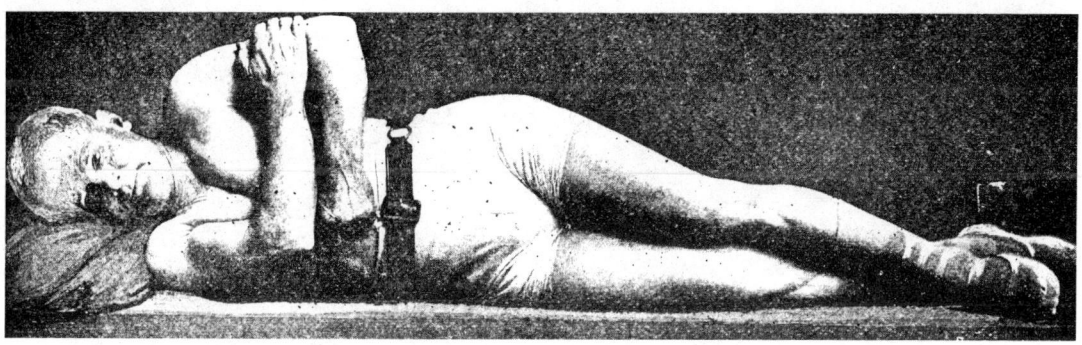

EXERCISE TEN
SINGLE ARM PULLING EXERCISE

1). Lying on your right side, fold the right arm across the chest, the right hand grasping the torso under the left arm.

2). Now lift the left leg, clasping the left hand around the left ankle. Pull the leg downward with all your strength, resisting with your hand. Hold the tension for a count of 6, then relax.

Repeat for 10 times, alternately tensing and relaxing the leg and arm. Increase to 25 as your muscles improve. You will find the tension of the shoulder muscles in this effort different from the preceding exercise, the tension being across the shoulders as well as downward. The muscles specially brought into action are those which make up the neck yoke, and those immediately around and bracing the shoulder sockets.

EXERCISE ELEVEN
PULLING EXERCISE FOR STRENGTHENING THE MUSCLES OF THE BACK AND LOINS

Lying on your side, clasp both hands over the left knee, as in the illustration. Stretch the left leg downward, resisting with your hands. Exert your full strength in a steady pull for a count of 6, then relax. Repeat ten times, alternately pulling steadily on the bent knee, then relaxing the tension. Increase the movements as the muscles grow stronger.

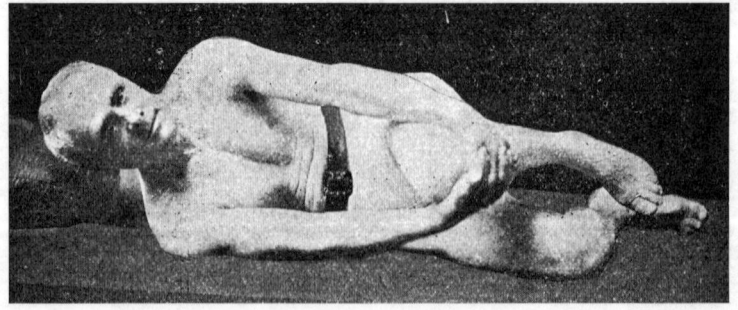

EXERCISE TWELVE

MASSAGE OF THE LIVER LYING ON THE SIDE

Still lying on your side, place your left hand over the region of the liver, which is located at the right side of the abdomen above the angle of the right hip bone and the edge of the lower ribs.

Incline the head slightly forward and bend the knees. In this position, the abdominal muscles will be relaxed and the liver inclined slightly forward. Press the ends of the fingers of the left hand, or the knuckles of the thumb, well under the ribs and massage or agitate the liver. While it is true that the first liver exercise lying on the back may be sufficient, yet this change of position seems to present another surface for manipulation, and both positions can be practiced with good results.

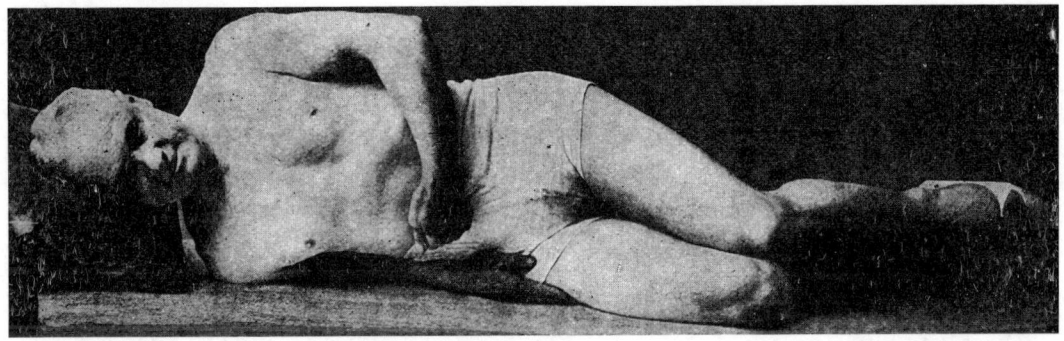

EXERCISE THIRTEEN

FOR THE DEVELOPMENT OF THE LEGS

Usually the legs, as they are constantly exercised in the ordinary pursuits of life, are proportionately better developed than the arms. But the mere exercise of walking will not specially develop the large muscles at the front of the thighs and in the calves, which I designate as the "climbing muscles." Walking or running, while either brings those muscles into action, docs not place any considerable tension upon them and, as a rule, neither pedestrians nor fast runners are notable for any unusual development at these point. On the other hand, bicyclists and "men of the hills" are almost invariably well developed there. The leg muscles of the runner are more elastic and capable of more rapid action than are those of the adept of the silent wheel, or the athlete of the hills. But the former soon tires under the strain of a steady climb, whatever his physical condition may be, simply because he has not developed the muscles then called into action. It is truly only a matter of training.

This, or any other athletic feat, is not so much a matter of natural ability as of the training of the muscles specially brought into play by the exertion. As a means of developing and adding to the symmetry of the legs, it is necessary to exert a pressure upon the ball of the foot, which can be accomplished very easily as you lie in bed.

Lying on your side, simply rest the ball of the foot against the foot board of the bed, and alternately press and relax.

ALTERNATE OR ADDITIONAL STEPS

Another and easier way—lying on your back, or partially on the side, as shown in the accompanying illustration, place the ball of the left foot on the upper part of the toes of the right. Tense the muscles of the right leg and foot so that it may afford support as you press the left foot against the right with enough force to straighten the left leg. Hold the stretch and tension for the count of 6, then relax. Begin with 5 movements, increasing later.

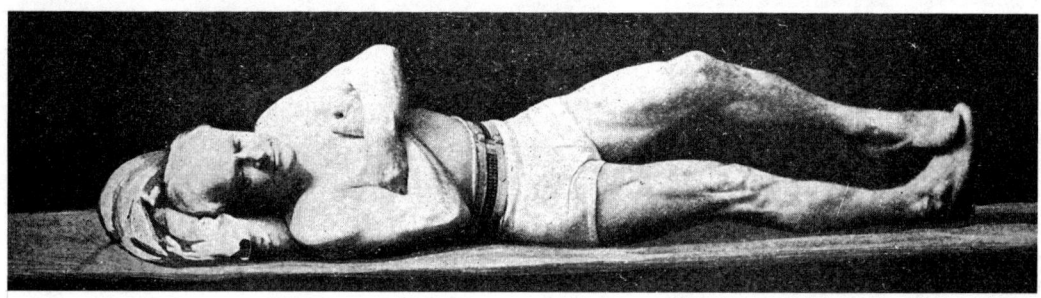

This alternate pressure and relaxation will actively exercise the muscles in question, will imitate the action of climbing with the leg so exercised and will bring no strain or possible injury upon the heart. The pressure exerted should be equal to that required in climbing stairs or a steep grade. This exercise, if persistently and regularly practiced, will surely improve the symmetry of the legs and give one an ability to ascend stairs and steep hills which can never be acquired by the same amount of walking or ordinary gymnasium running exercise.

In this similar exercise, while no pressure is applied with the ball of the foot, still the tension exerted is extremely effective for developing and firming flabby calf and thigh muscles.

Lying on your right side, drop the heel of your left foot downward and turn the toes upward. Stretch the left leg downward, tensing every muscle. Hold the tension to the count of six. Release, briefly relax and stretch again. Begin with 5 stretches, increasing as your muscles grow stronger.

EXERCISE FOURTEEN
TWISTING EXERCISE FOR DEVELOPMENT OF THE ARMS

This movement brings into action all the muscles of the arms, and is exactly like the exercise of fencing, in which the play of the foils necessitates this twisting motion. The benefits of fencing are well known, but as only the right arm is used by the fencer, that arm is often unduly developed while the left is neglected. He is, therefore, in this respect, usually ill balanced.

Lying on your right side, extend your left arm at full length parallel with your body, as shown in the illustration. Clench the left fist tightly and tense the muscles of the arm. Twist the left arm backward and forward as far as possible, alternately tensing and relaxing the muscles. Begin with 5 movements, increasing later.

EXERCISE FIFTEEN
RESISTANCE EXERCISE FOR DEVELOPING THE ARMS

Lying on your right side, grasp the left wrist with the right hand, as shown in the illustration. Pull upward with the left arm, resisting the pull with the right hand.

At each movement, that is, in the alternate strain and relaxation of the muscles, turn the left wrist slightly as it lies in the clasp of the right hand. In the one position, the front of the left wrist should meet the palm of the right hand. In the next, the side of the wrist should meet the palm of the right hand. This slight change, made by the turn of the wrist, will bring into action another set of muscles, and if you desire to thoroughly exercise the muscular system, do not overlook these apparently trivial changes in position.

Begin with 10 movements and increase as your physical condition improves.

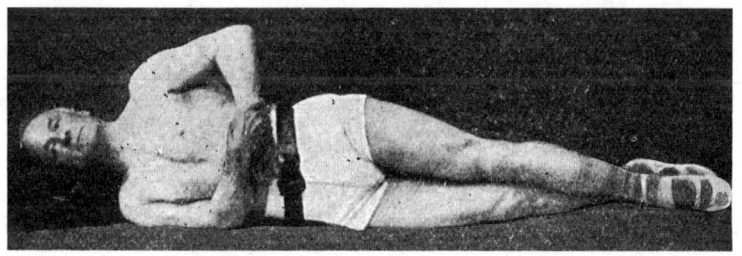

EXERCISE SIXTEEN
FOR DEVELOPING THE BACK AND SHOULDER MUSCLES

Bennett performs this last exercise using a lifting board, but it can be just as effective following the instrucions below:

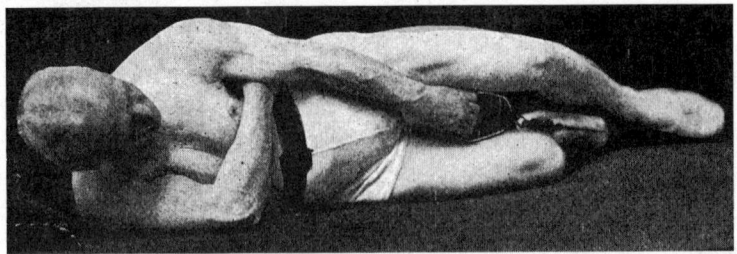

In the last exercise lying on the right side, fold your arms across the chest, the fingers grasping the outside of each arm. Bend the head well forward, tensing the muscles at the base of the neck. Exert full strength upon the folded arms and neck muscles, keeping the lower part of the body relaxed. Now slowly shrug the left shoulder up and down, alternately tensing and relaxing the large muscles of the neck and shoulders. Begin with 5 movements and increase to 15 as your muscles strengthen.

──────────── Now turn on your left side. ────────────

EXERCISE ONE

Throw the head backwards, then, with the thumb of the left hand under the chin to act as a restraining rod, bring the head forward until the chin touches the chest, resisting the movement with the thumb. Tense every muscle of the throat and jaws. When the chin touches the chest, relax the tension. Then, tensing again, move the head backward, still using the thumb. When the head is tilted backward again, relax. Alternately contract and relax the muscles of the throat as you move the head backward and forward. Begin with ten movements, increasing to fifty as the muscles strengthen.

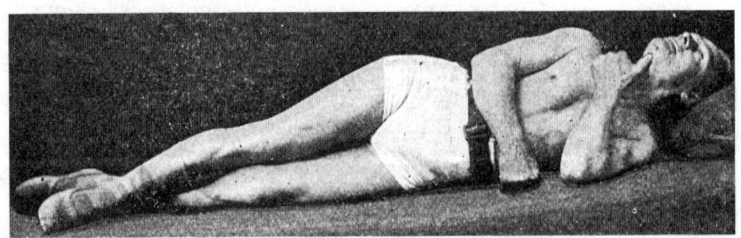

EXERCISE TWO

Lying on your left side, drop the heel of your right foot downward and turn the toes upward. Stretch the right leg downward, tensing every muscle. Hold the tension to the count of six. Release, briefly relax and stretch again in a kind of kicking downward movement. Pause and repeat. Begin with five stretches of each leg, increasing as your muscles grow stronger.

EXERCISE THREE

Fold the arms across the chest. Turn the chin as far as possible toward the upper shoulder, contracting the muscles on the sides of the neck and of the throat. Pull the right-hand corner of the mouth toward the upper shoulder as far as possible. Hold to the count of 6. Drop the head back to its original position and relax. Repeat for 5 times and gradually increase up to 50 as the muscles strengthen.

EXERCISE FOUR

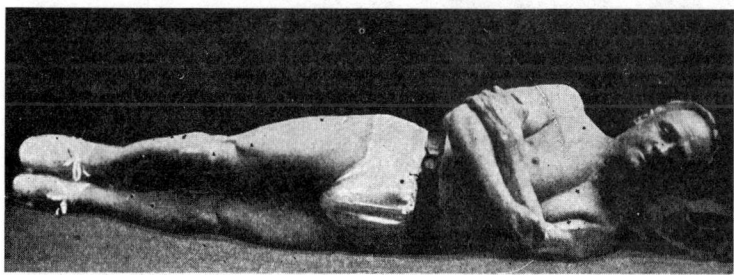

Fold your arms across the chest, grasping your elbows with your hands. Throw your head well back, exert pressure on the elbows, and stretch your body its full length, tensing every muscle until your entire body becomes rigid. Hold the tension only 2 or 3 seconds. Relax a few seconds, then repeat. Repeat only 3 or 4 movements. Gradually increase up to 10 times.

EXERCISE FIVE

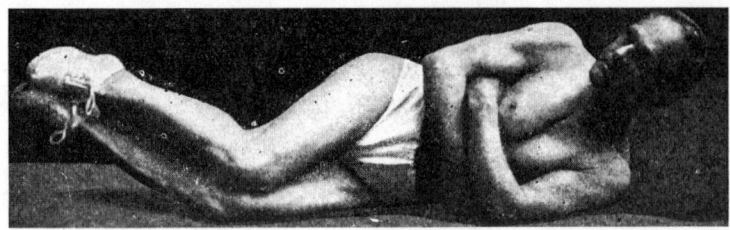

Fold your arms across the chest with your hands hugging the torso underneath the arms. Now raise your head and feet simultaneously, contracting the side muscles of the loins, the legs and abdomen. Begin with only 3 movements, gradually increasing up to 6 or 7 as you grow stronger.

EXERCISE SIX

Extend the right arm the full length of the body, folding the left arm so that the left hand rests beneath the right arm. Shrug your right shoulder, the tension being upward and forward as far as possible, and turn the chin upward. Hold the tension to the count of 6, then relax. Begin with 5 movements of the right arm, increasing up to 20 as your strength improves.

EXERCISE SEVEN

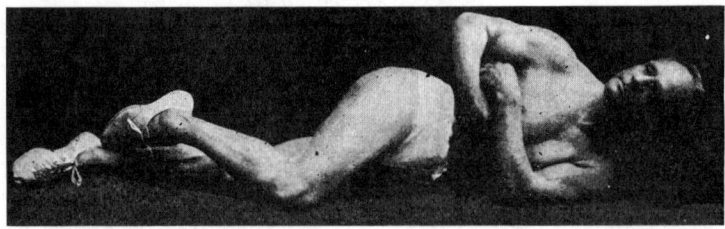

Throw the right hip forward by holding the left leg straight and bending the right leg, locking the right foot near the ankle of the left leg. Slightly twist the body. Fold your arms across the chest with each hand hugging the torso. Now pull your right arm backward as far as possible while twisting forward with the right hip, tensing the muscles of the loins and of the contracted arms. Allow the chin to turn toward the upper shoulder. Twist your upper torso backwards and your lower torso forward as does a chiropractor when giving a spinal adjustment. Relax and repeat 3 to 5 times.

EXERCISE EIGHT

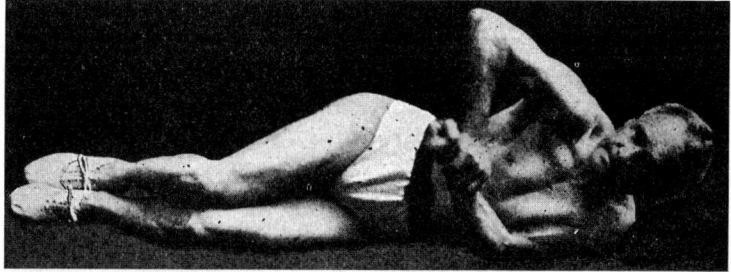

Grasp the wrist of your left arm with your right hand. With your right hand, attempt to force your left arm to the ground. Resist with your left arm. Press with your full strength downward to the count of 6. Relax and repeat. Begin with 5 movements, and increase later.

EXERCISE NINE

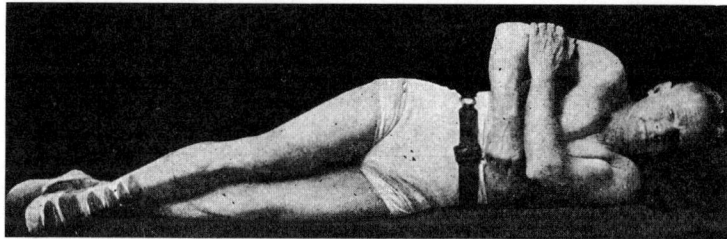

Firmly grasp the upper right arm with your left hand between the elbow and the shoulder. Pull backward with your right arm, at the same time resisting the backward pull with the left hand. Hold the tension to the count of 6, then relax. Begin with 5 movements, alternately pulling and relaxing the tension. Gradually increase to 10 times.

EXERCISE TEN

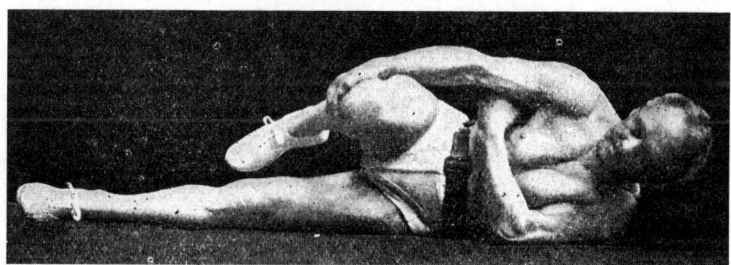

Fold the left arm across the chest, the left hand grasping the torso under the right arm. Now lift the right leg, and clasp the right hand around the ankle of the right leg. Pull the leg downward with all your strength, resisting with your hand. Hold the tension for a count of 6, then relax. Begin with 10 movements, alternately tensing and relaxing the pulling motion. Gradually increase to 25.

EXERCISE ELEVEN

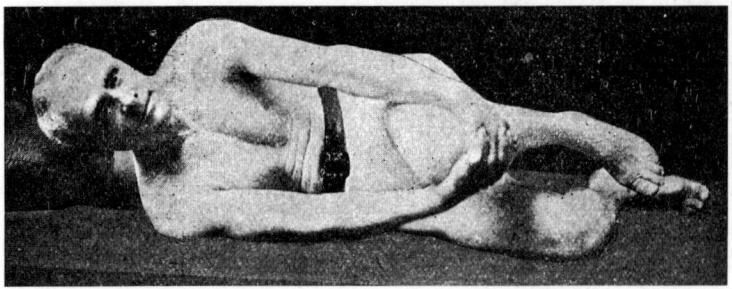

Lying on your left side, clasp both hands over the right knee. Stretch the right leg downward, resisting with your hands. Exert your full strength in a steady pull for a count of 6, then relax. The tension should focus upon the back muscles of the shoulders and the muscles of the loins. Repeat 10 times to begin, increasing the movements as your muscles improve.

EXERCISE TWELVE

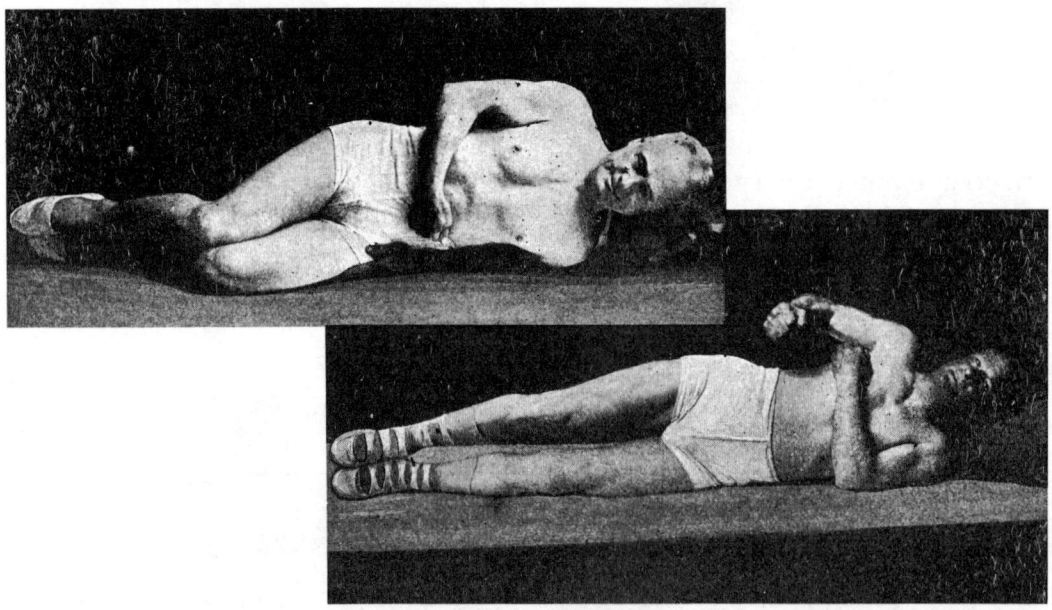

Place your right hand over the region of the liver. Incline the head slightly forward and bend the knees. In this position the abdominal muscles will be relaxed and the liver inclined slightly forward. Press the ends of the fingers of the right hand or the knuckle of the thumb well under the ribs and massage or agitate the liver.

Now clench the right fist and strike light but rapid blows over the liver. Begin with 20 light blows, increasing the force, and increasing to 100 as the muscles grow stronger.

EXERCISE THIRTEEN

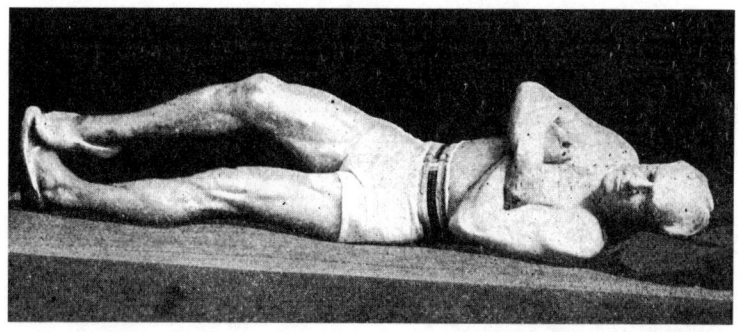

Lying midway between your back and the left side, place the ball of the right foot on the upper part of the toes of the left. Tense muscles of the left leg and foot so that it affords support, as you press the right foot against the toes of the left with enough force to straighten the right leg. Hold the stretch and tension for the count of 6, then relax. Begin with 5 movements, increasing later.

EXERCISE FOURTEEN

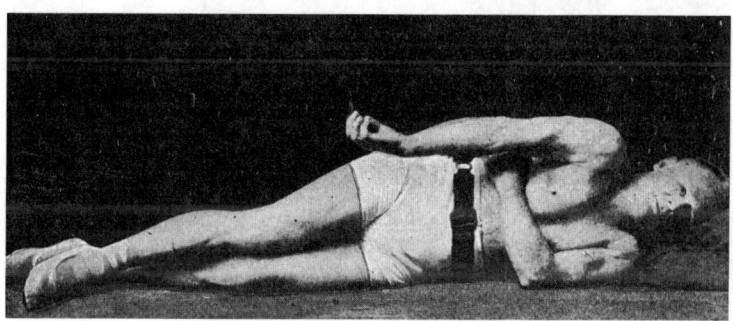

Extend your right arm at full length parallel to the body. Clench the right fist tightly and tense the muscles of the arms. Twist your right arm backward and forward as far as possible, alternately tensing and relaxing the muscles. Begin with 5 or 10 movements, twisting the arm backwards and forward 5 or 10 times. Increase as the muscles strengthen.

EXERCISE FIFTEEN

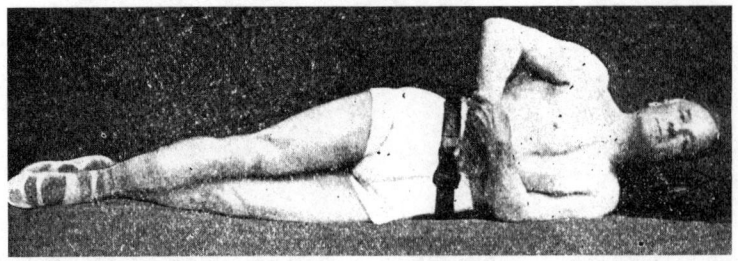

Grasp the right wrist with the left hand. Pull upward with the right arm, resisting the pull with the left hand and arm. At each movement, that is, in the alternate strain and relaxation of the muscle, turn the right wrist slightly as it lies in the clasp of the left hand. In the one position, the front of the right wrist should meet the palm of the left hand. In the next, the side of the wrist should meet the palm. Begin with 10 movements and increase as the muscles strengthen.

EXERCISE SIXTEEN

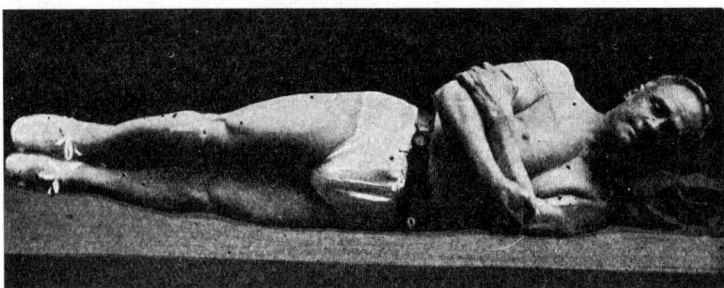

Fold the arms across the chest, the fingers grasping the outside of each arm. Bend the head well forward, tensing the muscles at the base of the neck. Exert full strength upon the folded arms and neck muscles, leaving the lower part of the body relaxed. Slowly shrug the right shoulder up and down, alternately tensing and relaxing the large muscles of the upper part of the neck and shoulder. Begin with 5 movements and increase slowly to 15.

This concludes the series of body exercises. In all the exercises, when the position is on the back, go through the series on the back before turning on the side. When the position is on the side, go through the whole series for that side before changing to the other side. I practice in the order of the descriptions and illustrations.

Doctor Chaney has prepared an extremely helpful cassette tape, guiding you through these exercises to attain their fullest benefit. Write to Astara for information.

CHAPTER 13
NATURAL WHOLISTIC METHODS, OLD HOME REMEDIES, AND YOGA

THE BIG BREAKFAST—A BOON OR A BOO-BOO

Nothing is quite so controversial as whether or not to eat a large breakfast. Nutritionists are avidly divided. Some feel that a hearty breakfast is the greatest thing in the world—the most important meal of the day. Others feel that stuffing the body early in the morning could be disastrous. They feel the body is attempting to eliminate many toxins in the morning hours and the system should not be clogged with an over-abundance of heavy foods.

I cannot, in all good conscience, join either of the groups. Some people badly need breakfast soon after rising because of low blood sugar. Others can well afford to wait until mid-morning or even skip breakfast altogether. I believe it to be a matter for each individual, obeying the instincts of his body needs. It very much depends upon your personal constitution. If you are hypoglycemic it may be well for you to eat at least a light breakfast of fruit and some kind of protein—perhaps yogurt—not too long after rising. But for all, a heavy "farmhouse" breakfast should be avoided, at least early in the day.

Absolutely nobody should go the heavy hearty breakfast routine—the fried eggs, pancakes, bacon, toast, potatoes, muffins, jelly, orange juice routine. And absolutely no one should go the coffee-doughnut route. These are both extremes. If one insists on a "heavy" breakfast, sufficient should be a glass of juice, two eggs, preferably poached, and a slice of toast—and of course, a cup of coffee for the coffee drinker. This traditional breakfast is, indeed, too traditional to change. And no wise teacher should insist upon it. I enjoy such a breakfast myself occasionally.

Early morning is when yoga should be practiced, when walking or jogging is best, when deep breathing is most beneficial. Therefore, if breakfast can wait a bit while the system continues to throw out its toxins, so much the better.

I'll share some of my breakfast ideas with you because I think, too, it could be the most important meal of the day. And because I think I have "evolved" some good and nourishing ideas.

I often begin with four ounces of fresh squeezed orange juice. I also eat the orange pulp out of the peeling once the oranges are squeezed which gives me fiber plus vitamin P interlining the skin.

Into the fresh orange juice I blend a teaspoon each of brewers yeast, whey powder, and lecithin—and sometimes the raw yolk of a fertile egg. Or I omit the egg yolk and eat five raw almonds with the blended juice. Thus I have a fresh fruit breakfast with the proper amount of protein. This breakfast—my favorite—does not overload my system yet it is packed with power. It is this type of breakfast I would suggest for most. Try it. You'll like it. Those who frown on juice may wish to eat chopped fruit instead, with perhaps a bit of yogurt or a topping of tahini, a sesame seed cream. Others may prefer plain yogurt topped with a handful of sunflower seeds, together with perhaps an apple, orange or peach.

Or try one egg, a slice of whole grain bread and an orange. Combining the vitamin C of the orange with the iron of the egg changes the iron into a form the body can assimilate. The combination increases the iron intake four or five times.

Compare these with a breakfast of canned orange juice, toast made from white bread and spread with margarine or commercial jelly, instant oatmeal or other cereal with white sugar and pasteurized milk or cream, and coffee with white sugar and cream.

This breakfast will rapidly elevate the blood sugar from the refined fermentable carbohydrates, then drop it rapidly because of the increase in insulin released by the pancreas in an attempt to normalize the blood sugar level. By ten o'clock, the consumer will be searching for a snack—or reaching for a cup of coffee with sugar.

The natural carbohydrates in the first breakfast—my breakfast—will digest slowly. The raw protein in the yeast, or seeds and yogurt, will allow the blood sugar to rise very slowly over a long period of time. Then it will level off and hold steady for many hours. With the proper diet there should be no more low blood sugar problems. The body chemistry will become better balanced from eating natural nutritional foods.

A word of warning: under no circumstances should you drink more than six ounces of orange juice at one time and preferably only four—at least in the beginning of your regeneration program. Sores may develop in the mouth and on the tongue if too much orange juice is taken into a system polluted with toxins. Once the body becomes purified and you've built up the chlorophyll and enzymes from the sulphur in your system, you may be able to drink as much orange juice as you desire with no ill effects. But while the body is regenerating, it is possible to experience a sore mouth even without eating oranges.

The sores in the mouth and on the tongue reflect the condition of the stomach. They indicate that toxins are pouring into the stomach, temporarily irritating the membraneous lining. Eventually the pure natural food program will heal the stomach and the irritations will go away, clearing up the stomach and the sore mouth.

The question often arises whether milk may be added to the orange juice drink of my favorite breakfast. Not if an egg is included. Mixing two animal proteins is never wise. It may even be that the mixture of whey powder and yeast powder is too much protein for you in the beginning. In that case, take them separately if a sore mouth develops—or begin in smaller portions.

Another delicious breakfast is steel-cut oatmeal cooked with raisins. I like to add just a touch of cream and perhaps a bit of honey. Don't eat this daily—the perpetual intake of cream could trigger a reaction of the gall bladder. But occasionally, such a breakfast is excellent.

Another delicious breakfast is the following *Super-Cereal* for those whose digestive system can handle a fruit-grain combination: Mix and store in the refrigerator in wide mouthed containers:

1 lb. sesame seeds
1 lb. almonds
1 lb. sunflower seeds
1 lb. pumpkin seeds
1 lb. chia seeds
1 lb. flax seeds

(Or any equal amount of each such as 1/2 lb.)

Store in refrigerator on a large turntable in covered containers:

1. rice polishings
2. raisins
3. shredded coconut
4. yeast - (Torumel or something similar)
5. bran flakes
6. granular lecithin
7. wheat germ

For Breakfast

Put two serving spoons of the seed mix in seed grinder, and then put the ground mixture in a large bowl with a serving spoon full of each of the other 7 ingredients.

Mix with carrot juice or milk, with honey to sweeten. Or select your favorite fruit juice to moisten the cereal. Add a chopped fruit—pear, apple, papaya, banana, apricot, etc.—if you desire.

Happy, healthy, holy day to you!

FATS AND OILS

Because of the current cholesterol scare, Americans have been urged to reduce their intake of meat, eggs, butter, cheese, milk, and all animal fats. And substitute polyunsaturated vegetable oils. As a result, millions of Americans now use vegetable oils for cooking, frying, baking and in salad dressings—and this is very good. But much confusion exists over what is meant by *saturated* or *polyunsaturated* oils.

A *saturated* oil is one that solidifies, such as: lard, margarine, and cooking shortenings. Saturated fats are also the fats of meat, poultry and dairy products. A "saturated" oil means that the oil is completely saturated with *hydrogen*, which breaks the double carbon bonds. Poly*un*saturated oils are those which are liquified—that is, they remain liquified at room temperature. They contain little or no hydrogen.

These liquified oils are the poly-unsaturated oils—sesame, safflower, apricot, olive, peanut, etc.—so popular with health advocates.

For the last fifty years the shortening industry has deliberately processed soft and liquid fats into solids, making them "hydrogenated" fats. The wholistic physician is well aware that these solidified, hydrogenated fats may well share blame for the present high level of arteriosclerosis, heart disease, arthritis and innumerable other ailments.

Saturated—or hydrogenated fats—include not only margarine, lard, shortening, but also ice cream, most peanut butters and bakery goods (since they also contain hydrogenated fats). If you insist on eating meat, be aware of the high fat content in beef, ham, bacon, pork, salmon, herrings, sardines and mackerals. Fish lowest in fat are the flounder, sole, trout, sea bass and cod. When buying beef, select that which is leanest. Trim that which is left before cooking. Especially, too, to be avoided are rich soups and gravies made with meat stock. Research clearly indicates:

1. The major cause of high cholesterol levels in the blood and arteries is not cholesterol-rich foods such as eggs, but rather the refined carbohydrates such as white sugar and white flour.

2. The main contributor to hardening of the arteries and heart attack is not cholesterol but a high triglyceride level in the blood, triggered principally by *sugar.*

3. A high fat diet—even when derived from vegetable oils—contributes to a high triglyceride level.

4. Many polyunsaturated oils quickly turn rancid unless they are preserved with harmful antioxidants. Thus they are also carcinogenic.

5. Thus, you should always look for *cold pressed unrefined polyunsaturated oils* because otherwise the processing has required heat, making even the vegetable oils dangerously rancid before you open them. *Unrefined oil* means it has been extracted by natural means and still possesses the raw ingredients of unrefined oil. If the label does not say *cold pressed unrefined*, it means the oil may be highly processed, chemicalized, and over-refined. They are extracted by either carcinogenic chemicals or high heat pressure methods, rendering them possibly carcinogenic.

When vegetable oil is heated to high temperatures, it becomes carcinogenic (causing cancer) thus all frying should cease. If you must fry some foods it is better to obtain a wok and saute-steam your vegetables in a small amount of water with a small amount of unrefined cold pressed vegetable oil. The mixture of water with the oil prevents to some degree overheating of the oil.

When cooking soups, beans, etc., oil should be added at the time it is served and not cooked with the food. If additional fat is needed, butter may be used in moderation, melted by the heat of the soup or beans when serving.

Since we need some fats and oils in our diet, we should eat nuts and nut butters. We should also include lecithin in our diet daily because it combats the fatty buildup in our bloodstream and arteries. Protein also aids in preventing fatty deposits from settling in the artery walls. A daily intake of fresh leafy vegetables also acts as a control over such deposits and in preventing calcuim deposits in the joints.

CASTOR OIL—
THE MIRACLE BALM

Edgar Cayce's use of castor oil is well known. Two of his most ardent advocates—both doctors—use castor oil for practically everything. But Dr. Som used castor oil also—for practically everything. Week after week and year after year, castor oil was his favorite remedy—and lemon.

First of all, he used it—castor oil—against allergies. He suggested putting pure castor oil into a small squeeze bottle with a top from which drops could issue. He suggested squeezing five drops a day under the tongue. During his years of medical practice, he had found it most effective against all types of allergy...and I must say that many to whom I have recommended the treatment report satisfactory results. This same "treatment" would overcome the toxins in the bowels and intestines known as "auto-intoxication."

He also suggested applying the oil to warts and moles—both morning and night—and rubbing it in well. He found it to be extremely effective in removing these troublesome appendages. He used it as eye drops to heal red and irritated eyes. He applied it to scalps twice a week for those who were experiencing thinning hair. It was applied in the evening, left overnight and removed the following morning with shampoo. He swears it encouraged a new growth of hair.

Here is his remedy for healing hemorrhoids: purchase a baby rectal syringe at a drugstore. Pour castor oil—perhaps four ounces—into a wide mouthed bottle and chop a garlic clove into it. Fill the baby syringe with the castor oil solution, insert it into the rectum and squeeze. This should be repeated several times a day and at bedtime, if the hemorrhoids are bleeding and serious. If they are more simple, then only after each bowel movement and at bedtime is sufficient—and later just at bedtime. I have never known a case of hemorrhoids to fail to be healed by this simple method.

To quickly relieve the pain of swollen hemorrhoids, Dr. Som recommended witch hazel applied with a cotton pat.

The castor oil packs, made popular by Edgar Cayce, were used constantly by Dr. Som. Placed over lymph gland areas, they seemed successful in healing all manner of human ailments—irritated and inflamed eyes, infected bruises, sprained ankles, exterior ulcers, acne, bursitis, hepatitis, gall bladder irritations, headaches, tonsillitis, vaginitis, ovarian cysts, and even pregnancy problems. The oil seemed to penetrate the cells of the skin and enter the lymph gland. From there, the lymph substances apparently carried the healing essences of the oil throughout the body, healing all manner of afflictions.

A castor oil pack can be made by simply soaking a cloth—preferably cotton flannel—in castor oil, and wrapping the soaked cloth in an outer protective covering. Placed over an afflicted area, or a prominent lymph gland, or at random over the lower abdomen, all manner of ailments responded favorably.

Som said the castor oil contained a substance that "took the poison out of poisons." I've even known him to apply it to a snake bite to "draw out the death-dealing venom"—and it worked. He called the mysterious substance "sodium ricinoleate," or "soricin." The soricin removed the toxic properties of the bacterial toxins and other poisons and left their other properties intact. Thus a toxin such as tetanus or diptheria, when detoxified by soricin, still retained the power to produce immunity even though stripped of its dangerous poison.

I'll share an experience of my own concerning castor oil which may be significant because it involved a violent reaction to penicillin. Some years back, while enduring a serious bout with flu, I contacted a doctor for medical help. Even though his records clearly stated I was allergic to penicillin, still he prescribed a penicillin derivative for me. Being ignorant of the fact that the tablets were related to penicillin, I began taking them.

Shortly after the first one, I noticed small red blotches appearing in a couple of areas on my skin. Unaware of their cause, I took a second tablet. During the night I wakened in dreadful pain. My body was swollen and had turned a fiery red from head to foot. The itching was agony.

Immediately I sensed what had happened. Since all efforts to reach the doctor failed, I contacted Dr. Som. He was at my bedside almost immediately. He took one look at me and out of his little bag came the castor oil. The itching was immediately relieved. For the following two weeks I applied the oil all over my body. Slowly the swelling diminished, the itching ceased and the redness vanished. So I owe a supreme debt to castor oil—and, of course, Dr. Som.

And I try to remember the five drops under my tongue daily.

ACIDOSIS

Som said that the term *acidosis* never applied to the blood. The blood never became acid. It never even became neutral. It must always remain alkaline. Actually keeping the blood alkaline could be the secret of eternal life—mortal life, that is. Certainly it could be the secret of eternal youth while mortal. So said Som.

The normal acid-alkaline balance in the body is 80 to 20—80% alkaline and 20% acid. The ratio is maintained by the potassium, calcium, sodium and magnesium salts in the bloodstream.

Som said we need not be overly concerned about it, except to be aware that we should not overeat acid foods which are all meats, cheese, milk, eggs, all cereals and grains, all legumes, nuts and almost all processed foods. The alkaline foods are vegetables and fruits—except prunes. Som taught that acid fruits such as oranges, grapefruit, lemons, limes, etc., did not produce an acid effect in the system, rather they reverted to alkaline ash (except in occasional rare individuals). So one must simply be aware of the importance of eating plenty of fresh fruit and vegetables to maintain the desired alkaline-acid balance.

Nor should one overeat protein foods, which are usually predominantly acid. When excessive acid foods are eaten, the blood must draw from the cells its needed supply of the minerals calcium, magnesium, sodium and potassium in order to maintain its alkalinity—thus robbing the cells of their own alkaline reserve. Adding kelp to the diet helps to supply both the blood and the cells with a rich source of the needed minerals.

WHAT TO DO FOR CHOKING

Have you ever witnessed someone

choking on food? Well, there are many different solutions offered by Dr. Som. One of the most reliable seems the most simple. Simply raise your arms directly over your head. Once the arms are raised, the throat muscles relax their grip on the obstruction. Then the food can be expelled easily.

Other suggestions are simply to pull on the tongue—a strong firm steady pull. With such a pull, the larynx moves upward at least an inch, providing space to reach down the throat with the finger of the other hand and dislodge the culprit. A napkin or handkerchief is needed to grasp the tongue which, otherwise, may be too slippery.

Another suggestion is to break a raw egg into an opened throat with the head thrown back. The egg creates gagging and vomiting.

BREAST ABCESS

When a woman cannot breast feed her child the milk has to be dried up so no abcess can form. Melt camphorated oil, rub breasts thoroughly and bind tightly (once a day) for 2 or three weeks.

EYE STYES

Place a cold wet tea bag on the stye 3 or 4 times a day—any kind of tea.

HIGH BLOOD PRESSURE

Making a tea from avocado leaves will drop blood pressure. Also—an Oriental method—using the fore finger of each hand, place one finger flat above the lips and the other below the lips. Rub backward and forward in a see-saw motion for eighty-four counts. The upper finger moves to the right as the lower finger moves to the left. This simple technique is amazingly successful. Use it daily if high blood pressure is a problem.

AFTER EATING—REST

Dr. Som always advised me to watch the animals if I would learn how nature intended us to behave. He pointed out that animals always curled up for a rest after eating. It may not always be possible for us to take a nap immediately after eating but we certainly don't have to become overly active. It's a good idea to lie down a few moments after a meal but if this isn't possible, try simply to relax and remain inactive for awhile.

The food you've eaten draws blood to the digestive organs, where it is needed to digest the food. All the digestive organs need an extra blood supply to complete the digestive process. When you immediately become active after eating, you draw the blood away from the digestive organs. If you begin mental work the brain will attract the blood from the digestive apparatus. If you begin walking or other physical activities the blood will revert to the legs, hands, or wherever the action is being applied. It is best to remain as quiet as possible for at least 20 minutes, preferably longer.

BEWARE OF TWO-IN-ONE-DRUGS

Very often a capsule will be prescribed to a patient combining a stimulant and a depressant in the same capsule. It can be extremely dangerous. The capsule may contain both an amphetamine (a stimulant) and a barbiturate (a depressant). The barbiturate is frequently added to the amphetamine to reduce such adverse effects as irritability, insomnia, and the jitters. The two-in-one pill greatly compounds the risk of addiction. Because some patients are not sensitive to the amphetamine, but are highly susceptible to the barbiturate, they may not realize they are receiving a barbiturate. Thus, if you are taking an amphetamine and are experiencing crying spells, anxiety and sleeplessness, check with your doctor. Your amphetamine capsule may also contain a barbiturate. The results could be an extremely toxic blood level of both amphetamines and barbiturates.

HICCOUGHS

Apply pressure upon the eyeballs. Or lie face down on the floor and relax.

THE PUBIC PARASITE

Many thousands of people become victims of the *crab louse* without ever being aware of the cause of their problem. This miniscule parasite is almost invisible to the naked eye. Technically it is known as the *phthirus pubis*. It infests many filthy public rest rooms and, using these rest rooms, one becomes exposed to these infinitesimal parasites.

This crab louse can leap many feet and hundreds of them can nest in the pubic hairs. The protective paper seat cover is no shield against these lice. One can also become infected through sex, poor hygiene, and crowded living conditions.

These crabs infest not only the street fighter and street walker, but also executive, society matron and debutante. Both male and female are contaminated. No one is immune from the problem.

The pubic louse usually makes itself known by the maddening itch it creates, usually in the genital areas, although almost any hairy part of the body is susceptible.

Dr. Som's method of removal was to apply generous portions of Campho-phenique to the pubic area, saturating the pubic hairs. It is best applied just prior to a bath or shower. The Campho-phenique will kill the lice and the shower or bath will wash them away. The treatment may need to be repeated for total effect. And it should be used after any exposure to a dirty public rest room.

TO KILL AN INFECTION WITHOUT AN ANTIBIOTIC

Here is Dr. Som's "remedy":
1. Send for a chiropractor
2. Fast on plain water and lemon water.
3. Take enemas night and morning.
4. Take a daily 15 minute tub soak. Add two cups of any kind of tea to the water. Drink one cup of hot tea while soaking to encourage perspiration.
5. Take *Echinacea* herb capusles (2) every two hours.
6. Take garlic capsules four times a day.
7. Take walks and breathe deeply if not too ill.
8. Go to bed and stay there (except for the walks).
9. Keep warm.

EMPHYSEMA

Emphysema is a strange disease that occurs when air can be easily inhaled but cannot easily be exhaled. To better understand emphysema, one should understand the anatomy of the lungs.

Consider first the bronchial tubes, beginning first with the nostrils and mouth. Both merge into a windpipe and larynx or voicebox. The larynx is located on top of the windpipe. The windpipe or trachea separates into left and right branches called the bronchi. These separate again into bronchioles, which divide again into tiny respiratory bronchioles. These are ultimately attached to the air sacs where oxygen is absorbed by the blood, and where the carbon dioxide of the blood is ingathered to be exhaled.

The principal function of the lungs and the entire respiratory system is to fill the blood with oxygen and to remove carbon dioxide from the blood. Because every set of lungs differs, the doctor frequently has difficulty in diagnosing whether or not a patient has emphysema. X-rays are of little help. His best hope is to fluoroscope the chest and analyze the motions of the diaphragm plus certain breathing tests and blood tests.

Emphysema can be caused by chronic infection, persistent exposure to harmful dust, air pollution or smoke. It goes without saying that most persons with severe emphysema are heavy smokers, or are the victims of persistent exposure to someone else's smoking.

The following are only a few of the many avenues for healing or improvement as offered by Dr. Som:

1. Change to a vegetarian diet with emphasis on raw vegetable and fruit juices.

2. Engage in an exercise program including vigorous walking.

3. Engage in persistent practices of deep breathing.

4. Take 2,000 milligrams of vitamin C daily, plus a vitamin B supplement.

5. Take 3 capsules daily of the following herb formula:
1 teaspoon each of Slippery Elm, Mullien, Comfrey, and Marshmellow herb powders. Occasionally add one half teaspoon of Lobelia. Mix thoroughly and fill capsules size 00.

REJUVENATION THROUGH HAND THERAPY

Dr. Som taught that the hands had a great deal to do with the character, and exercising and massaging points of the hands and the fingers increased particular characteristics. The thumb, for instance, was directly influenced by the will, and vice versa. Massaging the thumb increased will power and the ability to use logic. Massaging pressure points of the index finger, which was the finger of destiny, helped one to become more aggressive. Massaging the middle finger increased the ability to teach and instruct others, to clarify points, to illustrate properly. Massage of the third (ring) finger increased the ability to love, to express compassion and empathy. Massage of the little finger stimulated the emotion of sex and physical love. Overstimulation could lead to lust. So said Som.

He encouraged the following hand therapy:

With the arms bent at the elbows, completely relax the hands and shake them vigorously, making them perfectly flexible at the wrist. Shake them up and down and in circles until a strong electric current vibrates throughout your hands and finger tips. Then rub the hands vigorously together, not only pressuring the palms and "wringing the hands," but the back of the hands as if you were drying them.

Then press the fingers together, then the palms, inward and outward. Now, move the palms away from each other, but leave the fingers and thumbs pressing together. While holding them thusly, stretch and expand the distance between them so that it is an effort to keep the tips touching.

With the fingers and thumbs pressed together, stretch the thumbs downward. This strengthens not only the thumb but the will power.

Once one recognizes the attributes of the fingers, it becomes easy to analyze the characteristics of an individual. Dr. Som said that one who folds the thumb under the other fingers when making a fist is a person with weak will power and poor health. And it also may indicate that he is a congenital liar.

By studying the hand postures, observe which fingers are pressed together. Such acts emphasize the attributes we have just ascribed to them. If the fingers are folded against the palm, then observe which fingers are extended.

To release energy all over the body, fold the third (ring) finger down into the palm to establish the pressure point. Press on this point with a pencil eraser or the top of a lipstick or cosmetic brush—repeatedly pressing and releasing. Repeat on the other hand.

PADMASANA AND ITS PRACTICAL BENEFITS

All the nerves are attached to the spinal column, either directly or indirectly. Thus all circulation ultimately relates to the spine. Circulation problems, backache, varicose veins and many other human ailments are caused because millions spend most of their day sitting in a chair with their legs dangling beneath the spinal column. Continuation of this unnatural sitting puts great stress not only on the lower limbs, but the heart muscle.

The blood circulating throughout the arterial system can return from the legs to the heart only by contraction of the leg muscles—which is to say, that if the blood is to be returned from the legs to the heart properly, the legs should not be dangled below the spine for hours. Blood reaches the legs through the arterial system, with the pumping of the heart muscle forcefully behind it. But it returns upward to the heart through the venous system and must make its way upward without the forceful heart beat behind it. Only when there is contraction of leg muscles can blood be successfully squeezed back upward toward the heart.

When you sit in a chair by the hour—such as do secretaries, executives and innumerable other millions of people—your body is under an unnatural stress, since the blood must battle its way back up to the heart through the circulatory system without aid from the leg muscles. Blood forms into "pools" in the lower legs, eventually causing varicose veins, hemorrhoids, blood clotting, and poor circulation.

The same is true for those who stand all day, such as factory workers, barbers, hair dressers, etc.

Dr. Som believed it advisable to sit in a "tailor style" cross-legged position as much as possible. Such a position, tentatively blocking the flow of blood freely into the legs, is a tremendous aid to the circulation system, especially the heart, because it reduces the distance the blood must travel back upward to the heart and prevents pooling in the lower limbs. One need not adopt the full lotus Padmasana posture. Simply sit cross-legged, tailor-fashion, preferably on the floor. But even when sitting in a chair, try to draw the legs into a cross-legged position occasionally and continue your "sitting down" activities for awhile in this position to give the heart a rest.

FUNGUS—THE FRIGHTENING INFECTION

If you've ever suffered from athletes' foot, from ringworm infection that infests underarms, the groin area, or the scalp, or suffered from some mysterious malady affecting the lungs, bronchial tubes, or ears, then you may have been the victim of a fungus infection about which medical science knows appallingly little.

There are approximately 200,000 acute cases recognized annually, but millions of mysterious maladies could have been unrecognized fungus infections. Many victims are hospitalized and hundreds die.

Many strange fungal illnesses are misdiagnosed since they mimic the symptoms of pneumonia, tuberculosis, meningitis, brain tumors, or even insanity.

Dr. Som declared that submitting to antibiotic treatment was the worst possible approach to healing, since antibiotics only destroyed the body's own normal bacteria and did not in any way affect the fungus. Once this normal protective bacteria was destroyed, the fungus infection really settled in.

During the war in Vietnam, up to 70% of our troops developed a strange type of ringworm—a type of infectious fungus. Many suffered with inflammatory ringworms covering almost the entire body. The carrier of the fungus turned out to be rats. The reason it is difficult to recognize and treat is because it frequently begins with fever, coughs, sore throat, nausea and other symptoms that would indicate the common cold, flu, pneumonia for which antibiotics are usually prescribed. Dr. Som advised that anytime a mysterious ailment strikes you, demand a sputum test immediately from your doctor. It could reveal the presence of a fungus. Thus your doctor would know immediately not to treat your ailment with antibiotics.

Dr. Som was skeptical of the wisdom of ever submitting to antibiotics anyway, so he suggested that should these symptoms attack you, before rushing to your doctor for an antibiotic, approach the symptoms first from a natural healing standpoint.

He always reduced food intake, prescribed alkaline vegetable juices (carrot, celery and a bit of beet) and suggested massive doses of vitamin C, principally through warm lemonade. He squeezed the juice of one lemon into a glass and filled it with lukewarm, pure water. He added a teaspoon of raw natural honey. It was to be sipped regularly during the day. He also rubbed lemon juice on any skin lesions that developed. He rubbed the chest with castor oil mixed with turpentine, or with straight DMSO. He advised soaking the feet first in hot then cold water. ending with cold. Then he rubbed the feet—especially the soles—with castor oil and turpentine. He advised a vaporizer near your bed. If massive doses of vitamin C were required longer than four days, he began giving a B-complex vitamin tablet because, he said, continued excessive intake of C leached vitamin B from the cells.

He said that since billions of fungus spores float around in our environment it is well to make a habit of drinking this warm lemonade fairly regularly. Extremely dangerous fungus frequently inhabit chicken roosts, turkey roosts, pidgeon droppings, the dust of horses, fields of hay and areas where hunters delight.

Although fungi are usually recognized as an occasional hazard in nature, they are also becoming recognized as a hazard even in our hospitals all across the land. According to researchers, advances in medicine may be partially responsible. When checking into a hospital, it seems almost automatic that you be given all manner of drugs and antibiotics which could trigger a latent fungal infection. Those particularly susceptible to reaction to a hospital journey are cancer patients receiving antibiotic treatment, leukemia victims, organ transplant cases, diabetics, burn victims, those with eye injuries or open wounds.

Once the antibiotics you've taken destroy the body's normal complement of bacteria, the fungus goes into action. So be wary of ever taking antibiotics.

Medical science is striving to develop a vaccine against ringworm and histoplasmosis, a dreaded fungus infection of the lungs and inner organs. But wouldn't it be better to find some more natural solution? Surely nature has provided a method. Try the trusted lemon (or garlic).

For an outbreak of fungus in the ears, Dr. Som prescribed equal parts of rubbing alcohol and white vinegar. The rubbing alcohol stops the itching. The acid in the white vinegar attacks the fungus. This will stop ear-itching almost immediately and heal the fungus before it can spread. Apply with a cotton swab.

For a fungus infection between the toes, such as athletes' foot, apply raw natural honey directly to the area at night, covering the feet with sox, preferably pure cotton. Wash and dry feet thoroughly the following morning. Apply apple cider vinegar if you wish or simply put on fresh sox. Applied only at night, the honey alone will heal the fungus within a few days.

ANTI-PERSPIRANTS

The public is finally becoming aware that it is not safe to use a commercial deodorant. The purpose of a deodorant is to block the flow of perspiration, thus also sealing off the escape valves of toxic poisons—the armpits being a principal area of release.

Sealed inside, the toxins must go elsewhere to make their exit. Finding no other "elsewhere," they often settle into the body as embedded toxins which crystalize and congest. Never, never,

never, use any of the popular deodorants.

There are now more natural products on the market—products containing chlorophyll which is a natural ingredient. It does not suppress the flow of waste from the body but does remove the odor, which is all a deodorant was ever meant to do.

Even the Food and Drug Administration has seen fit to remove some extremely dangerous anti-perspirants from the public market, realizing the deadly effect on the human system. They not only blocked the flow of natural waste, but their ingredients entered the body through the pores—resulting in additional, even deadly, poisons and toxins in the human system.

Chlorophyll tablets may even be popped into the mouth to discourage mouth odors, or added to a glass of water and gargled for a mouth rinse.

Some persons, after using anti-perspirants, develop a vague illness—pains in the stomach, vertigo and nausea. But, not realizing the source of their problem, they continue to use the harmful product. Even when made seriously ill, they are not apt to connect it to the use of their anti-perspirant. Visiting a doctor and complaining of ailments, one is apt to be given a drug to hopefully combat them, which only compounds the problem, until the patient is caught in a vicious circle of medicines and illness, drugs and illness.

So if you suffer from some vague disease with an unknown cause, try throwing away your anti-perspirant. It may be the hidden culprit, especially if it is a spray, liquid or roll-on deodorant containing *zirconium*. It is a definite health hazard. The inhalation of miniature zirconium particles could result in all manner of chronic lung disease. It has produced inflammatory swellings which impaired lungs in animal experiments in the laboratories.

Dr. Som recommended this formula as an excellent homemade deodorant:

1 tablespoon plus 1 teaspoon vegetable oil, preferably sesame oil
2 tablespoons cornstarch
2 tablespoons baking soda

Mix ingredients together and heat on the stove until thoroughly blended. Store in a small container and use when needed.

NOSEBLEED

Dr. Som said a nosebleed could be overcome by taking vitamin C, since it promotes blood clotting. For immediate help, he suggested stirring approximately 1/2 teaspoon of cayenne pepper (capsicum) in a glass of water and sipping it.

He also suggested holding an ice cold knife blade against the back of the neck or between the shoulder blades—a blunt blade of a dinner knife, not a kitchen knife. Or cold keys if no knife is available.

HAY FEVER

The following was often prescribed by Dr. Som:

1. Stop all foods except fruit, emphasize citrus fruits.
2. Take up to 1,000 milligrams of vitamin C each hour and take one or two capsules of Propolis, available from a health store.

3. Drink Comfrey, Alfalfa, or Red Clover tea.

4. Using an eye cup, wash the eyes in a solution of EyeBright herbal solution.

Often just taking the Propolis capsule will suffice, especially if the patient must continue daily activities and cannot submit to the diet listed above.

PROSTATE

One with prostate problems should eat sunflower seeds or pumpkin seeds, which contain zinc, plus many other valuable nutrients—or take zinc tablets. Zinc is required by the prostate gland in order to maintain health. The culprit causing the prostate to lose zinc is the intake of sugar—white sugar. Eliminate it immediately from your diet, whether or not you have prostate problems. If you already have them, eliminating white sugar can go far in restoring the prostate to normalcy. That is, if you will also take zinc supplements or eat pumpkin and sunflower seeds.

THEN THERE IS DMSO

I heard about DMSO many years ago but realized that it, like so many other "good" drugs, was being kept from the public by the FDA for some strange reason.

It was brought forcefully back into my awareness in 1980 by two things:

1. A book "DMSO—the Persecuted Drug" by Pat McGrady.

2. The powerful television program "60 Minutes," which exposed the FDA as bureaucrats who prefer to keep off the market a drug which could ease the pain of millions rather than admit to serious misjudgment.

But Dr. Som was using DMSO "away back when." I saw him rub or pat a clear substance that looked like water on many a patient and pain was gone in a matter of minutes.

"What is that you're using?" I once asked.

"It's DMSO," he whispered furtively, "but if anyone asks, I just tell them it's horse linament."

"But DMSO is illegal!" I reacted. "Where do you get it?."

"From various sources," he replied, "but mostly from Mexico. As you know, I'm dead against the use of drugs. But this one is different. It's really *not* a drug. It's a natural product. Comes right from trees, you know. It's derived from lignin, a sticky substance that penetrates the cells of trees. It's kind of like the sap or resin in trees and it's packed with healing power."

Dr. Som explained that DMSO would help any disease in existence—*any* disease, he said, because the substance, once applied, immediately penetrated the skin and was flowing throughout the blood stream in seconds. If it was applied to bursitis in the shoulder, it might also heal an inflammed ankle muscle because of its penetrating power. When it departs the body as waste, it carries with it many dissolved and undesireable chemicals which would otherwise harm the body.

"That's what is known as "chelation," Dr. Som enthused. "It means it has the ability to draw chemicals such as lead right out of the system, to dissolve it—DMSO is a solvent, you know—and then to carry the dissolved essence right out of the body. So it not only relieves pain immediately, but it has a high potential for curing the ailment causing the pain."

I was puzzled. "If it's so great," I asked, "why doesn't the FDA approve it for public use?"

"Big fight going on," he replied. "The FDA makes such demands in testing a drug, it costs many millions to satisfy them. So drug companies will not spend it to test the drug because they see little profit in it. It costs only about $4.00 to produce a quart of it and, once on the market, it would outsell many high priced drugs now making millions for them. They actually don't want the drug widely distributed—it would be too popular. Its sale could undermine the sale of any of the high priced drugs now available. Who wants a cheap drug on the market? Not the drug companies! So we doctors are forced to be criminals, forced to break the law if we want to really help our patients."

Dr. Som relieved many of my headaches by simply applying DMSO to my forehead and the back of my neck. I've seen him heal bursitis, tendonitis, arthritis, sprained ankles.

I've seen him apply DMSO to a sore throat only to have pain in the knee disappear immediately. And I've seen him apply DMSO to arthritic joints in the fingers only to have congested sinuses open up within five munutes. And I've seen him apply DMSO to bald heads to see if new hair would grow—and it did!

Sore joints and inflamed muscles stopped aching, rheumatism vanished, paralyzed arms or legs were reactivated, chronic backaches were relieved, acute bursitis healed, sprained ankles and wrists stopped their pain and swellings vanished almost immediately, and pinkeye—well, that was a mystery.

One day I saw him working with a patient with red eyes. First, he asked her to splash aloe vera gel all over her face, making sure the eyelids were moist. Then he very carefully touched each closed eyelid with DMSO.

"'But the instructions clearly say to avoid the eyes!" I protested.

"I *am* avoiding the eyes," he smiled. "I'm treating the eyelids"—he knew perfectly well the essence of the DMSO would penetrate the skin of the eyelids and vicariously effect the eyes. "Dorothy here has pinkeye. It will be gone by morning. She also had cataracts, scheduled to be removed, but she doesn't have them anymore."

"Not only that," piped in Dorothy, "but he is removing my wrinkles. First I splash my face and throat with water and leave it on. Then I cover my face and neck with a thin layer of vitamin E oil. Then I pat on DMSO with a pat of cotton. My wrinkles are slowly vanishing just like my cataracts!"

Dr. Som explained: "Sometimes I experiment with aloe vera and jojoba oil instead of the vitamin E oil. But the face must be moist with water first. The DMSO will take the moisture right into the inner layer of skin cells where moisture rightfully belongs. Actually it should be pure distilled water—not the regular faucet kind. Or it can be just boiled water. But I do believe I've discovered the way to keep the skin wrinkle-free.

"Of course, one *does* need to be careful of direct contact with the eyes.

DMSO should be applied very carefully, always with the eyes closed, preferably patted on the lids with a cotton pat. But if direct contact is made, I just splash the eyes immediately with cold water and drop water into them with an eye dropper."

"I really don't believe one should use DMSO around the eyes without a doctor helping." I was still cautious and skeptical. "But sooner or later, I'll be a candidate for a wrinkle-free face."

"You're absolutely right," he warned. "If you ever get pinkeye or cataracts, let *me* do the treating."

Fortunately I've never found such treatments necessary. And I've yet to try DMSO for wrinkles. But I shall one day. I haven't the slightest doubt Som will be watching from heaven, overseeing my efforts to find the eternal "fountain of youth."

GEROVITAL—
THE YOUTH TREATMENT

Back in 1951, a tiny female doctor in Bucharest, Rumania, made medical history. Dr. Anna Aslan, faced with the problem of alleviating pain for an aging patient, injected him with procaine plus other ingredients and found a response far greater than anticipated. So miraculously did he improve, she began using the same treatment on all her aging patients—only to discover she had stumbled upon a medical miracle.

Her formula included procaine hydrochloride, Benzoic acid, potassium metabisulfite and disodium phosphate—and her aging patients began not only to lose their pain but also symptoms of old age. As news of her treatment spread, her clinics were filled with many seeking the restoration of youth. Her treatment is now known as the "youth drug." It is called Gerovital—or GH3—and is now famous worldwide.

Proven effective for almost 30 years, it is still not legal in the United States, where doctors, for some unexplainable reason, still insist it must undergo further "testing." Yet no vigorous testing program has ever been widely publicized. The treatment is available only in the state of Nevada. There the state legislature has licensed the Rom-Amer Pharmaceuticals, Ltd., to distribute the treatment.

Americans seeking the benefits of this promising treatment must either travel to Rumania, to Nevada, to the Philippines or some European clinic. It is sold by the package all over Europe, England, South Africa and Mexico. It is available in vials for injection or in pill form.

It has proven effective in aiding arthritis, diabetes, ulcers, new hair growth, heart disease, sexual impotence, high blood pressure, arteriosclerosis, Parkinson's disease, aging appearance—and in simply restoring a feeling of buoyant youth and well-being.

I have been fortunate enough to occasionally receive a gift package from some friend returning from Nevada, Mexico or Rumania and have experimented with both the injections and the tablet. I've already spoken of my incredible energy at age 63 and of my total feeling of well being. Perhaps I should also mention that my hair is as dark as in my youth—no gray. As for a youthful appearance—well, let's just say that out of my eyes there peers a soul well pleased with life. That's a sure sign of at least "feeling" young.

No doubt on my epitaph, Sita will have engraved the following "testimonial":

Here lies Mama, in spite of Propolis, ginseng, Gerovital, DMSO, and castor oil.

As for Dr. Som, I suspect he obtained and used GH3 during all the latter years of his life. He certainly remained young. He lived well into his nineties and was still giving chiropractic treatments up until the day of his easy and sudden departure for higher realms—yes, and still scolding about becoming a vegetarian and giving up "that old sex."

WALKING FOR PHYSICAL REGENERATION

There is no one physical exercise that can benefit the human body more quickly than plain old fashioned walking—said Dr. Som. Not jogging. He didn't approve of jogging. Said it wasn't as "natural" as walking, and could be injurious, especially for the bladder and feet. He thought all females should avoid jogging—it could cause the uterus to fall and could prolapse the breasts. A prolapsed uterus could make childbirth precarious. But walking could only bring benefits. Walking became one of my first exercises in my days of Beginning Again.

I started with a walk to the end of the block and back, but as the weeks passed I steadily increased it to two full city blocks which were quite extensive. Some of the walk involved deep breathing and, take my word for it, I noticed an immediate upsurge in well being from the very first day.

Walking is as natural as breathing and it is to be regretted that man no longer walks except in the case of dire necessity. There is a proper technique to obtain the greatest benefits, however. It should be smooth and effortless, not quick and jerky.

Begin by practicing the standing technique. Simply stand for a few moments with the feet apart, the shoulders down and relaxed, the arms hanging loosely at your side. Breathe easily, concentrating your attention two inches below the navel. Hold your tongue upward against the palate and breathe slowly and easily. Now begin your effortless walking. Be sure the body weight balances on one foot at a time. Continue to hold the body straight, loose, and relaxed. Keep the tongue placed lightly against the palate the better to stimulate saliva while walking.

Keeping your attention concentrated on the abdominal chakra just below the navel causes great charges of prana to begin radiating from the lower abdomen outward and upward throughout the entire body. The body should not be restricted with girdles or binding bras. Women should wear a "sport" bra to hold the beasts firm without binding. One must have free-flowing garments and comfortable low heeled walking shoes—shoes especially padded and constucted for proper walking. If a beach is available, walk barefoot in the sand.

The body should be free swinging, the spine, neck and head held erect. The head should not be bent forward with the eyes surveying the ground. The bent-neck walking posture defeats the benefits. Make sure your head is up and eyes straight ahead, or surveying that which is before you and above you, not that which is on the ground, which tends to create a slouch in the shoulders. Certainly it impedes the flow of life force into the brain, face and eyes. So make sure your shoulders are squared back, head up, eyes forward, arms free swinging and legs and feet clipping off a brisk measurement so that by the time your walk is completed, there is some degree of enforced deep breathing.

Your weight should be balanced equally between the legs, which swing freely from the hips. It helps to walk with some kind of musical rhythm, chanting or counting. Deep breathing or breath control is important. Count as you walk, one, two, three, four—sniff, sniff, sniff, sniff, as you inhale to the count of four. Then exhale either sniff, sniff, sniff, sniff through the nose or with the mouth slightly pursed. Either way is beneficial. One must choose that which is most comfortable. But the breath should be inhaled to a comfortable count, held to a comfortable count, exhaled to a comfortable count, held to a comfortable count and then the inhalation begun again—all the while concentrating on the navel chakra and holding the top of the tongue against the palate. Use breath control, concentration and counting only until you tire. Then spend the rest of your walk just enjoying nature and your surroundings.

Remember that the closer you can get to the magnetic currents of the earth itself, the better will be your physical benefit, whether it is in walking, running or just sitting or lying under trees. Choose an area away from cement or asphalt when possible—directly on the ground.

Even walking up and down stairs is of great benefit. So is uphill walking and sand walking. Wholistic physicians now encourage their heart patients to stair walk, realizing the heart exercise is of extreme benefit, proven to reduce the chance of more heart attacks and strokes. Walking can also remove a headache. It will improve your total well-being.

The beauty of walking is that it can be performed by anyone, old or young. It's a natural procedure and requires no bending, stooping or painful breaking in of sore muscles. If space and circumstance prevent your daily walk, then perform it in your bedroom, walking-in-place briskly—that is, stand in one spot and walk without going anywhere. Be sure, however, that doors and windows are open to allow fresh air breathing.

THE MEDITATIVE WALKING JOG

There is a deliberate yogic discipline Easterners use as a meditation exercise. Dr. Som taught me the technique. It begins as a walk but, with deliberate practice, can evolve into a gliding jog if desired. It is not done for physical exercise, but for meditation. Those who choose the walking meditation over the sitting meditation feel that the movement of the body calms the mind and helps maintain the mental discipline necessary for successful meditatation.

There are rules to be followed:

1. The eyes should focus straight ahead, not being distracted by environmental surroundings.
2. The body should be held erect

but relaxed. The head should not be bent forward but should also be held erect so that the eyes will look straight forward. Arms should hang freely at the sides.

3. The tongue should be held against the palate. This serves several purposes. For our purpose, it creates increased saliva which, when swallowed with air, is transmuted into creative power in the abdominal chakra.

4. The mind should concentrate on breathing in the navel chakra two inches below the navel.

5. The walking step should be a little higher than the normal walking step though not an exaggerated step.

6. Relaxation of the entire body should be maintained so that a sensation of lightness can be achieved.

7. The strides taken should be slow, long and rhythmic. As the walk continues, one gradually ceases to be aware of the body or to be distracted by any surrounding circumstances. The attention is focused completely on the breath in the abdominal chakra.

With walking, circulation of the blood is increased, the oxygen supply is increased and prana invigorates and restores the body to wholeness.

When first beginning meditative walks, they should be of short duration and gradually increased. Walk daily. Tiredness will be experienced in the beginning but it will gradually disappear as the body adjusts to the habit.

Eventually you may wish to begin with a slow walk and increase the momentum, being sure the gait is smooth and not jerky. Gradually you will begin to feel a sense of buoyancy, of ingathering vitality in the abdominal chakra. As your walks continue the inflowing energy will begin radiating throughout your entire body.

The legs will begin to move forward in a smooth, light, rhythmic dancing glide rather than a disjointed walk. As with swimming, the beginning swimmer splashes with little breath control and wasted energy. The accomplished swimmer floats with buoyancy upon the water, gliding effortlessly through it and using the water actually as an aid. Swimming energizes rather than tires and the expert swimmer can float endlessly with no effort. Similarly the proficient meditative walker finds himself blending with the prana in the air, using it as a cushion upon which to walk. His body feels increasingly light and buoyant until the walk, becoming more like a smooth jog, is performed with little effort and actually energizes rather than tires.

The "slow walk" is often employed to bring mind and body to a state of quietude and serenity. For best results in meditative walking, the breath must be synchronized with the steps while the mind is held concentrated in the abdominal chakra. If it is difficult to hold the attention on the abdominal chakra, two inches below the navel, and count your steps with your breathing, then simply be aware that you are inhaling slowly and exhaling slowly in conjunction with the walking.

This is the technique used by the long-walkers of Tibet, who can travel endless miles in a day. Their consciousness passes into a light trance state and their bodies, responding to increased energy in the navel chakra, defy the law of gravity and seem to slightly levitate as the legs glide forward. You may not be able to achieve such a state, but you *can* achieve increased energy, mind power and a higher level of pranic voltage in your total being.

MEDITATION

The ancient tabernacle in the desert, designed and erected by Moses, symbolized the three planes of mind with its three courts—the outer, the inner and the holy. The outer court symbolized the "religion" of the profane or the world. It represented the world of material mind or of waking conscious mentality.

The inner court was known as the holy place of worship where the masses gathered to pray and receive outer instructions concerning religion, morals and ethics. This "church" court represented the subconscious mind, in that it was the medium through which messages were transmitted to the mass mind, or world consciousness, or the waking conscious mind.

The inner court was known as the *Holy of Holies*, representing the purified inner shrine of the superconscious mind. A veil hung over the entrance to this innermost Place of Light, no one being allowed to enter but the high priest, and he only for the purpose of making atonement for himself and asking forgiveness for the actions of the masses.

In the Holy of Holies was placed the Ark of the Covenant—a chest containing sacred furnishings of the tabernacle. This chest was both lined and covered with gold plate. On its top were two cherubim kneeling and facing each other. Between the cherubim on the cover was an upraised altar known as *the Mercy Seat.* It was also known as *the Holy Shekinah.* This altar was the focal point of God's presence in the temple.

The silence of meditation is drawing aside the veil to the inner temple and entering the Holy of Holies at the sacred center of one's being. There in the midst of the silence one may become imbued with Universal Wisdom. Obvious or not, the soul receives instructions or a blessing.

Dynamite is concentrated, crystalized energy. Man, when focused and one-pointed in mind, becomes like dynamite—concentrated, crystalized energy. This dynamic mind force has a driving power that can penetrate and transmute that upon which it is focused, much as the focused sunray can transmute its objective.

Energy rays of the sun fuse or diffuse the object on which it is focused. Mind should also be used for fusion and diffusion. When focusing on fusion, the mind concentrates on electromagnetic attraction, cohesion, crystalization, manifestation. When focusing upon diffusion, the mind concentrates upon seeing the object scattered, vaporized, disintegrated.

A thought ray, together with a word or decree of affirmation, projected with Holy Breath, always completes its cycle, returning to the sender in manifested objective form. When focused upon diffusion, the thought ray, together with the word power, "sees" the object disintegrating and slowly vanishing away.

When focusing such a mind power for the purpose of concentrating upon or seeking the answer to a personal prayer, one should approach the silence filled with sincere earnest desire for good—for the "betterment of all involved" in any situation, and a will to do that which our divine Father-Mother God would so will.

Such mind creativity may be used to attune to inspiration, to command the subconscious mind, to acquire wisdom, knowledge, power, abundant supply, business success, the power to heal, cosmic consciousness. Consciously using such mind force and mind control results in a frequent display of extraordinary power through Holy Breath, prana, magnetic life force.

The superconscious mind is a great storehouse of light, love, wisdom, power and life force. The purpose of entering the silence is to make a "Cosmic Connection" with this powerhouse of sacred energy—to be charged with the Thought of God, the Holy Breath of God, much as electric storage batteries are charged. Thus in the silence one gains wisdom, energy, health and electromagnetism.

The mind is like a razor blade. It possesses penetrative power because it has an extremely fine, sharp cutting edge, rendering less resistance to the molecules of substance than would the blade of a blunt, dull edge. The concentrated mind, like the razor blade, is one-pointed, sharp and penetrative, piercing the molecules of substance, dissolving and disintegrating that which appears to be impossible to change.

Many a mystic, involved in the business world, has turned the tide of failure into success by devoting time to meditation daily inside his business establishment before opening it to the public. Thus he establishes two purposes—he attunes himself to his inner business "Partner," and he charges his place of business with the pranic presence of electromagnetism, which acts as a magnet to draw people to him.

Every mystic recognizes that he is an epitome of all law, force and manifestation in nature—the telephone, the radio, the camera, the television, the airplane, the missile, the satellite, the far distant star. It is true that the greatest study of mankind is man. He is a child of God—with all the potential of Godhood seeded within, waiting to be released, waiting to mature.

MENTALIZING AND BLESSING YOUR FOOD

"And He shall bless thy bread and water."

Exodus 23:25

The influence of the mind upon the body is well known but it manifests rapidly in eating. Often you are admonished not to eat when you are depressed, angry, irritated, upset. Your thoughts should be constructive, happy, relaxed. Food should be eaten with happy anticipation. Your mind should be tranquil and at ease.

Certainly it is most proper and desirable to say grace before partaking of food. This sets the pattern for the mental thought waves during the meal. Most of us prefer that each individual bow the head in a personal blessing of one's food. Form a habit also of thinking love thoughts in connection with food. Love the food, love the God who produced the food and love your body which it is nourishing.

Before beginning your meal, hesitate a moment and think to yourself, "This food is most excellent for just what I need to make me well and strong." Allow the mind to flash occasionally with thoughts of absorbing purifying food, powerful life food—mentally projecting throughout your body the thoughts that you are imbibing life and power and that whatever ailments you may have noticed are being completely healed and overcome.

The glands of the mouth and stomach change their chemical secretions under the varying stimuli of mental impulses. The type of thoughts you think about food affects the salivary glands and the chemical combination of the saliva. If thoughts of power, purification and life force are projected upon or about the food, the salivary glands produce a chemical combination of saliva to correspond with the digestive requirement of the food to be eaten.

This is another reason we should masticate slowly and maintain an attitude of health toward food—especially thoughts of love and appreciation for the "sacrifice" made by the plants which are sustaining you. You should also hold a most positive thought that you will be able to digest everything you eat. Thus you most certainly can make food your "best medicine."

Invoking the blessing of God upon food before partaking is a custom as old as time. Earliest man sensed that a divine transaction occurred between himself and the Giver of the food which sustained life in his body. Invoking the alchemical power of Spirit added something . . . LIFE that only the Father-Mother of mankind knows how to "mix and make and give."

Blessings used for centuries contain thoughts found in the simple words known to many: "Come, Lord Jesus, (or Blessed Mother), be our guest! Breathe thy blessing upon us. Bless this food that it may bring health to our bodies, clear minds to serve Thee, and clean hearts filled with devotion to God. For all our blessings we do thank Thee, Father-Mother. A-men."

A *Pythagorean Grace* (said to be used at the tables of Orders founded by Pythagoras):

"Holy God, we bless Thee and thank Thee for this good clean food, procured without injustice. Grant that we may be as clean inwardly as we are outwardly, that the inner man and the outer man may be one, and that we may be one with Thee. A-men."

A simple favorite of mine is:

"Holy God, bless this food to my physical use and me to Thy spiritual service. Transmute this food to my highest good—spiritually, mentally, physically. Amen and I thank Thee."

CHAPTER 14
THE HEALING MIRACLES OF ACUPUNCTURE

I heard vaguely about acupuncture and its healing wonders, as did everyone else, as knowledge of its art and science began to seep into the consciousness of Americans through various sources of the media. But I came face to face with its wonders when, one day, I arranged for an appointment in the beauty salon of Bullock's Wilshire department store in Los Angeles.

My operator was Margit Nilsson, my hairdresser for many years. I first came to know Margit when Sita, our daughter, was still an infant. Margit had just arrived from Sweden, and I employed her as Sita's nurse in our home. She lived with us in this capacity for almost three years, during which time she was studying to fulfill the necessary requirements to become a hairdresser. Thus, as a live-in nurse and companion to Sita, and a member of our family, we came to know and love her dearly. The warm relationship continued through the years, long after she left us to be employed in the beauty salon at Bullock's Wilshire.

On this particular day during my hairdressing appointment, she confided that she was experiencing pain in her right arm, which was becoming so severe she feared it might necessitate resigning her occupation as a hairdresser. The tendonitis seemed to result from the constant need to raise her arms—and at that time she could barely lift her right arm. I did not see Margit again for several months, at which time I inquired concerning her tendonitis problem. It had utterly disappeared. The pain was gone and she was now able to raise her arm gingerly above her head.

"How in the world did this healing come about?" I inquired.

"Through acupuncture," she confessed, and then related the complete details.

She had sought an acupuncturist in the city, and had submitted to several treatments, plus specially prescribed herbs. After each session, her arm improved until finally she no longer found treatments necessary. Her tendonitis had completely disappeared.

I was tremendously impressed! As a result of this startling interview, I sought out the same expert and began treatments. He was a Japanese master acupuncturist, very skilled in his occupation. It was obvious that he certainly achieved many healings, but often the needles were painful. So busy was he, proceeding from patient to patient, there was no time to sympathize or adjust for individual discomfort. Although I dreaded each treatment, I continued to submit, realizing they were indeed improving my health.

It was about this time—the year must have been 1974 or '75—when Robert, my minister-husband, was invited to teach classes in Christian Mysticism at the College of Oriental Studies, near our church in Los Angeles. I attended the sessions with him.

On the evening of the first session, we met a member of Astara (our church), who was in training at the college in the art of acupuncture. Learning that I was undergoing acupuncture treatments, he introduced me to the master acupuncturist teaching classes at the college. It was thus that I met wonderful Master Sehan Kim and his lovely wife, Doctor Kyoo. He readily consented to give me acupuncture treatments.

and Dr. Kyoo were from Korea—indeed he was one of Korea's finest acupuncturists. Dr. Kyoo, his wife, was a medical physician, having established several important clinics in Seoul. I found—to my total surprise and delight—that acupuncture treatments under his gentle hands were not at all painful. With the insertion of each needle, he very carefully noted whether or not there was a slight twinge of possible pain. When so noting, he immediately withdrew the needle and inserted it in a less painful meridian point. Thus I came to realize that treatments from this amazing soul would be even pleasure, certainly not painful—pleasure in that I could immediately discern incredible results. He was simultaneously prescribing a combination of Oriental herbs for my hypoglycemia and its attending problems, principally headaches.

I began steadily to improve in health. The headaches totally disappeared. I

Dr. Kyoo and Master Sehan Kim

This mild, marvelous master was totally different from the practitioner with whom I had been a patient. He

began to add weight to my thin frame, color to my skin, and to experience increased energy. Simultaneously I was pursuing other methodologies such as sauna baths, massage, walks, diet, tub soaks. But I must credit my greatest benefits to acupuncture treatments. As life began to assume new meaning for me, I came to know Master Kim and Dr. Kyoo intimately. They became and have remained two of my dearest friends. I learned that Master Kim had been an acupuncturist in Korea for 35 years before coming to the United States. Suffice to say that under his skillful treatments, my health returned completely. It was as if I had never been ill. I have continued to this day to seek acupuncture treatments from him at the least sign of an approaching health problem, and each time the problem disappears.

At this present writing—at age 63—I truly feel better than at age 25. I believe

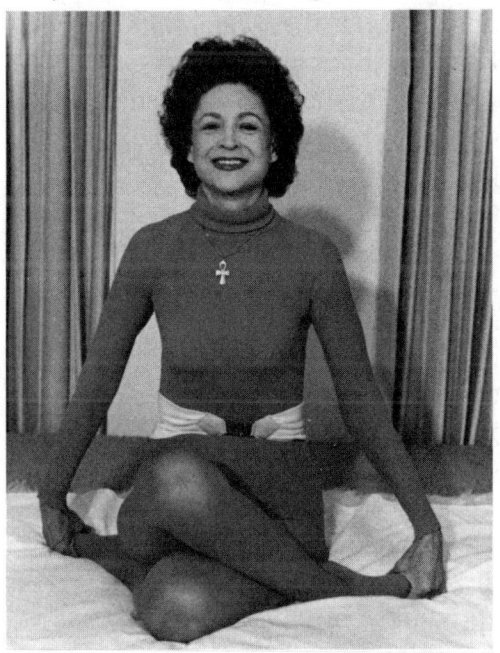

I exhibit as much or more energy than the usual person. My day begins around 4 a.m., when I waken and enter meditations. My actual writing for the day begins around 8:30 a.m., and lasts the entire day, and often into the evening. I usually retire around 11:00 p.m. Occasionally, I nap during the day, but as a rule I do not. I seldom feel tired. The many hours of work seem only to rejuvenate me. Although my diet and daily exercise play an important part in my continued well-being, I must also credit the acupuncture treatments of Master Kim for my incredible energy. I could become quite "wordy" in my praise, but the statement just made seems sufficient.

In the interim years, I have attended many of his classes, learning much about acupuncture and Oriental herbs. Let me share some of my learnings with you.

Master Kim believes thoroughly in the existence of *the etheric body*, familiar to all seekers of new age teachings. Astarians—and most seekers who are enrolled in Mystery School teachings—are familiar with the function of the etheric body. Briefly, it is the underlying "battery body" of the physical form. Indeed, without the etheric double, the physical form would be lifeless. It is the etheric double that is the vessel for pranic life force within the physical form.

CHI

Master Kim believes—as do I— that all illness results from a malfunctioning of the link-up between the physical and the etheric form. When, through wrong diet, lack of exercise, wrong thinking, wrong doing, the physical form displays illness, it simply means it is in a state of *imbalance*. The physical and the etheric forms are out of alignment. The life-force is impeded from flowing through from the etheric into the cells, muscles and tissues of the physical. The positive-negative aspects of a universal energy called *chi*—which many call the *yin* and the *yang*—are imbalanced. There are dammed up meridians in the physical form through which the chi (prana) cannot flow. To Master Kim the art of acupuncture is simply removing these blockages in the meridians so that the chi life force can flow through from the etheric into the physical. It requires balancing the yin and the yang—the positive-negative life force—throughout the form. Once the yin and yang forces are flowing in balanced distribution, illness disappears.

This life force presumably flows throughout the universe, and is vaguely related to the five elements of wood, water, metal, earth and fire. To the Oriental, chi is a form of pneuma, "breath," or ether. Chi, to them, is the "breath of life" flowing freely within a person, a special concept of "air." We western mystics would call it *prana*, an unseen, unrecognized form of ether flowing abundantly throughout our universe and indeed throughout our bodies, indrawn through the breath and the chakras. Illness is usually an imbalance of forces in the body. This kind of illness responds to treatment by acupuncture. It aids the body to resist disease by promoting the body's natural reactions to invasions of viruses and pollutions.

MERIDIANS

Meridians are described as a circulatory system in the physical form, linked with the nervous system but separate from it. It is the nervous system of the etheric body, and it is composed of etheric substance. It is recognized that a substance circulates in this meridian system. This is what the Oriental healers call *chi*. Again, the esoteric western healer would probably call it prana, mana, or life force.

The insertion of acupuncture needles relieves by releasing congestion in the lines of communication between the meridain points in the body. These meridian nerves should be pulsating with energy constantly. The energies released and balanced relate directly to the individual and his vibratory frequency. It is the blocked-up energies that create physical deterioration. Blood and nerve energies cannot function correctly unless the meridian nerves are opened and the pranic life force is flowing through. Prana—or chi—is required to nourish and energize the cells of the body. Once the meridian points are dammed up, the chi force cannot flow and the cells deteriorate.

A skilled acupuncturist frequently diagnoses the ailments of his patient simply by listening carefully to the pulse points in the wrists, in the throat and in the solar plexus. The pulse points reveal which meridian points are dammed up, which points are deteriorating and which need a flow of life energy. The expert acupuncturist knows well that there is a connection between the etheric body and the physical. He knows the meridian points are terminals of communication between the nervous system of the physical with that of the etheric. He knows they are probably electrical lines carrying life currents.

Such an acupuncturist is fully aware of the chi forces vaguely connected with air, fire, water, earth and metal. Unblocking the meridian points, he realizes full well that he is charging both the physical and etheric bodies with these important elements. He knows which meridian point to stimulate to increase fire, for instance, in a certain area of the body. He knows when a certain area needs cooling because it already has too much fire. He knows what needle to insert and where in order to attract the water element—or that of metal. Such approaches to healing are far beyond the understanding of most medical doctors in America. They are too accustomed to a different type of needles—that of injecting drugs. To many of them, this is the only logical approach.

Probably the greatest mystery concerning acupuncture is the relationship between a diseased area and its corresponding meridian point. For instance, one seldom heals a headache by inserting a needle in the head. It is usually inserted elsewhere in the body, perhaps in the lower leg near the ankle, or even in the hands. A disturbed liver may require stimulation of a meridian point in the foot.

Needles introduced into one part of the body produce an effect in another part of the body. The art is for the skilled acupuncturist to know the effective point. He must know that insertion at that particular point will produce a particular effect in another part of the body, and upon which part. Thyroid operations, for instance, require a needle inserted one inch deep into each forearm at a point about four inches above the wrist. Other acupuncturists prefer to insert needles in the neck and the back of the wrist to perform thyroid operations. Thus there is more than one point to be considered.

The skilled acupuncturist must not only be acquainted with the meridians and their essential points of insertion, but he must know the proper depth of the needle insertion. The point must be penetrated only to a particular degree and properly manipulated, or twirled, if the proper results are to be realized. Often the operator will rotate a needle in a clockwise movement, a counterclockwise movement, or a slight pumping action. It is this seemingly irrational approach which so disturbs the western medical scientist. He simply cannot conceive such vagaries.

On some occasions, the acupuncturist may apply a process called *moxubustion*. Moxubustion is the application of heat to either the upper point of the needle or the meridian point directly. The heat treatment employs the use of a special herb called *moxa*. The moxa, like strange smelling "dust," is lighted and applied, for instance, to the projecting needle head. The heat, moving through the steel, enters the meridian point and accomplishes its effective result. The heat in no way disturbs the comfort of the patient but, in the hands of a knowledgeable acupuncturist, it does add significant benefits to the treatment.

YIN AND YANG

The *yin* and *yang* concept further presents the idea that all matter and energy is continuous in the universe. It is chi, a universal substance, in motion, but always in a constantly changing balance of opposites. The chi forces that are positive and negative are not actually opposite and separate, but are really different aspects of a greater unit. Thus the yin and yang, or positive-negative flow of life energies, must be balanced. It is the flow of chi, or this life-giving energy, through the body along the internal network of meridians, that link the 12 vital organs of the body. The meridian channels lie close to the skin surface.

The purpose of acupuncture is, again, to balance the flow of life force. The able acupuncturist, from a pulse diagnosis, realizes which meridian point requires sedating because of too much chi, or energizing because of its lack. He or she also knows which meridian points are blocking or damming up the flow.

Yin represents the feminine-negative principle—darkness, passivity, cold—the waning moon. Yang, on the other hand, is the masculine-positive principle—representing light, heat and activity—the sun. The yin and yang forces are biologically present in our bodies flowing along the meridians. Disease results when imbalance occurs between yin and yang forces disrupting the orderly flow of chi throughout the body. In specific acupuncture terminology, this translates to mean that a patient's condition is either chronic or acute. If it is chronic, it is long term, or yin. If it is acute, it is short term, or yang. The life energy, chi, is controlled by yin and yang, which is the Taoist concept of universal opposites, existing throughout nature.

Following this theory further, the major body organs—12 in all—are divided between yin and yang. The liver, spleen and heart are yin, while the gall bladder, large intestine and stomach are yang. The chi life energy flows from organ to organ through the meridians—a network of 12 channels beneath the skin, running on either side of the body. There are two extra meridians, one along the center of the front of the body, and one in the back. Spread along the network of meridians are between 500 and 1000 specific acupuncture points where the life force can become blocked. The acupuncturist must learn the location of these points and how to pierce them with his needles to correct imbalance in the flow of chi.

These etheric meridians are not readily discovered by western science. Acupuncturists claim that acupuncture points lie on these mysterious meridians, or where the meridians cross and intersect. The meridian channels connect with, but are not necessarily attached to, the physical nervous system.

Ancient Chinese knowledge of anatomy maintains that there is access to each organ within the body from some definite point on the surface. The concept of yin and yang does not compare in any way with the western idea of good and evil. To repeat, it relates to the flow of positive and negative life forces. Yin and yang complement each other. The acupuncture needle is an attempt to restore balance between yin and yang, either by blockage of the overabundant one or the increased release of the one deficient. Again, it is this kind of vague thinking that creates incredibility among western physicians. They find it difficult to accept such unscientific logic.

Witnesses—even doctors and reporters from America—on a visit to China during 1973, observed delicate brain operations, deep chest surgery and complicated abdominal operations conducted on fully conscious, alert and talkative patients. Their only anesthetic was a few wire-thin needles inserted at various points on the body far from the site of the surgery. The observers watched in awe and amazement. They simply could not comprehend what was happening.

Returning to America, these reporters and doctors released reports via the media concerning their observations. Because the doctors were highly respected in the medical field, many previously skeptical evinced an interest in pursuing research concerning this unique approach to healing.

Acupuncture therapy has spread slowly throughout the United States today, and many doctors are now using it. Some attempt it without being the least skilled in its practice. Experiencing failure, they widely report that acupuncture is "not a tool for modern medical practice." The truth is that acupuncture is only successful in the hands of skilled acupuncturists who have often spent years delving into the science and art of this mystical approach to healing. Since it does not involve the physical form, but rather an esoteric, hidden "body"—the etheric form—many modern physicians tend to scoff at its credulity. Not so, the Oriental acupuncturist. He knows clearly he is dealing with vague and indescribable aspects and terminologies, yet he has seen the science work so many times it is not possible to doubt its validity.

In recent years, the AMA with the Institute of Medicine and the National Academy of Sciences has sponsored a United States trip for a delegation to visit China and contact Chinese doctors. They toured various medical research centers to exchange information. Research is being carried out by the Sloan-Kettering Memorial Cancer Center, after having contacted Chinese doctors.

ACUPUNCTURE NEEDLES

The acupuncture "needle" is not actually a needle. To call them needles is a misnomer. They are long thin slivers of stainless steel—so thin they can pass through the eye of an average sewing needle. They are like a very fine wire-like pliable string. They are not hollow, nor do they transport any fluids into the body. The word pliable must be applied, because they are not stiff, as is a needle. Thus their insertion can be and usually is quite painless, unless they inadvertently hit a very sensitive meridian point—in which case, any compassionate acupuncturist will immediately withdraw them and insert them into a less sensitive point. The patient will then experience the same benefit with less and needless pain.

I think the application of acupuncture needles is often painless or painful according to the skill or consideration of the acupuncturist. Certainly some are more skilled than others, and some are operators to whom pain and the patient are secondary to the work being performed. Most are like Master Sehan Kim, who earnestly strives to make the treatment as painless and comfortable as possible.

Western physicians never stop to consider whether or not an injection with a hypodermic needle is painful. They simply know that a certain fluid must be injected into the blood stream, and the hypodermic needle is the only direct approach, regardless of whether or not it is painful. Acupuncture needles cannot be compared in any way with the hypodermic needle, and patients in the western world must realize this. They are accustomed to pain usually following the insertion of a hypodermic needle, thus they are mentally programmed to believe that anything called a "needle" must be painful.

Acupuncture needles vary in size from half an inch to several inches in length. They can be inserted into any one of the several hundred specific points in the body. Depending upon the location and type of illness, the needles may be twirled, vibrated or tapped into strategic nerve centers. To repeat what has already been said, the acupuncturist must know not only where to place the needles, but he must be aware of the depth of insertion. He must also be knowledgeable as to how they are twirled to obtain the desired vibratory effects. A skilled acupuncturist is able to judge by the familiar feel of the needle—how tightly or how loosely it twirls. He must know, too, how long it should remain inserted. The needles are often connected to a 6-volt or 9-volt battery, with a timer and rheostat in the circuit. The machine delivers tiny electrical impulses at the rate of about 120 a minute.

EAR ACUPUNCTURE

There seem to be specific points in and around the ear which, stimulated with acupuncture needles, accomplish incredible healings for various diseases.

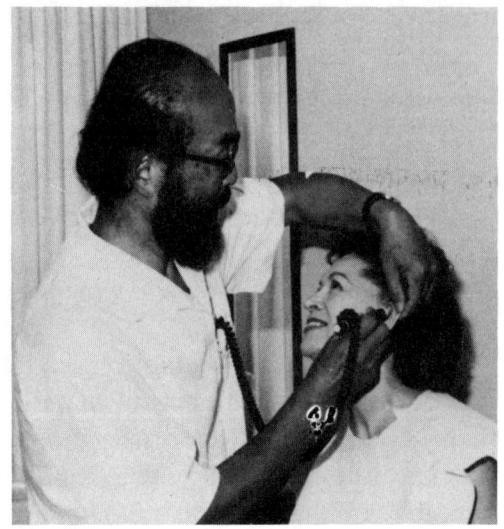

Dr. Earlyne tries ear acupuncture.

The human ear possesses the fetal outline, the embryonic shape of a developing fetus. If the human ear is placed over a miniscule human fetus, the points of organs within the body relate to points of the human ear. That is, the embryonic shape of the ear corresponds exactly with the joints and organs of the body. The head-down position of the fetus during late pregnancy corresponds with the lobe of the ear—the lobe paralleling the head. Outlining the ear clockwise causes each fraction of an inch of it to relate to a specific area in the human body. Thus if an acupuncturist diagnoses an ailment in a specific area of the human body, he can treat the ailment by inserting an acupuncture needle in a corresponding point on the ear.

The ear possesses more than 200

separate acupuncture points directly related to sites on the body far removed from the ear. Acupuncturists employ the use of an "ear map" displaying the points on the ear that correspond to the various organs in the body. Needles are inserted in the particular points indicated resulting in improvements or cures for the organs that correspond. Spectacular results have followed in curing chronic conditions. The method is called *auricular medicine.*

The International Acupuncture Association has released a report from China covering a 10-year study and involving more than 20,000 patients. Ear acupuncture played a major role in their research. Sensational cure rates of better than 90% were achieved for

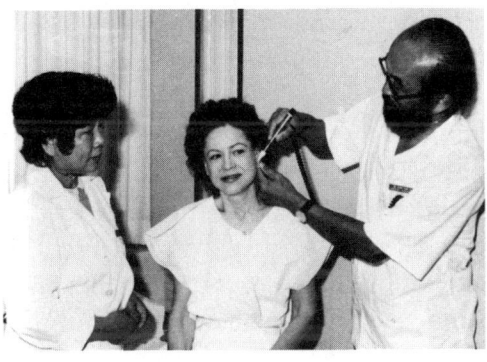

many ailments including migraine headaches, cystitis (bladder inflammation), enteritis (intestinal inflammation), chest pain, nausea, indigestion, constipation, painful menstruation, and insomnia. Its greatest success is in connection with arthritis, impotence, hypertension, allergy diseases, hearing loss, high blood pressure, ulcers, asthma, bursitis, lumbago, tendonitis, paraplegic cases, paralysis following strokes, lame or paralyzed legs, rheumatism, backaches, gall bladder and kidneys, spinal discs, diabetes and liver toxicity.

It is widely claimed that acupuncture can aid a *heroin addict* in overcoming his habit within three days, with none of the horrendous withdrawal horrors. The needles are usually inserted in the ears and hands. Master Kim states he has accomplished such feats.

Addicted smokers are aided in overcoming the tobacco habit through the science of acupuncture. Master Kim's usual treatment is to insert a tiny "thumbtack" needle in the tissue of each ear. It is covered with a small piece of surgical tape and left in the ear several days at a time. When a desire for smoking approaches the patient simply presses on this needlehead gently but firmly. He must use a rhythmic on-and-off pressure continuously for three minutes at a time. The stimulated ear point causes craving sensations to

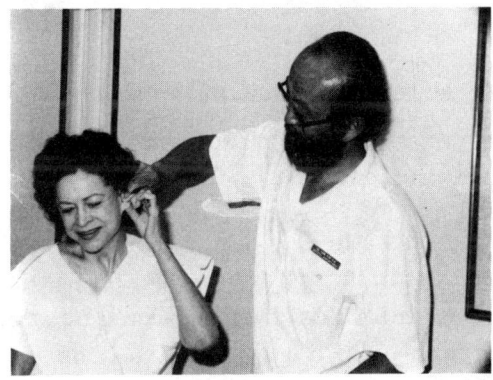

subside. The treatment must be repeated at least three times a day and more often if the craving for a cigarette approaches. The needle is removed after about a week. If further treatment is required, another needle is inserted at a different ear point, and the process continued until the habit is completely overcome.

Jiggling ear staples also aids in overcoming alcoholism. The jiggled ear point stimulates the glands which control blood sugar, causing a sudden release of the needed sugar and reducing or nullifying the need for alcohol—which is a hidden need for blood sugar.

It is widely reported that acupuncture needles applied to specific ear points will aid in *weight reduction*. Again, tiny thumbtack needles are inserted in the ear, covered with tape and left indefinitely. When symptoms of hunger approach, the patient is told to manipulate the needle, which presumably kills

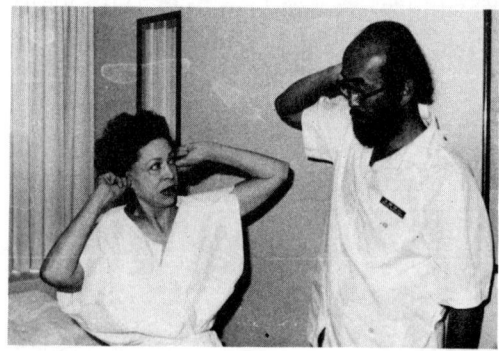

the appetite, enabling the patient to lose weight. Implanting needles semi-permanently in the ear is called *staple-puncture*.

For deafness, Master Kim inserts needles in or near the ears and into the arms and hands. He twirls each needle until the patient winces with discomfort, signaling the proper timing for stimulation. He says he has restored hearing even in those born deaf. "But it requires treatment for many months—perhaps even a year," he stipulated, "and then booster treatments may be necessary to maintain the status of hearing."

He makes no claim to cure cancer. But I've known several patients who had malignant lumps in the breasts to disappear. And he confesses he cured cancer patients in Korea. And he has used methods for pain control with several cancer patients I've known. He has great success in treating asthma, ulcers, sciatica and chest pains from heart disease, and countless other ailments.

He treats even those with emotional and mental problems, and severe depression. For these, his favorite point is the ear near the auditory canal. These patients, treated twice a week usually, soon cease their visits to psychiatrists and toss away their tranquilizers and sleeping pills.

SONO-PUNCTURE

Acupuncturists now claim incredible cures with a new kind of acupuncture that uses painless sound waves. It is called *sono-puncture*. The technique employs the use of a thin metal tube which shoots ultra-high frequency sound waves through the same points which would ordinarily be pierced by needles. No needle is used in sono-puncture, only the high frequency

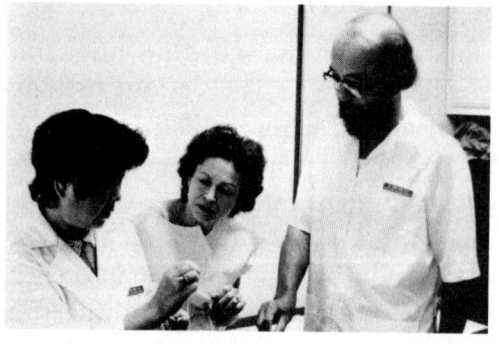

sound waves. Apparently they stimulate the meridian points, bringing the same results as that experienced with needles. Applied to patients in an effort to cure colds, for instance, sound waves are projected through points around the face and ears for approximately 30 seconds each time. The patient feels and hears nothing. The treatment usually requires less than three minutes, after which the patient experiences relief

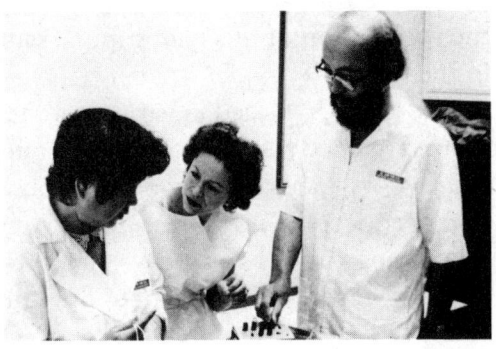

from body aches and stuffiness usually apparent with the common cold. There are no side effects. Sono-puncture is now being employed in relieving numerous other painful ailments including headaches, sinus congestion, menstrual cramps, diarrhea, sciatic nerves which cripple through the hips, muscle pains, low back pains, stiff neck. if the sono-puncture method "catches on," it could become extremely popular since many patients are frequently reluctant to undergo the needle treatment.

ACUPUNCTURE AS AN ANESTHETIC

Acupuncture is already recognized, though little understood, as an anesthetic. No one, not even the Orientals themselves, claim to understand how the application of needles in specific points blocks pain receptors in the body which relay signals directly to the brain. The only really understandable theory is that, even though acupuncture needles may initially produce some discomfort, they simultaneously anesthetize. They block nerve impulses, relieving pain for hours, even after the needles are withdrawn.

Such an approach to anesthesia eliminates the inherent risks frequently attending the toxicity of general anesthetics, many of which involve a certain percentage of mortality. In other words, general anesthetics occasionally create so much toxicity, death results. For many patients, such a methodology as acupuncture offers tremendous help. Because of a diminished physical resistance, they are not able to undergo surgery because their bodies will not withstand the onslaught of the typical anesthesia. Certainly, even for the patients who cannot accept it as the total anesthesia, acupuncture may well be used to reduce the dangers or difficulties inherent with drug anesthesia alone

In anesthesia, two different methods of acupuncture may be employed. One is simply to insert the needles and leave them in the body approximately 20 minutes. Another system involves twirling the inserted needles—either by hand or by low voltage electric current. Either method stimulates two kinds of nervous systems.

Two types of nerve fibers enter the spinal cord. One is a small fiber system conducting the feeling of pain to the brain. The other is a large fiber system that channels the feeling of touch. There is believed to be a gate-controlled cell in the dorsal horn of the spinal cord and the fiber systems act upon this gate-control cell. The needles apparently block pain impulses coming through the small fibers. This theory—often called *the spinal gate theory,* or *the gate control theory*—is the theory of blocking pain through the stimulation of the large, so-called A-delta fibers in the sensory nerves. This stimulation presumably closes a hypothetical gate in the spinal cord, blocking pain impulses from reaching the brain. These impulses travel along a set of smaller nerve fibers, extending up the spinal cord to the brain.

However, this theory seems inadequate, since it would only block pain traveling along the peripheral nerves leading to and from the spinal cord. It does not explain how acupuncture needles would reduce pain in surgery related to the abdomen, or the extraction of teeth, etc.

Sehan Kim believes, as do most American scientists, that acupuncture works by activating a natural pain suppression mechanism in the brain. American scientists, striving to understand the mechanism of acupuncture anesthesia, tend to follow this belief. Those testing the phenomenon suggest that the acupuncture needles stimulate nerves deep in muscles, causing the pituitary and other brain structures to release a substance called *endorphin*—which inhibits the brain cells that respond to the pain message. Endorphin, produced naturally in the brain, is 400 times more potent than morphine.

When scientists removed the pituitary of a test animal, acupuncture no longer had any effect, which led them to suspect that endorphin, produced by the pituitary, could normally block transmission of a nerve signal to the brain cells that respond to pain. Blood tests have shown increased levels of endorphin in blood in the brain during acupuncture treatment and for a considerable time afterward. It is recognized that the human brain emits *endorphin*. Attempts to understand the mysterious function of acupuncture as an anesthetic causes many practitioners to believe that acupuncture stimulates the production of this pain suppressant in the brain.

The needles, placed in various points around the body, stimulate certain brain centers or glands, which release these potent endorphin hormones. If research now being carried out proves such to be the case, acupuncture can be accepted as a scientific procedure, thereby achieving full medical recognition and respectability.

An occasional medical scientist still insists the acupuncture effects are due to hypnosis, even though time after time he sees the practice of acupuncture effective in animals which cannot be hypnotized. To suggest that hypnosis is the underlying approach to acupuncture anethesia ignores the fact that serious surgery is seldom performed on patients through hypnosis. Even mild surgery requires that the patient experience several hours of initial training and specific instructions covering a period of days or weeks. Such is certainly not applied when a patient undergoes surgery with acupuncture anesthetics. Patients undergoing such surgery talk spontaneously, sip tea, display an interest in the ongoing operation, and are even given food to eat.

Acupuncture as an anesthesia works just as well on animals as humans. Veterinarians report that many horses, mules, donkeys, cattle and pigs have responded to the "needling," which should offer some evidence that it is not the result of hypnosis.

Acupuncture has been proven safer than traditional anesthetic methods. It also speeds up the patient's recovery. The normal mortality rate following serious heart operations is from 25 to 30%. The mortality rate with acupuncture is normally 8%. The use of drugs and narcotics in such operations hinders heart muscles. It is well recognized that many heart operation deaths are caused by drugs damaging the heart. The use of acupuncture eliminates this danger.

Usually major heart surgery requires the use of eight inch long stainless steel needles. The patient frequently experiences some discomfort during the first ten minutes when the needles are electrically vibrated. But the presence of the needles brings about a gradual deadening of pain as the patient becomes anesthetized, remaining fully conscious. The usual meridian points are the ears, the throat and the forearm. Two needles are usually placed in each ear, one on each side of the thyroid in the throat, and one on each forearm. A very low voltage of electric current is then passed through the needles. The vibration of the electric current deadens all pain. The patient, remaining conscious, can converse with the doctor at all times, and realizes full well what is occurring.

Patients usually require only five or six days of recuperation, whereas with drug administered anesthesia there is a lingering recovery of from six to seven weeks. An estimated one in every five thousand administrations of general surgical anesthesia proves fatal. Also, some anesthetics pose a risk of kidney and liver damage. In comparison, acupuncture is relatively safe. Neither does it reduce blood pressure or depress breathing, as general anesthetics often do. Also there is no nausea or post-operative aftereffects with the use of acupuncture. Pain control—especially in the case of accident victims, post-operative pain and pain caused by inflammation and bone fractures—requires insertion of the proper needle at the proper meridian point. It can stop the pain in a few moments. Used as an anesthetic, it is discovered that relatively few needles are necessary—placed in appropriate meridian points. Many anesthetization points are in the ear. Occasionally electrodes are attached to the needles that are inserted in the points used for anesthetization. After the needles are inserted and attached to an electrode, usually about 20 minutes' wait is necessary for anesthetization to take effect.

One of the most astonishing aspects of acupuncture anesthetization is that patients are able to walk away from complicated operations. There is little after-pain, few medications are required and the risk of infection is minimal.

My own theory of how acupuncture needles block the sensation of pain is simply this: if needles inserted in certain meridain points can *unblock* the dammed up meridian allowing life force to flow through it, why can it not work in reverse? The application of a needle in a certain meridian point twirled in the hands of a skilled acupuncturist, or attached to an electrical device, may well *block* the flow of life force through the meridian channel. Thus, if the life force being blocked cannot reach the brain cells carrying the message of pain, then pain is temporarily suspended. Consciousness is not blocked out, as is the case with the usual anesthethic procedure, but the pain is blocked because the flow of pranic life force is temporarily prevented from reaching the brain cells which would signal pain to a certain area of the body.

This, of course, is over-simplification, and much more may ultimately be learned. But at least this is a step in the right direction. Somehow, some way, the message of pain does not reach the brain cells which register the pain message. The application of the needle obviously is producing some form of blockage preventing the pain message from being received in the brain cells.

It all relates to recognizing the presence of the etheric body interpenetrating the cells of the physical form. Perhaps the application of the needles at the meridian points temporarily disconnects the etheric body from the physical body. Perhaps, then, we must realize it is the etheric body that is the carrier of the life force, not the physical form itself. Therefore, temporarily disconnecting the lines of communication between the etheric and physical form would block the pain message from reaching the physical brain cells. This—together with the released hormone or endorphin—could be the answer. Again, though oversimplified, this may be a consideration. Ultimately, western medical science must recognize the presence of the etheric body. By so doing, many medical mysteries may be understood.

DIAGNOSING

Master Kim describes a difference between western and Oriental medicine. In western medicine, often an ailing patient submits to all manner of expensive tests in an effort to arrive at a correct diagnosis of a health problem—and the physician is still uncertain. Often he still must guess at the cause of an illness. Not so the Oriental acupuncturist. The wrist pulse test can immediately reveal to him the places in the body where the flow of life force is impeded.

He does not need to give a name to a disease or illness. He calls all disease simply *imbalance*. He knows from his pulse test where best to insert the needles to release the meridian blockages and restore a free flow of chi throughout the body, and to stimulate the proper endocrine glands to distribute their outflow of hormones.

For instance, if a patient complains of an eye problem, the western physician immediately prescribes stronger eye glasses—whereas the acupuncturist begins eye treatments to correct the vision so that, hopefully, glasses can be discarded. He believes it necessary to direct a stronger flow of chi to the eye—and he does it through stimulating the area best suited to that end. Master Kim says even emotions can cause poor vision—fear, anger, stress or meloncholia can prevent the energy flow from reaching the eyes. Acupuncture, he says, is a positive method of unblocking the tensed meridians and restoring chi to the eyes. A paralyzed arm, says Kim, is an excellent example of a part of the human anatomy from which the chi is cut off.

Western doctors customarily check one pulse, the heart, when examining a patient. An acupuncturist checks twelve pulses—six points in each wrist. These points are associated with each of the body's twelve organs. Some acupuncturists also check pulses in the throat and in the solar plexus. The pulses in the wrist, however, connected with the body's twelve organs, register the pulse rate of any indicated organ. A knowledgeable acupuncturist can determine if an organ is low in energy, is too high, or is normal. Needles are inserted at points along the flow of energy—the meridians—involving the afflicted organ.

A skilled acupuncturist begins diagnosing a patient immediately upon contact—eye contact. He searches for such things as the color of the skin, the tone of the muscles around the mouth. At a glance he is often able to diagnose an immediate problem. The patient's tone of voice and the way he breathes also tells him much. Some even consider the aroma of a person's body in making their unique diagnosis. When checking the wrist pulse points, the expert acupuncturist listens for such sounds as *bird pecking* or *shrimp swimming*. He is capable of interpreting these unusual sounds emitted by the various pulse points in the wrist and in the solar plexus.

ACUPUNCTURE AND NUMEROUS AILMENTS

Regardless of the health problem—whether it be arthritis, headache, heart, multiplesclerosis, deafness, menopausal problems, menstrual pain, labor pains, whatever, acupuncture has been shown to be effective. It seems it is a far safer procedure than the drug route taken by the usual medical physician, from which patients have experienced so many horrendous side-effects that they are ready to view acupuncture with credulity. Certainly it must be realized it has not the side effects often experienced with drug therapy.

In Headaches and Arthritis

Migraines and arthritis seem to be two of the major ailments responding to acupuncture with amazing results. Migraine sufferers report incredible results. Some have suffered practically a lifetime, and have found relief only through acupuncture treatments. Arthritics have gradually improved to the point of discarding wheelchairs and crutches. Even though the Orientals themselves seem not to be able to offer a scientific explanation of how the miracles happen, the point is, miracles *do* happen. and one who has suffered long with migraines or arthritis is not particularly concerned with "how" the method works. All they know is that they no longer suffer pain.

Acupuncture and Backache

Acupuncture should be the first type of therapy for those with back problems. Usually they are referred by their doctor to a spinal specialist, who turns out to be a surgeon, often too anxious to apply the knife. There is an astonishing percentage of success in curing backache and back problems through acupuncture, and it should be sought as a first approach rather than the last. Back problems are usually the result of kidney distress, muscle strains, tendonitis, or nerve inflammation. All these respond remarkably well to acupuncture treatment. The approach to be avoided, if at all possible, is back surgery. A great percent of such patients never fully recover, nor is the surgery ever as successful as hoped. Many suffer even more agonizing pain following surgery. On the other hand, if acupuncture is sought first, surgery is often never required.

Acupuncture and Childbirth
Acupuncture is also performed on many women about to give birth. They have their babies with no pain and with no anesthetics. Usually there are only two needles inserted during childbirth—one near the ankle and the other in the wrist. Often, electrodes are taped on the abdomen. The vibration of the electrodes is controlled through an instrument called *Acupuncture Anesthesia Machine* which is powered via a low voltage battery similar to that of a flashlight. Anesthesia through the needle insertions, plus stimulation through the electrodes, enables a woman to have her baby without pain or drugs. She is on her feet within an hour after delivery with no drug side effects and usually feeling happy, relaxed and excellent. *Electro-acupuncture* is also being used to aid in abortions when they are indicated to save the life of the mother. They are replacing dangerous salt infusions frequently used for late-stage abortions.

Anesthetics should seldom be used in childbirth, since they increase the risk to both mother and child. Acupuncture seems an excellent alternative. Chinese clinics have been quick to point out that acupuncture, if improperly used, can cause sterility. Such knowledge should alert the American medical profession that the insertion of staple-type needles in the ear could be an answer to birth control. Along the mysterious meridians there are also some twenty "forbidden" points, including one in the abdomen that can cause a pregnant woman to abort. There is another forbidden point under the arm that, ignorantly probed, could cause death.

Acupuncture and Deafness
Acupuncture has been attempted in curing nerve deafness, which is a common form of hearing loss. Nerve deafness cannot be cured by surgery or other modern forms of medical treatment. The deafness usally occurs from damage to the hearing nerves, resulting in distress, injury or infections and inflammations early in life. Nerve deafness is the only kind which can actually be helped by acupuncture. The success of this type of treatment comes as a surprise, since the medical profession in America offers no cure for nerve deafness. A needle about 3-1/2 inches long is usually inserted a half inch into the skin behind the ear to stimulate the auditory nerve that carries sound signals from the ear to the brain.

Doctors in China report that they have been successful in 90% of the cases of deafness when the affliction is the result of a childhood disease. They have even obtained striking results with deaf mutes. The needles are inserted into ear points for quick results and into the arms and hands for slower but more permanent results. Acupuncture stimulates the nervous system and adjusts the hearing nerves in some mysterious way. Even deaf mutes often obtain good results within six months. Most cases usually require at least a year. The results come even more slowly where deafness was caused by brain injury or inflammation. But reports from China report a definite cure for nerve deafness, and some deaf mutes, following their treatments, are placed in ordinary schools where they are treated as normal children.

The reports of people having hearing restored through acupuncture treatments are so astonishing as to sound almost sensational. Master Sehan Kim, through his years of practice, claims a good percentage of cure rate for deafness. Some had hearing only partially restored. Master Kim claims that hearing is connected with central brain functioning. He says that when the meridians are unblocked and energy is flowing through the brain cells, the effect is upon the whole person—who sees better, feels better and has better memory function. Master Kim uses needles in the ear a lot, claiming that the ear meridian points often directly affect energy flowing through the brain.

I have witnessed hearing improvement in several I have sent to Master Kim for treatment. I have known people to remove their hearing aids. I have witnessed some who began treatments to experience partial restoration of their hearing, and then ceased their acupuncture treatments, only to revert to their previous state of deafness. It is in the case of deafness that I would personally like to see considerably more research. I truly feel acupuncture to be substantially effective in this field.

ACUPUNCTURE IN DENTISTRY

Acupuncture is used by many dentists for both light dental work and complicated surgery. It is performed by inserting a needle in a spot on the webbed area between the thumb and the forefinger. This point is called *the hoku point*. Many serious dental surgeries are performed with the insertion of this sole needle.

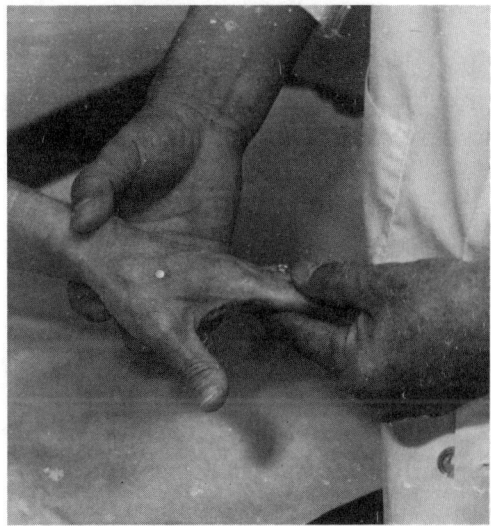

The hoku point is also used to treat headaches, abdominal cramps, toothaches and sore throats.

ACUPUNCTURE IN GENERAL

I have focused on only a few diseases now being treated with acupuncture. It assuredly has a great future in the treatment of many other human ailments. One is in the treatment of mental illness. The use of acupuncture could totally eliminate the use of shock therapy. It could also aid in rehabilitating criminals with mental problems. Patients with emotional problems are also being successfully treated. It removes mental confusion, improves insomnia, relaxes patients with severe depression, replaces tranquilizers, improves the power of concentration and memory recall.

It is important to place acupuncture within the framework of modern medicine, attempting to remove or correct false and exaggerated impressions. It is being used widely in Europe, especially France. It was brought to France from China in 1934. It has been practiced and taught since then by the French medical profession and is, at present, an accepted form of therapy paid for by the national health insurance.

It was brought to the Soviet Union around 1959 and is now an important adjunct in their medical schools.

Researchers agree on one thing— acupuncture works. It works for enthusiastic patients in China, Japan, Korea, England, France, Germany, Russia and, to a limited degree, in the United States. Many American physicians, reluctant to accept the mysterious Oriental method since they can discover no scientific logic for its performance, either refer to it as "mumbo-jumbo," as "hocus," as "primitive," or as "unscientific." Patients who have been cured are not the least concerned with any of these "words." They only know that they have been released from pain and cured of ailments.

It is pointless for the American Medical Association to withhold the marvelous functioning of acupuncture until arriving at a satisfactory explanation of "how it works." Such a lengthy procedure could delay for years acupuncture's introduction into the American medical system. It has been proven applicable over hundreds, perhaps thousands, of years in the Orient. And it assuredly would not have enjoyed such a sustained record of benefit without some degree of success. Pain can be alleviated, many chronic diseases overcome, and health restored through properly administered acupuncture treatments *while* investigations of how it works are continuing. Since the Chinese have been using it for at least hundreds of years, and still do not understand how it works, why should American doctors withold its benefits until *they* can arrive at some logical explanation of how the human body responds. Research on how it works could proceed at the same time patients are receiving relief from pain and the restoration of health. Once medical science does unravel the mystery of its function, perhaps the entire medical community throughout the world may take a basic "leap forward" into the Aquarian Age, since they will have uncovered a completely new realization concerning the human body.

It is nowhere suggested that medical scientists give up their medical procedures in lieu of acupuncture. It is only strongly suggested that one use his technical knowledge in conjunction with acupuncture to achieve what his allopathic drugs alone cannot. Combining both therapies could be a tremendous source of healing therapy for a suffering humanity.

Western medical science must adapt its concept of healing to include balancing energy flows through such techniques as acupuncture, kirlian photography, energy radiations from the body by electrical sensing devices (biofeedback), and by ultimately recognizing the presence of the etheric form—permeating and penetrating every cell of the physical. Many of the new age type doctor, including the holistic approach to healing in his modalities, already is aware of the unfolding mystery of man before his very eyes. Others remain devoutly skeptical, refusing even to "see" that which is directly before them. Such has it always been and such will it ever be, until acupuncture ultimately proves to be so effective it can no longer be ignored in the progressive march toward human immortality.

Since it has received such wide publicity of a sensational nature, it is easy to think of acupuncture as a panacea, especially since there have been numerous reports of patients experiencing a complete cure after only one treatment, but these are the exceptional cases. No one—not even the most skilled acupuncturist—claims that it is the sole approach to diagnosis, surgery and well-being. What is claimed is that it should be used as an adjunct to ongoing medical research. It is the concensus of opinion that acupuncture can never totally replace other methodologies of healing. Its remarkable effectiveness as an anesthesia will not replace the usual medical approach. It may only partially do so in selected individuals. In the future it assuredly should occupy a place in the management of pain problems. What it can and cannot do should be firmly established. The Orientals usually use it in conjunction with Oriental herbs. Often they place as much importance on the herbal therapy as upon the acupuncture.

It must be readily admitted that western medical science has proven unsuccessful in many illnesses—certainly it blatantly announces there is no cure for arthritis when many an acupuncturist has brought about astonishing recoveries. Migraine headaches are another. There are so many illnesses the western physician is unable to benefit. He simply tells his patients to "learn to live with it." The acupuncturist, on the other hand, has brought about incredible cures or partial cures in diseases the American doctor cannot yet benefit. Therefore, acupuncture could very well occupy an important place in treating many of these "incurable" diseases. Certainly many patients are now weary of the total drug approach of allopathic medicine.

Some American doctors now practicing the Chinese art of acupuncture claim that many American doctors are opposed to acupuncture because it could lower high medical costs. They claim that many doctors fear it might affect their incomes. Be this as it may, there is no way to hold back a methodology whose time has come, and certainly acupuncture is becoming widespread and effective enough to be applicable universally. When enough patients begin demanding acupuncture therapy, the pressure of public opinion will cause the hesitancy to give way, as more and more doctors learn the necessity of its application in their practice.

In defense of the American doctors, however, it may be said that they will ultimately outdistance the ancient Chinese method. They will ultimately discard the thin wire needles now used by Oriental physicians and begin experimenting with infinitesimal laser beams.

Once learning what meridian point controls a particular disease, they will use electrical charges and avoid the insertion of needles, or they will use the application of a laser beam. Either method is not painful to the patient and is certainly more desirable than with a needle even though it be only a thin wire-like needle and usually not painful.

The usual needle treatment requires 30 to 45 minutes. The insertion of the needles is occasionally painful and certainly fear on the part of the patient makes them undesirable. The laser treatment can be accomplished in a matter of minutes. It is extremely effective and the patient is subjected neither to fear nor to pain. The laser acupuncturist uses a pen-shaped point-finder through which a thin red shaft of light is beamed at the acupuncture points. The laser beam directs energy at blocked meridian points. It stimulates the body's resistance, enabling it to fight a particular condition. Also, it unblocks the energy field, allowing the pranic life force to flow through, just as does the needle procedure. The American doctors, becoming skilled in this ancient art, will find many ways to improve the ancient techniques.

Doctors or researchers wishing further reports from the research work now being done may write directly to the following address: American Academy of Acupuncture Medicine, 2718 Dryden Drive, Madison, WI 53704

Ancient Chinese texts that are now being translated by qualified researchers reveal the belief that China was once visited by space beings and that it was from these aliens that the Chinese learned acupuncture. A contact with space aliens was made by a philosopher named Mo-Tzu over 2,300 years ago in the 4th Century B.C., according to the translated ancient Chinese texts. Mo-Tzu was then 82 years old. Asking for immortality from the superbeings, the aliens gifted him with 25 volumes of medical information which were all written on white silk. The texts describe how Mo-Tzu went up a mountain to contact a certain superman and communicate with him telephathically.

The texts, now being transcribed, say that the aliens provided Mo-Tzu with detailed information on drugs, herbs and acupuncture therapy. It was they, too, who taught the Chinese concerning the five elements—wood, fire, water, earth and metal—on which traditional Chinese acupuncture is based. Although Mo-Tzu may not have been granted permanent immortality, it is reported that he lived to be a wise old sage, at least three hundred years old. The report suggests he may never have died at all. There is no report of his death nor where he is buried, if at all. Perhaps the space alien came back for him and escorted him to higher planes without his ever experiencing the phenomenon we call physical death—Quien Sabe?

ACUPRESSURE—
A SELF-ADMINISTERED
TREATMENT

A treatment similar to acupuncture may be self-administered. This is the technique of *acupressure*, or pressure upon certain meridian points with the fingertips rather than puncturing the skin with needles. Acupressure is becoming widely known as a method of relieving a variety of aches and pains. Certainly it is safe, with no side effects. You simply find the point related to your own problem and either press upon it and hold the pressure for from one to three minutes, or press and release for the same amount of time.

Better than the tip of the finger, Master Kim suggests any kind of rounded small pointed object—such as the blunt point of a make-up brush,

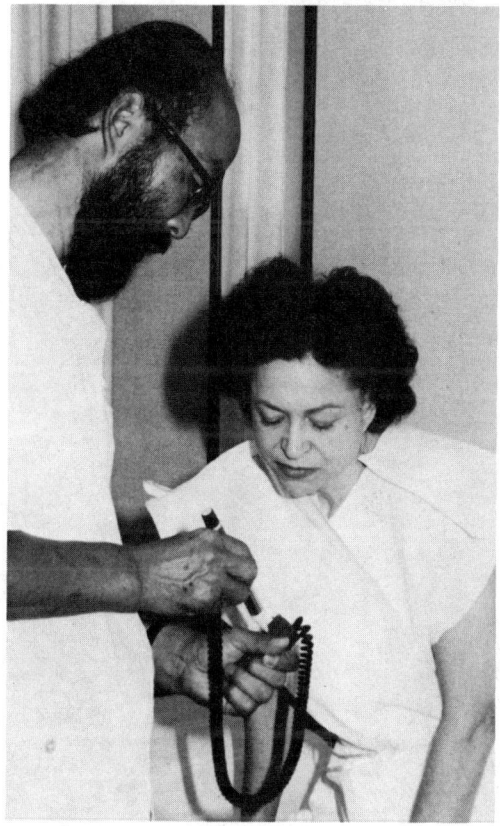

perhaps a lipstick brush. The point should not be sharp, and should never penetrate the skin. It is not designed to bring about a specific cure, but it will assuredly relieve pain. Cure must be brought about by whatever caused the problem, but alleviation of pain can be brought about by acupressure. Ailments benefitted by acupressure include: headaches, toothaches, foot pain, impotence and frigidity, nervous tension, menstrual cramps, kidney blockages and disorders, respiratory problems, indigestion, allergy, arthritis, tendonitis, bronchitis, backache, sciatica, neuralgia, migraines—and face lifts.

For Flu, Colds, to Reduce Phlegm, to Relieve Allergies

Colds—with a pencil eraser or point of a make-up brush, press on the inside center pad of the third finger and hold it for three to five minutes. Also press on point #4, just under the knee, outside the shinbone.

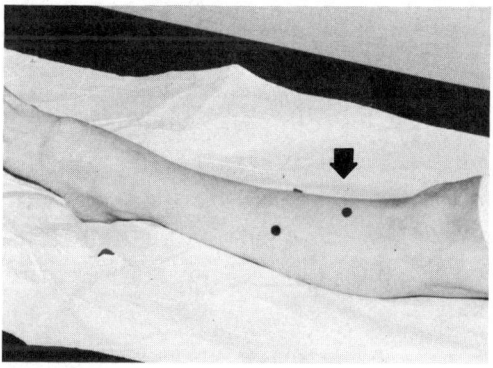

For a Racing or Skipping Heartbeat

Kim advises ear squeezing—also for chest pains. The squeezing slows the heartbeat and reduces blood flow by stimulating the vagus nerve. Cover the entire ear with the open palm of the hand, with the fingers pointed toward the midpoint of the neck. Squeeze the entire ear for 10 to 20 seconds, much as you would a sponge. The vagus nerve begins in the brain and branches to both ears and the heart. Squeezing the ears sends a "slow-down" message to the heart.

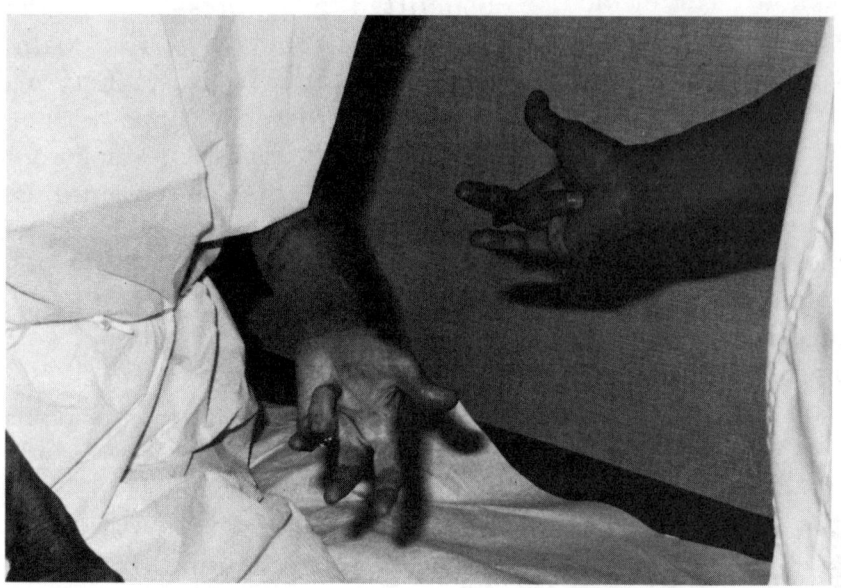

Fatigue, Tiredness and Stress

First close your fingers down into the palm. Where the ring finger strikes, press on that point. Then press the thumb of the opposite hand on that point. This is the Palace of Tiredness—the Nokung point. Recharges the entire body.

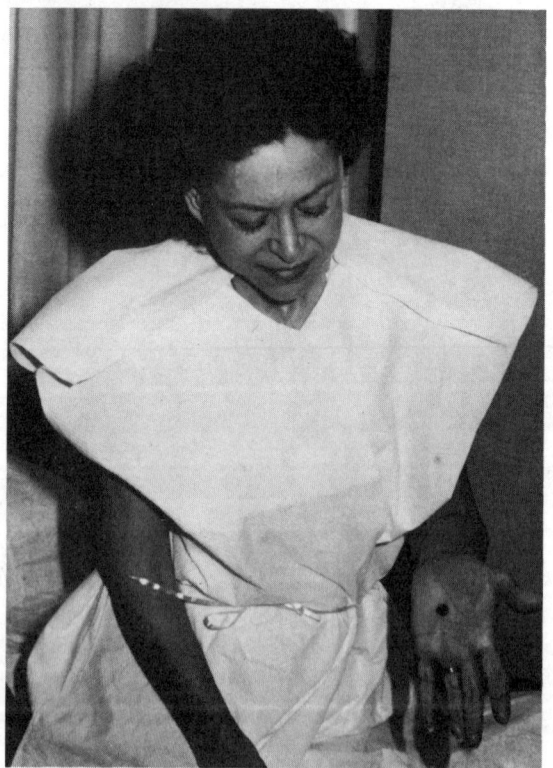

Ovarian Cysts

Press on each side of the nose where the bone and cartilage meet in the nasal cavity. Press between the nose and the upper lip.

Arthritis

Press on the back of the knee.

Hoku Point

For insomnia, tranquilizing, dental surgery, diarrhea, constipation, sinus congestion, headache, muscle spasm, facial pain, earache, eye ache, or anything connected with the face or head, toothache, abdominal cramps, sore throats, tooth extractions, tonsillectomy, headache.

Antibiotic Point

On the elbow, press and release for infections. Also for inflammation, fever, arthritis.

Migraines

Press on the soft spot on the head, an inch into hairline. Press on each side of the brow midway between high point of the eyebrow and hairline. Press on each temple. Press behind each ear on a level with the bottom of the ear.

Weight Control

Pull out on the flagus of the ear, then release. Press and pull out. Repeat the procedure for three minutes.

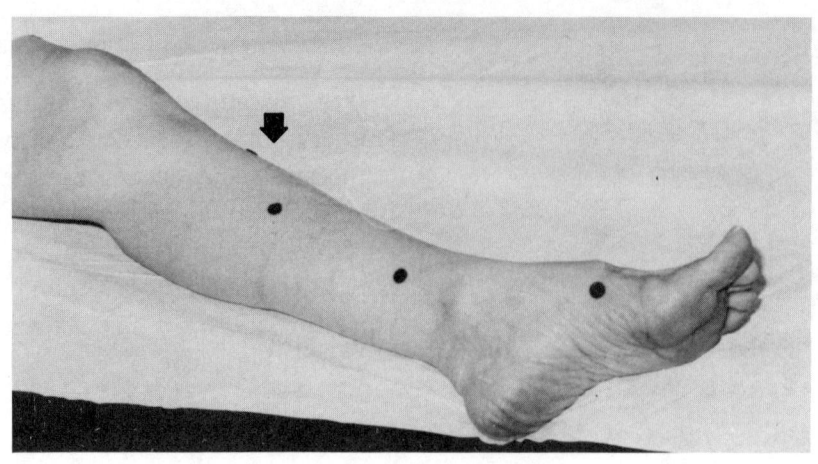

Nookok Point

For hypoglycemia and sugar control, press Nookok point on the leg, on the inner side of the shinbone, halfway between the ankle bone and just below the knee.

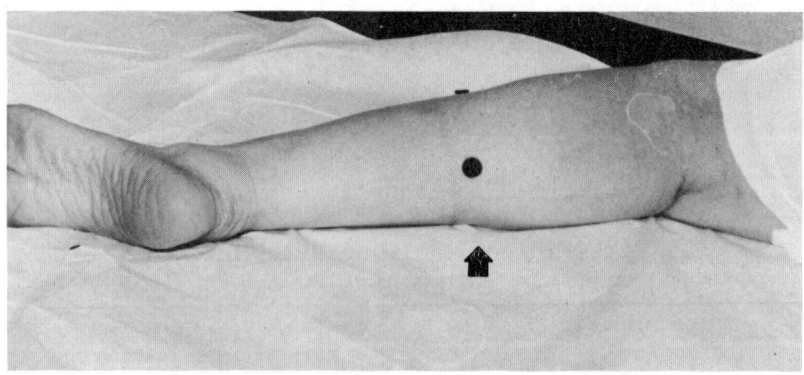

Sunsang Point

Women's cramps and muscle cramps. Press and release for three minutes, or press steadily for three minutes, on calf muscle back of leg.

COSMETIC SURGERY AND ACUPUNCTURE

Leading plastic surgeons throughout the western world are now eyeing acupuncture as a means to benefit their clients. Many are already applying the method now used in France, which enables the surgery to occur without the use of novocaine or drugs as anesthesia. Needles are usually inserted in the ears and hands. They are connected to electrodes which operate on a low voltage charge of electricity. This enables the client to undergo surgery anesthetized only with the acupuncture needles. Surgery using this method enables the patient to sit upright, reduces bleeding to a minimum, eliminates considerable swelling, and gives the physician a greater potential for correcting facial wrinkles and structure. Plastic surgery using acupuncture will probably become increasingly popular as we move into a new drugless era of medicine.

FACE LIFTS USING ACUPUNCTURE

Acupuncture creates a balanced glandular system, particularly stimulating the thymus gland, which is directly related to youth and anti-aging research.

A conventional face lift costs from $2500 to $7500, perhaps even more. The operation is usually conducted under local anesthesia, requiring from three to four hours. Unless the face lift is performed using acupuncture as an anesthetic, there is normal bleeding and considerable swelling, requiring an extended recovery period. A face lift via acupuncture requires from 10 to 16 treatments, with no surgery. The treatments are comparatively pain-free and last no more than an hour each. The total cost ranges between $500 and $800. Admittedly the best candidates for acupuncture face lifts are women under 50 years of age, or those with relatively small wrinkles. But all clients, regardless of age, can experience considerable improvement. Older persons may not realize the desired extent—especially if they are inclined to have deep wrinkles. A favorable aspect concerning acupuncture face lifts is that there are no side effects.

TECHNIQUES FOR ACUPUNCTURE AND ACUPRESSURE FACE LIFTS

Long before a face lift via acupuncture became popular, Sehan Kim had admitted to me that he was an expert in the technique. I say "admitted" because he is so modest I had to coax the information from him.

I was continuing to have acupuncture treatments from him on a regular basis long after my health had "normalized"— just as a preventive measure. One day I said, rather in jest, "If acupuncture releases life force into muscles, why couldn't a technique be developed that would cause an inpouring of the force into facial muscles and perhaps tighten the skin—something like a face lift?"

I saw Sehan Kim and his wife Dr. Kyoo, exchange glances. Then they began to speak in Korean. I couldn't understand a word they said. This continued for a while. It was Dr. Kyoo who finally said:

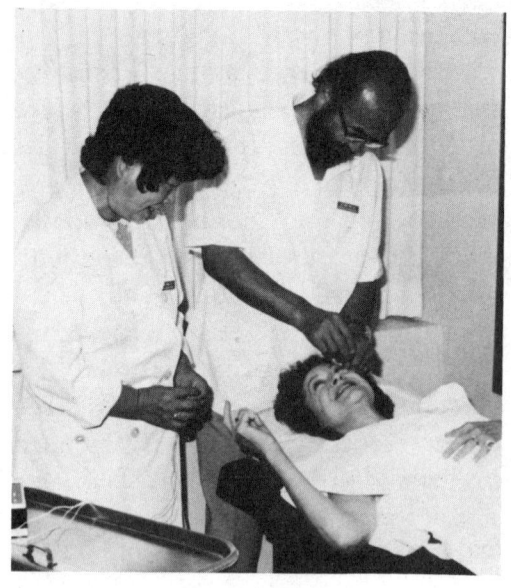

Dr. Earlyne experiments with face lift via acupuncture.

"There certainly is already such a technique—and Sehan is an expert. In Korea he used it often, and taught the technique to acupuncturists in clinics in Korea. Also when women want a face lift by surgery, he can insert a few staple-needles in the ear, which, remaining there during surgery, will prevent bleeding and swelling."

"You mean he *can* give a face lift by acupuncture?"

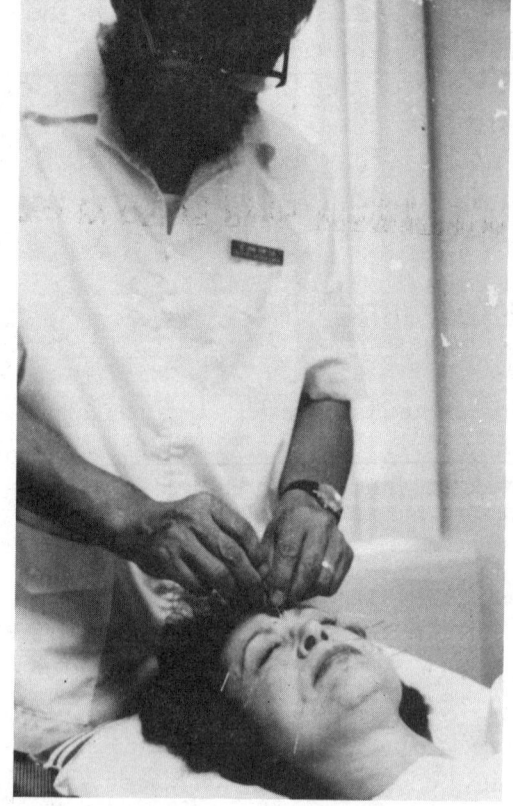

* Sehan Kim's address is 7080 Hollywood Blvd., Hollywood, Calif. 90028.

"Yes—but it requires seventeen treatments, given twice a week, and many women do not want to give the time and trouble to return so often."

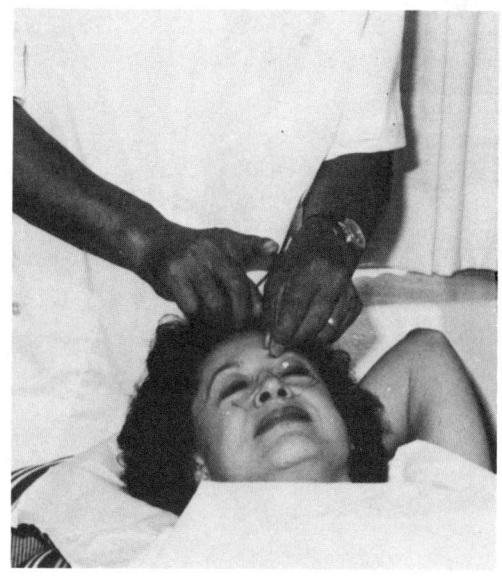

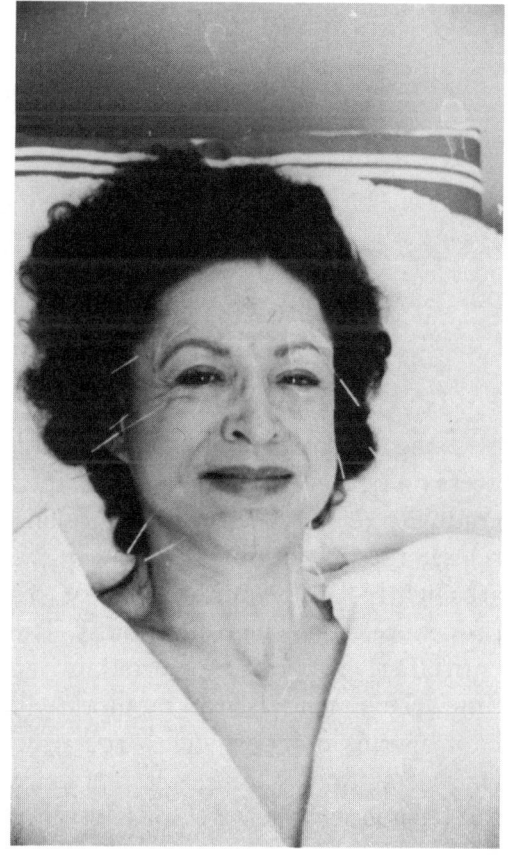

"Oh, but many *do!*" I replied, and asked that since I was already having general acupuncture once a week, he apply the face technique just for fun. I must confess I did not continue the full course of treatments so cannot be sure my facial muscles responded enough to say I had an acupuncture face lift—but others I have sent to him for this purpose have enthusiastically reported excellent results.

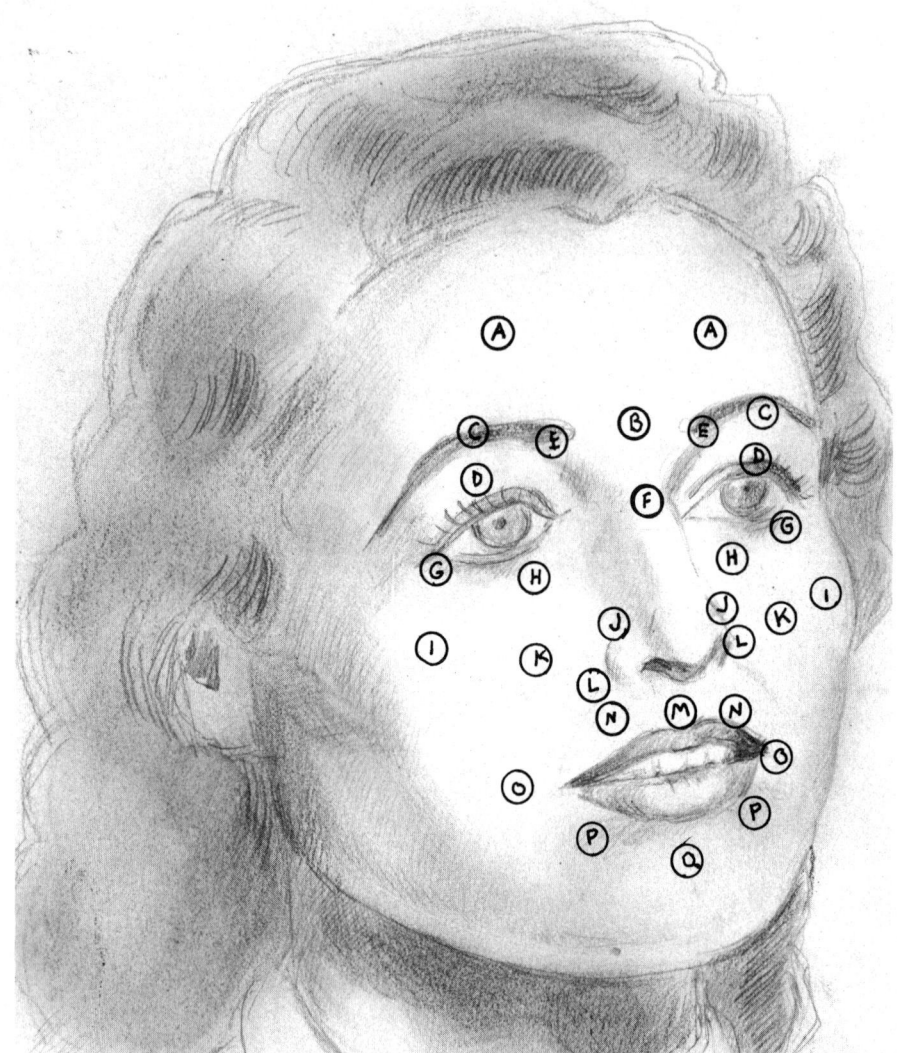

Sehan also taught me how to give myself home treatments for a face lift via acupressure.

I am including a chart he supervised, using both acupuncture needles and the home method of acupressure. As for home treatments, do try the techniques Sehan has offered in this book. Again, many have experienced results—some have been amazingly successful, others only partially so. But all have been satisfactory.

Using the forefinger of each hand, press on points A for ten seconds, then gradually release. Repeat pressure and release for two minutes. Then tap the area lightly for one minute. Repeat this procedure on all the other points. The entire face need not be treated at one time. This acupressure method will banish wrinkles if persistently practiced for several months. Suggestion: practice this technique while watching television.

AFTERTHOUGHTS

This being the final retrospection on health, healing and Holy Breath—and the Book of my own Beginning Again—many thoughts rise into my consciousness as I write these words. I wonder about the results to be gained if these instructions and teachings are followed. The product of my pen will be justified in your improvement if you've gained the most important things for a happy journey on this Earth—a healthy body and a peaceful mind through rational living, wholistic healing and Holy Breath.

My thoughts go back through history to great souls of the past. I think there is not one among them who did not apply the natural laws much as have been indicated in this book. I think, were this not so, they may never have gained the stature of their greatness. Whether or not those of us applying "the rules" now attain their stature is not important. It is only important that we live the highest and best, mentally and spiritually, and the purest, physically, in order that the soul, incarnated for the purpose of betterment, accomplishes that purpose. If these writings have offered guidelines toward that goal, then the love and the labor involved was well worth while.

We make much of the dawn of the Aquarian Age, the coming of a better time for the human race. Assuredly the human race cannot long endure the present mode of living. Could we not see evidences of the coming dawn and occasional glimpses of the Light, Earth as it is now would be well nigh unendurable. Food industries poison our foods. Crime rates are at an all time high. Our rivers, oceans and atmosphere are polluted and blessed mother Earth groans under the treatment she has received from her children.

But through it all we see glimpses of the dawn and glimmers of the coming Light. We are establishing better health through the wholistic approach, better happiness through our meditations, and a change in our attitude towards success. We are reestablishing a consistent philosophy of life as the Great Ones who came to earth long ago meant it to be established. We understand the identity of eternal elements as creative intelligence, space and matter. We are well aware of the emanation of God's great power and the goal of human destiny becomes ever clearer.

In this dawning of the Aquarian Age

there are many pathways to God—perhaps as many as there are living people on the Earth—but they all eventually merge into the one path leading to the true God. That one path must be illumined by every individual's own soul. To every soul there must eventually come the divine message which many consciousnesses have failed to interpret. Until now it has died in its inception.

All my writings—including this present book—have led, step by step, toward the ascent human consciousness has been traveling until it becomes united with the One Reality. They have been given in plain, simple language that even he whose eyes are closed may read and understand. There is an emerging Order of human souls now in the vanguard to establish perfect order and government upon this Earth. We try to live in one breath of love, prayerfully working toward the day when competition, war and destruction shall be abolished from this planet.

My writings have admonished many times that if man is to understand life he must first understand himself. This book has been an attempt to bring you further toward that goal. Pray now that the higher Creative Intelligences guide you further. Their fingers are always pointed in the right direction—upward.

Hold always to your faith in a Supreme Power.

SUMMATION

"Blessed is the lion which the man eats and the lion will become man; and cursed is the man whom the lion eats and the lion will become man."
(Apocryphal Gospel of Thomas.)

This saying implies that through self-conquest, right use of free will, "crosses are turned into trines." Since it is in the kingdom of the body that we eat the bread of many initiations, it requires the daily walk upon the razor's edge.

True, food serves you, not vice versa. But more important than eating meat or abstaining from meat, is the curb and rule over emotions and thoughts. For truly, eating or not eating meat cannot undo the harmful effects of negative venom which pours into the blood stream by outbursts of anger, silently nursed hatred, unrestrained negatives of all kinds. Of no avail the careful diet when countermanded by worry residing uppermost in mind. Hence self-conquest of "the whole person" is sooner or later mandatory in the soul who knows his destination is "into the fullness of the stature of Christ."

There is an old Indian fable told in the *Panchatantra*. It concerns a mouse who was obsessed with fear of a cat. Every moment of his sleeping and waking moments were imbued with fear and anxiety. He couldn't eat properly, he couldn't sleep. His dreams were filled with fear and trembling. Always he saw before him a vision of the vicious cat.

So his master—a magician—took pity on him and transformed him into a cat. "Now your fearful days are over," said the magician. "Go forth as a brave and beautiful cat."

But, instead, as a cat the mouse became afraid of a dog. His entire consciousness focused upon the same anxiety. The only thing changed was the object he feared. Once it was the cat, now it was the dog. The anguish continued, the fear remained unabated, the dream still rampant with anxiety and trembling.

So the magician, out of pity, changed the cat into a dog. But the mouse inside the dog immediately became afraid of the tiger. The fear remained, the anxiety remained, the wakefulness, the trembling, because the dog became afraid of the tiger. The magician changed the dog into a tiger and the tiger immediately became afraid of the elephant. The fear and trembling continued because the elephant became anxious about the hunter. In the mammoth body of the elephant, the mouse consciousness remained. He cowered and crouched the whole day long trembling in fear of the hunter.

So the magician turned the mouse back into a mouse. "It is no point to keep changing the outer form," he explained. "It is the mouse consciousness that must be transformed. The fear remains fear, the anxiety remains anxiety, regardless of the outer form. So you may as well live through the state of negativity in the form of a mouse. Changing the outer being does not help until the inner consciousness is transformed."

And so it is toward the inner consciousness and the transformation thereof that this book ultimately must be planted. It does no good to be obsessed with the outer transformation of the body—through food, clothing, behavior, meditations, prayers—unless the inner is equally transformed. Many disciples lose the way, lose sight of the Path because they become obsessed with the outer transformation. All day long they think of nothing but food. They can't eat this or they can't eat that, and they think of nothing else. Their consciousness is on the level of the mouse. They are fearful and anxious over food and they become extreme bores to their friends and fellow travelers on the Path. No one truly enjoys the companionship of such a disciple. No one wants to hear him speak constantly of food.

It is equally disastrous to become obsessed with all manner of techniques and behavior patterns. Neither does anyone want constantly to hear of "the proper discipline," the restrictions, of constantly keeping the eyes glued to and the consciousness focused upon always and eternally following "the rules." Obviously I am not saying that one should not be aware. Awareness is essential. Because I believe so strongly that the outer consciousness should be aware is the reason I have given time to writing this book, pointing the way towards purification, both physical and mental.

But, beloved, never lose sight of the fact that in transforming the outer, the mouse consciousness within must become the cat, the dog, the tiger, the elephant, giving equal or more thought to the inner transformation. The one who remains balanced, giving equal thought to outer purification and inner serenity, will become the teacher. The one who does not become balanced becomes only that—an imbalanced disciple. Certainly not a teacher. His principal focus will be upon how dreadful it is to drink a cup of coffee.

So while you are applying the teachings and guidelines offered so lovingly in this book, do be aware that you must, at the same time, be transforming the mouse consciousness into that of the elephant and, with the elephant consciousness, move forward into love, light and enlightenment. The balanced disciple, becoming the teacher, is a delight to all who contact him. The inner self, transformed, will radiate outward, making of this one a teacher to be sought—a soul to be followed—a living example of true transformation.

Selah!

A VITAL BOOK TO HELP YOU TOWARD SELF-REALIZATION
KUNDALINI AND THE THIRD EYE
by Earlyne Chaney & William L. Messick

Discover the Inner Fire of the Ancients! Go beyond yoga, beyond ESP! Discover truths and secrets that were taught by the Mystery Schools in highly advanced civilizations of long ago.

Seekers of truth are becoming enlightened Initiates in the fast-dawning Aquarian Age. Find answers you need to help you on your personal journey as your soul unfolds to this New Age challenge.

You will find many once-secret teachings concerning special yogic practices, breathing techniques, transmuting of sexual energies; how to stimulate and equalize the centers that create the connection between the personality and the Oversoul. Tells the nine secret steps taught to disciples in ancient Mystery Schools to prepare them for initiation into the great order of Melchizedek.

Discover the Cosmic Connection of Kundalini and the Third Eye to the ceremonies and rituals of the ancients. Become aware of how you can use this same vital energy to open your all-seeing, superconscious Third Eye, purify your psychic "passageways," tune your awareness to hear the Divine Sound Current and safeguard each step of your inner growth toward Higher Consciousness.

This extraordinary book is 8-1/2" x 11", has a four-color Lexitone cover, with 70 half-tone illustrations.

About the Authors

Earlyne Chaney is a teacher to thousands. Studies of mysticism and esoteric philosophy flow from her pen into the lives of Seekers around the world.

Her "cosmic connection" began with psychic experiences as a child in a lonely Texas town, then came frequently to the surface of her life during an acting career in Hollywood. Psychic and mystical experiences surged into full expression in her life following the tragic loss of a loved one, and since 1951 her work has gained worldwide recognition through her authorship of a series of Lessons known as Astara's Book of Life, mystical studies published by Astara, a New Age Church and Mystery School of international scope which she co-founded in 1951.

William Messick recently retired from the Federal government where he was a Foreign Service Officer in the Middle East and Asia. He holds the U.S. State Department's highest award for heroism and was decorated by Secretary of State Dean Rusk for "bravery under fire, aiding the wounded, and saving a life" in Viet Nam.

It was during Mr. Messick's Asian tour of duty that he began to study Oriental philosophy and mysticism. As a student of a Chinese Zen Master he had a life-changing mystical experience—a journey in cosmic consciousness, a momentary "flash" that changed him from an agnostic to a mystic, a searching seeker after Truth.

Remembering

THE AUTOBIOGRAPHY OF A MYSTIC
By Earlyne Chaney

Earlyne Chaney whose quest for truth led through Hollywood to world-wide prominence as a teacher of mysticism.

REMEMBERING is . . . a story of life after death . . . and love beyond death . . . the story of a quest for a love from a past life whose eyes haunted her dreams . . . of contact with a Great Being from the Other Side whose influence brought illumination to one in search of Light.

Do you believe unseen beings guide our lives?

Do you believe unseen beings sometimes guide and guard those whose destiny is marked for greatness? *Remembering* tells of such a being — his appearance and his prophecy to a girl whose search for God led her away from orthodox religion and into mysticism . . .

Do you believe in life after death?

Do you believe our loved ones can, under certain circumstances, return to bring solace and guidance to their bereft? *Remembering* tells of the pilot whose death in a plane crash changed the life of this same girl — how she turned from a career as a movie actress to search for the meaning of life and death and immortality. And how he returned to tell her he still lived . . .

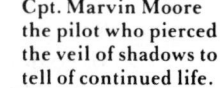

Cpt. Marvin Moore the pilot who pierced the veil of shadows to tell of continued life.

Do you believe you have lived before?

. . . and that you can dream dreams of the one whose love endured from the past? *Remembering* tells of the girl's lonely search for the beloved and how the pilot, from the Other Side of life, guided her to find the eyes that haunted her dreams.

This autobiography of a mystic is a true story of life from a humble beginning to a film career, then to eminence as one of today's outstanding authors of mystical teachings whose writings are sought by mystical seekers the world over.

Remembering by Earlyne Chaney is a life-changing experience. A journey through its pages is an upgoing path into the starmists of your own soul searchings, vague rememberings of other lives, other loves, other hopes, your own yet-to-be dreams.

Robert Chaney whose love, haunting her dreams of a long-ago life, guided her way into a new light.

". . . a philosophically guided tour past the treasured milestones of memory in the romantically inspiring life of the modern mystic, Earlyne Chaney."
—Harold Sherman, author of *How to Make ESP Work for You* and *You Live After Death*

At your bookstore, or order from
Astara, Upland, CA 91786

How soon do you want to feel better?

Immediately?
Then try the
LIGHT AND LIFE COOKBOOK
By Jan and Alan Pearson
Created with Earlyne Chaney

A forty-day transitional diet to vegetarianism.

.....Can you smell the aroma of *Cheddar Cheese Cutlets* glorified with *Sweet Basil Tomato Sauce*, followed by some *California Orange Cake?* (See Day 10.)

Can you taste the bright goodness of *Yin-Yang Stuffed Tomatoes* and *Wok Tossed Greens?* (See Day 3.) Or *Light Asparagus Souffle* with *Honey Glazed Carrots?* And *Peasant Corn Pones?* (See Day 31.)

Are you daring enough to try *Walnut Rounds*, waiting under *Parsley Sesame Gravy* to tempt your taste buds? (Day 26.) Or *Broiled Avocado in Half Shell* with *Tomato Coconut Sauce*, perhaps followed by *Papaya Orange Smoothie?* (Day 28.)

And above all, can you feel the surge of energy, know the strength and stamina, experience the inner physical cleanliness and alertness of mind which result from a natural, full-of-health diet? The *Light and Life Cookbook* guides you in Aquarian Age eating adventures that are nearly as exciting as they are healthy.

OVER 300 PAGES OF HELP

The *Light and Life Cookbook* contains forty days of complete menus — breakfasts, lunches, dinners — all nutritionally balanced for providing the greatest possible amount of food value.

Each day's menu leads you a step further toward the healthiest vegetarian regime, but allows you to stop at any point most appealing to you. You can become a "not-quite" or an "all-the-way" vegetarian according to your personal inclinations. Even if you do not wish to be a vegetarian, these dishes will be a welcome relief from the high cost and boredom of meats.

There are dining room tested recipes for all the menus. The recipes are for servings of from one to four persons, easily reduced or increased depending on the number to be served. Natural, healthy ingredients are featured throughout.

At your bookstore, or order from
Astara, Upland, CA 91786

Shining Moments of a Mystic

Earlyne Chaney

Those with a troubled heart often seek the solitude of a peaceful hilltop; a lonely heart, the light of the stars; a grieving heart, a sad refrain. But the troubled, the lonely, the grieving — and the happy heart, all find solace, peace and fulfillment in Cosmic Poetry. Such are these writings.

Let the breath-taking beauty of this superb book of shining moments inspire you now and forever. Let it fill the moments of your own cosmic loneliness and searchings with lingering thoughts of hope and light.

Share your "shining moments" with those of Earlyne Chaney. You will cherish "Shining Moments of a Mystic" for those intimate moments when you need inspiration, encouragement, consolation, and healing. You will see Light — in a world of darkness.

MAKE IT AN ADVENTURE

By Marcus Bach

Whatever is happening to you — good or bad, expected or unexpected, wanted or not — is part of a venturesome enterprise so great it nearly boggles the mind. Most people are unhappy, afraid, failing at the enterprise of life because they don't know the simple way to turn it around and make it an adventure.

But every once in a while one comes upon an "alchemical idea" that transforms life wondrously. Just such an idea was used by Dr. Bach to overcome dreaded malaria. He found that others used the same idea — whatever the land or language, or the purpose — with equally incredible results.

The lives of these people, from the most obscure to the most prominent, appear on the pages of this book with a radiance that will illumine your life, too. If you will but note the obvious principle which recast their lives, and incorporate it into your own, you will count this book as a treasured classic.

Learn to shape your desires and your abilities, grow in mind and spirit, rid yourself of daily irritations, discover your potential talents, and gain new vistas of satisfying achievements. Start a new way of life today with **Make It an Adventure.**

ABOUT THE AUTHOR

Dr. Bach has lectured around the world. He has also *listened* around the world . . . and has put the wisdom gathered from the humble and the great into two dozen books and thousands of lectures, articles and seminars.

He is the founder of the *Fellowship for Spiritual Understanding,* is considered the foremost authority on contemporary religious movements, is listed in *Who's Who in America* and in *Who Knows — And What,* and believes that your body, mind and spirit comprise a total person who can find much more in life if only you will make it an adventure.

At your bookstore, or order from
Astara, Upland, CA 91786

CREATIVE SELF-TRANSFORMATION THROUGH MEDITATION

A SIX WEEK COURSE
by Swami Parampanthi

To really change yourself in a creative way, to bring forth your inner potentials, go directly to the source of your highest inspiration and creativity... your own inner being.

Softbound

Swami Parampanthi helps you discover that, without realizing it, you have actually been meditating all your life — and that by the application of a few simple self-disciplines you begin to utilize your own natural powers in a self-creative way, integrating your normal consciousness with its higher counterpart. To gain spiritual insight, or to become more creative, competent or capable, or to achieve any of scores of personal benefits, you will find that *Creative Self-Transformation* offers you the path towards greater success, self realization and fulfillment.

Swami Parampanthi realizes that the meditation practice which helps one person may not be best for another. He therefore provides alternatives and suggestions which enable you to originate variations of special benefit to your goals, circumstances and requirements.

In this compact soft cover volume you are given a goal for each week of instruction. You are then presented ideas, exercises and disciplines which traditionally have led to the realization of those goals, along with suggestions about ways to personalize them for your individual requirements and purposes in your world today.

If you want to be your *real* self, use the order coupon for *Creative Self-Transformation,* a treasury of instruction on the world's oldest and most helpful personal science available in one book.

ABOUT THE AUTHOR
Swami Parampanthi

... was born in the shadows of the Himalayas in Assam, India, in 1928. His religious training began at the age of five under His Holiness Swami Muktananda Paramhansa, the family guru. After graduating from Hindu College, he studied six more years at Viraj Religious Institute, then did personal research throughout India and in the Himalayas with many teachers. He has taught and lectured throughout the United States since 1958 at universities, seminars, churches, clubs

At your bookstore, or order from
Astara, Upland, CA 91786

ADVENTURES IN ESP

by Robert Chaney

Would you like to focus your inner sight on visions of other dimensions, or on scenes a thousand miles away? Or know the history of an object, or its owner, simply by touching it? Could you use a time-tested formula to improve your intuition?

Adventures in ESP is a guide to fascinating inner areas of your Self . . . areas that hold all the promise of the Aquarian Age person.

You'll find it a clear, compact study of ways to develop the three psychic faculties most frequently used in the waking state — *Clairvoyance, Psychometry, Intuition* — plus additional chapters on *The Art of ESP* and *The Aquarian Age Consciousness*.

Here is a book of new age ideas, lessons and development exercises to help you use Extrasensory Perception, ESP, in your daily life . . . to help you solve problems, be more creative, harmonize your relationships with others, improve your business or profession, and experience a deeper and more enriching inner life.

Adventures in ESP is not a book of academic, technical material related to the usual laboratory experiments and group testing of research scientists. Rather it's an instructional manual of individual development for the person who already understands the theory and philosophy of ESP and wants to do something about it in his own life. It's a concise, compact workbook . . . one you will recall daily as your own experiences correspond to the principles and teachings it presents.

ABOUT THE AUTHOR

Robert Chaney left the business world in 1938 to use his psychic talents on behalf of others. He engaged in spiritual healing, demonstrated and taught numerous aspects of psychic phenomena.

Through lectures, classes, demonstrations and writings he has brought knowledge, comfort, peace of mind and personal attainment to thousands. His personal biographical data is found in *Who's Who in the West, Who's Who in California,* and in *Men of Achievement.*

At your bookstore, or order from
Astara, Upland, CA 91786

UNFOLDING THE THIRD EYE

by Robert Chaney

The central powerhouse of all psychic and spiritual perception is the Third Eye—that mysterious sense faculty that sleeps like a dormant cosmic television station in the center of the brain.

Does it lack a charged battery to make it function?—a cosmic sound track?—an attunement to a higher wave length of receptivity? If all beings possess it, how does one cause the incomparable cosmic station to begin "receiving" the "messages" obviously bombarding the ethers of space? How does one bring the cosmic camera into focus?

When the seeker begins to activate the pituitary-brow chakra through meditation techniques, light impulses pulsate outward toward the sleeping pineal-crown chakra. This radiating force begins to arouse the cosmic fires of kundalini in the root chakra at the base of the spine.

The chemical fires, rising up the spine, enter the third ventricle of the brain, contacting the positive-negative forces of the brow-crown chakras—and the All-Seeing Eye opens, lifting the seeker into the very heights of spiritual ecstasy.

Unfolding the Third Eye is an exciting adventure into the superconscious realm of the Self. Step-by-step methods are described to achieve this supreme attunement to divinity. The book is fully illustrated to guide you toward the illumination every serious disciple seeks.

At your bookstore, or order from
Astara, Upland, CA 91786

THE INNER WAY
By Robert Chaney

Special meditation for healing, self-confidence, stability, creativity, and numerous other everyday needs and activities.

If your life is crammed with many things to do, problems to meet, little time for leisurely contemplation — then you are the person Robert Chaney had in mind when he wrote *The Inner Way*.

He deliberately wrote much of the book in the waiting room of American Airlines at the Los Angeles airport, for there he could make actual contact with persons "hurrying to or from life's important matters."

He visited with them at random and learned that business, illness, life and death, intimate personal situations, dreams and aspirations, were constantly thrusting problems into their lives, as into yours. He also learned that while "outer" solutions weren't effective, the "inner way" produced results in meeting the problems.

So if you've had a problem today, if something "went wrong," if you've needed strength or understanding, or inner healing for an illness or sorrow, if you wished your mind could have been more alert, then *The Inner Way* would have served you well. Send for your copy now — it's a book you can really use every day of your life — immediately effective.

ABOUT THE AUTHOR

Robert Chaney is a mystic who understands we are *in* the world though not *of* it ... a minister who realizes that personal order may be found even in the midst of confusion ... and a teacher whose objective is to make the subtle evident and the complex simple.

He left a business career to enter the ministry in 1938, and soon thereafter gained a nationwide following as a psychic, lecturer, spiritual healer and the author of numerous books and lessons. In 1951 he and his wife, Earlyne, founded *Astara,* whose lesson studies and other publications reach seekers in some 90 countries.

At your bookstore, or order from
Astara, Upland, CA 91786

Psalms
Prayer Power for Your Problems

* The Psalms in metre, photocopied from an 1856 Bible
* Indexed for use with specific goals and problems such as success, protection, freedom from anxiety and pain
* Additional text on how to use the Psalms by Carrie Pevarnik and Robert Chaney
* A dozen simulated woodcut drawings
* Simulated antique pages
* Beige Lexotone cover, simulated leather grain

The Book of Psalms has been a source of comfort and strength to readers for centuries—what is different about the Psalms as included in *PSALMS: Prayer Power for Your Problems* is this: you don't just read them, like a novel. You *use* them, and bring to life their immense power of transformation and transmutation.

In addition to historical background and helpful suggestions on how to become more receptive to the vibrations of these scriptures, *PSALMS: Prayer Power for Your Problems* gives you a categorized reference list—specific Psalms for specific problems.

Do you need Higher guidance in making a difficult decision? You're led to the special version of Psalm 25.

Do you need encouragement to finally accomplish a long-held goal? You're directed to the special version of Psalm 138.

Whether you're standing at a bus stop, waiting in a doctor's office or washing the dinner dishes, you have the tool of vibrational Psalm power at your command. *PSALMS: Prayer Power for Your Problems* shows you how to use it.

At your bookstore, or order from:
Astara, Upland, California 91786

Suddenly the answers become crystal clear ... facts, figures, policy decisions, new ideas spring to life with

PSYCHO-DYNAMIC SYNTHESIS:
The Key to Total Mind Power

- Manage yourself, your business and your affairs more effectively
- Use "higher level thinking"
- Discover and use unsuspected inner potentials and resources
- Reduce pressure and strain
- Set and achieve your goals
- Expand and improve your environment
- Transmute troubles into assets
- Establish good family relationships
- Treat frustration creatively
- Use what you've forgotten, even though you can't remember it
- Expect a lot from yourself — and get it
- Change your past — yes, change your past
- Select the best objectives for you — and attain them

MYRON S. ALLEN

Dr. Myron S. Allen is Director of the Creative Growth Center at Los Gatos, California, and is also Director of Technical Service Research—consultants in physics and industrial psychology. He has been Professor of Physics at Long Beach City College, and Visiting Research Associate, Psychological Laboratory, University of Southern California.

He is widely known for his lectures to executives from major corporations, covering his unique methods of quick reasoning, communication, business planning and personal growth.